ISBN 978-0-483-69895-6
PIBN 10446549

Valley Herald.

F. E. DU TOIT Proprietor. TERMS, $1 50, Per Annum.

VOLUME 8 CHASKA, MINNESOTA, FRIDAY, DEC. 3, 1869, NUMBER 15

The Valley Herald

Official County Paper.

BY F. E. DU TOIT,

CHASKA FRIDAY DECEMBER 3 1869.

CORRESPONDENCE.

BELLE PLAINE, Nov. 26th 1869.

By previous arrangements, the merchants of Scott County met at Spicer Hall and organized by choosing H. W. Stone of Belle Plaine, chairman, and J. M. Spicer of Belle Plaine Sec'y. There were present:

H. W. Stone,	Belle Plaine.
C. T. Metzner,	"
A. V. Heydovstadt,	"
I. P. Black,	"
James M. Sprague,	"
M. M. Carson,	"
Wm. Henry,	"
John Schlitz,	"
J. M. Spicer,	"
I. N. Dean,	Blakely.
W. W. Strait,	Jordan.
F. Nicolen,	"
O. Zillert,	"
E. Holmes,	Carver,
P. Thompson	"
H. R. Denny	"
Henry Young,	Chaska.

The object of the meeting was pronounced to be the consideration of the expediency of perfecting an organization for mutual protection in business interests.

Peter Thompson of Carver by request presented a copy of proceedings made by the merchants of Carver Co.

I. N. Dean presented copy of proceedings of meeting of merchants of Sibley County, pledging co-operations with any organization here affected. After free discussion a motion prevailed to organize a Merchants Protective Union for Scott County.

Messrs. Metzner, Dean and Nicolen were appointed committee on permanent organization who reported for President, H. W. Stone; Treasurer, W. W. Strait; Secretary, J. M. Spicer.

Motion to accept and adopt report, carried.

Messrs. Nicolen of Jordan, W. H. Anderson of Shakopee and I. N. Dean of Blakely were appointed a committee of correspondence with other person and organization interested in the movement.

Messrs. Dean, Black, Strait, Metzner and Nicolen were appointed committee on Resolutions who reported the resolutions of the Carver County organization simply changing time of collection of outstanding debts from December 1st 1869 to Jan. 1st 1870, which report was accepted and adopted.

Whereas, The present financial condition of the Country demands the attention of every business man, in order that he may adopt his circumstances thereto, and

Whereas, The merchants of Scott County have heretofore been accustomed to do a heavy credit business with their customers, which accommodation has in many instances been abused by those receiving it. And,

Whereas, We find ourselves in pressing need of money, being compelled to pay our debts when they are due, therefore.

Be it Resolved, That we are forced to call upon those who are indebted to us to settle their accounts before the first day of Jan. next, and unless payment is made within said time, the same will be collected by law.

A motion prevailed authorising the committee of correspondence to provide such number of circulars as may be required by the members respectively and adopting the form of the Carver County Circulars.

A vote of thanks was passed to the merchants of Carver Co. for courtesy and assistance.

Adjourned to meet at Jordan on Thursday December 2nd at such hour as may be designated by the committee of correspondence.

J. M. SPICER, Sec'y.

Miss Kate Field,

A Boston correspondent of the Anti-Slavery Standard says:

Last week's lecture before the Parker Fraternity was given by Miss Kate Field who presented herself to the audience as one of "Murray's fools, and discoursed on "Life in the Adirondacks." She chose to give her lecture sitting instead of standing, the result of which was that a good many of the audience heard her but imperfectly. So far as your correspondent heard (in a seat favorable for hearing), the lecture sounded as if it would make a pleasant impression on being printed and read. But the apparent purpose of the speaker to impress the audience by her person, her attitude and her dress, (which presented in an extreme degree, all the offensive peculiarities of this year's fashions), was felt to be a considerable drawback on the effect which the lecture unadorned would have had.

HON. I. DONNELLY,

His Views on the Red River Revolution

Hon. Ignatius Donnelly has written the following letter in response to an invitation to address the Chamber of Commerce on the subject of the Red River revolution:

MERCHANTS HOTEL,
St. Paul, Nov. 23, 1869.

Ossian E. Dodge, Esq., Sec'y Chamber of Commerce, St. Paul:

DEAR SIR—I have the honor to acknowledge the receipt of your favor of this date in which, in the name of the Chamber of Commerce of St. Paul, you invite me to be present at the next meeting of that body, on Monday evening the 29th inst.

It will give me great pleasure to comply with this invitation.

I am thoroughly convinced that if the proper course is pursued by the American people, the present moment is fraught with the weightiest consequences.

As our form of government is simply organized liberty our liveliest sympathies must go out to every people who seek to relieve themselves from oppression and injustice. We have nothing in common with the ludicrous and burlesque aristocracy of Canada that is trying to prove anew in the wilds of the Red River, the old doctrine of feudalism that "some men were born saddled and bridled, and others are born booted and spurred to ride them."

The geographical necessities of Minnesota require that the great valleys of the Red River and the Saskatchewan shall be thrown open to unrestrained American settlement. Minnesota should be heard at this crisis; and the capital of the State is the spot from which its voice should go forth.

Such a state of feeling should be aroused in the nation as will prevent General Grant from giving permission to the red coated soldiers of England to cross the soil of our State to reduce to subjection men whose aspirations are for liberty, and whose entire sympathies are with the American people.

If the revolutionists of Red River are encouraged and sustained by the avowed sympathy of the American people, we may, within a few years, perhaps months, see the Stars and Stripes wave from Fort Garry, from the waters of Puget's Sound, and along the shores of Vancouver.

I have the honor to be,
Very respectfully, yours,
IGNATIUS DONNELLY.

Boutwell's Plan.

A new York correspondent of the Chicago Times claims to have ascertained that, after consultation with leading New York bankers, and also with western financiers, Secretary Boutwell has decided to submit, at an early day, probably in his annual report, the following programme for a return to specie payments, to the consideration of Congress:

1. The National Banks to redeem their notes for greenbacks by July, 1870.
2. The government to redeem its greenbacks in gold after June 1, 1871.
3. Free banking for all parties upon bonds bearing interest at 4 per cent in gold.
4. This point is not quite settled.—There is some division in regard to the question whether the banks shall be permitted to issue notes, as notes, or whether the United States shall take charge of all the circulation by the issue of greenbacks by a plan somewhat similar to that of the Bank of England. It is, however, understood that no greenbacks of a smaller denomination than $5 or $10 will be issued.

Do the Farmers Like It?

The World has a comparison of the prices of wheat and other products of the farm, in the New York market, on the 20th of August and 12th of November—wheat being $1 60 in August and only $1,35 in November—showing that the Western farmer has lost during the period embraced in the above dates over $25 on 1,000 bushels of wheat. The World continues:

He has to pay the same price for his leather goods, for his iron articles, for his woolen and dress goods, for his coffee, tea, and sugar, as if his wheat would still fetch him $1,600 for 1,000 bushels. But why has the fall of gold not had the corresponding effect on manufactured commodities? Simply that an oppressive law, subsidizing a corrupt monopoly, forbids us to buy our iron in England, where it costs only $14 gold a ton per pig, but obliges us to pay home manufacturers $37 to $38 currency per ton for it. It is the same with blankets, alpaca, leather, steel, glass, and a thousand other articles.—The nearer we approach a healthy state of currency, the more keenly will the oppressed and robbed producers of the soil feel the oppression. The present shrinkage in the price of products abundantly proves that the greatest hindrance to the restoration of specie payments is the existing tariff. In the meantime, our farmers are deprived of fully one-fifth of their year's labor; which, we fear, will have an immense influence on the commercial prosperity of the country.

HOME ITEMS.

HERALD AGENT CARVER—G. A. DuToit.

PATRONS OF HUSBANDRY.

An organization of this order was affected in our village at the Court House last Saturday. Some 20 odd names were enrolled, mainly through the effort of Mr. John Koch, and officers nominated and elected.

The meeting was called to order by Mr. Koch, whereupon Fred E. Du Toit was chosen temporary Secretary. After which the following gentleman were unanimously elected officers for the ensuing year.

Master, John Koch.
Lecturer, J. A. Sargent.
Overseer, Henry Young.
Steward, Peter Weego.
Asst. do Henry Koch.
Chaplain, Freeman James.
Treasurer, John Dunn.
Secretary, Fred Henning,
Gate Keeper, B. Salee,

After which upon motion F. E. Du Toit and Peter Weego were appointed a committee to procure the use of the Court House Hall for meetings of the Grange, from the County Commissioners.

It is expected that a special deputy from the State Grange, will visit Chaska in a short time to install the officers elect and set the order in motion.

COMPLETED. The alteration of the Chaska & Waconia road is completed and the town supervisors have accepted the same. This is an important road and its completion insures a much heavier trade for Chaska than ever enjoyed heretofore in the direction of Waconia. The long, steep and almost impassable hill near town is avoided and an easy grade secured. This year has marked a new era in the history of Chaska. New and costly roads have been built that will in due time tell heavily in our favor. The new road, including the two bridges cost $800. It is a good investment.

Wm Brinkhouse was contractor and H. J. Chever superintendant; to them there is due much praise for the workmanlike manner in which the work was executed.

DESTRUCTIVE FIRE.—We inadvertantly omitted to mention the fact that Mr. John M. Troll sustained a serious loss last week in consequence of loosing his hop ware house and some 65 or 70 hundred pounds of baled hops. It took fire at two o'clock in the morning and when discovered had gained such headway that it was impossible to extinguish the same or save anything. Loss $3,500 insurance $2,500. The Underwriter or N. Y., carried the risk.

SOCIAL RE-UNION.—Mr. Jos. Schaaf, John Ess, Jos. Ess, E. Schneider and Jos. Winninghoff with their families met at the Chaska House, Frank Ess proprietor last Sunday evening and enjoyed a very pleasant evening. This was an annual gathering and was attended by a number of invited guests. A bountiful supper was provided by Mr. Frank Ess and lady, which was done ample justice too by those partaking.

SNOW.—We were visited by a light fall of snow on Tuesday evening which made sleighing passable.

OUR STORES.—Chaska can justly boast of her stores and merchants.

Messrs. Linenfelser and Faber have one of the largest Stores in the Valley and probably as well stocked.

Henry Young, and Lucien Warner have also large and well approportioned stores. Besides we have Mr. Thies and Bennett. We advise our farmers to consult their interest and trade at home.

FANCY ARTICLES.—Mr. Bennett, of drug Store fame, has received a fine lot of perfumery &c. Call and see his show case.

PERSONAL.—Mr. E. Holmes, and H. R. Denny, of Carver made our city a short visit on Wednesday evening last.

Mr. Austin Brown of Shakopee also made our village a call on the same evening.

HARPERS MAGAZINE.—We have before us upon our table Harpers Monthly Magazine for December, one of the best and most interesting numbers we ever read. It is replete with good solid article, both instructive and entertaining. There is an interesting historical article upon "The First Œcumenical Council" and another upon the 'Life and Services of Frederick the Great" In fact every article are well worthy perusal. Address, Harper & Bros., Franklin Square, N. Y.

WATCHES & CLOCKS.—Chas. Marx, the new jeweler, has just received a new assortment of Clocks & Watches He also does repairing to order. Call at his place of business in Schroer's Boot and Shoe Store.

GRAIN.—Grain is still declining in price. Wheat brings 55 cents per bushel, while barley only commands 60 cents. Hard times for farmers.

WANTED.—Wood to apply on subscription or debts owing the HERALD office. Bring it in at once and settle your accounts.

SCHOOL BOOKS.—Mr. Thies will hereafter keep a full supply of school books on hand. His store is next to Youngs.

Bad enough to look and feel bad yourself; but no excuse for having your horse look and feel badly, when for a small sum you can buy Sheridan's Cavalry Condition Powders, which given in grain two or three times a week, will make him look and feel well.

STILL AHEAD.—That Star Spangled Banner, which for several years has "waved" to the great satisfaction of its many thousand readers, and to the dissatisfaction of all swindlers and rascals generally, is even more wide awake than ever. It has at an immense expense secured the services of an eminent artist, and the result is that it propose to give away a splendid engraving entitled Evangeline to every subscriber for 1870. This superb work of art is one and one-half by two feet in size, and is equal to the best $3 engraving ever offered.—The Banner is a large eight-page, forty column paper, overflowing with splendid reading of all kinds and costs only 75 cents a year, which is very cheap for the paper alone, but the publishers propose giving every subscriber a copy of their elegant engraving gratis. The paper and its publishers are reliable and it will pay to send for specimens to The Star Spangled Banner, Hinsdale, N H., or they can be seen at this office.

Winter is now fairly upon us, and the teams are hastening to the lumber woods in various parts of the country. Our advice to every man who goes to the woods, be he captain, cook, teamster, or any other man, is to take along a good stock of Johnson's Anodyne Liniment, and Parson's Purgative Pills Many months of labor (in the aggregate) may be saved by this precaution.

Patrons of Husbandry.

Cor. Rochester (Minn.) Post.

Noticing in your last issue a communication relative to organizing Farmers' Clubs, let me call the attention of the farmers to the organization known as the Patrons of Husbandry. This is a secret association which secures a fraternity and already has in this State some forty subordinate branches, and it is through such an order only, that the farmers can hope to obtain those advantages they desire. History proves conclusively that ordinary farmers' clubs and associations are too isolated in their efforts to accomplish much, but through the order of the patrons they can work in unity Establish them in every town in our State and the result will be unity of action. The order has now been before the public for several years and is gaining an immense membership in all parts of the country, north, south, east and west. Organize granges instead of clubs.

Cheap Transportation and the Price of Wheat.

The Madison, Wis., State Journal, of a recent date, in quoting the low price of wheat now paid throughout Iowa, makes the following sensible suggestions:

Had we a steamboat channel from Prairie du Chien to Green Bay, wheat could be taken from Mississippi river towns to lake Michigan for ten cents a bushel.

We find, on looking at the market reports, that wheat was worth from twenty five to forty cents less at McGregor and other towns on the Mississippi than it was in Milwaukee and Chicago on Nov. 11th. This difference, we take it, represents the cost of transportation.—Putting the surplus crop of wheat in Iowa at 20,000,000 bushels, and ten cents as the highest figure for river and canal transportation, it seems fair to say that there would be a saving of fifteen cents per bushel in the transportation of Iowa wheat to the lake if we had a canal. It would be $3,000,000 on this crop and enough on return freight to actually save in one year the entire sum necessary to make the improvement.

Estray.

Came into my enclosure in the town of Hancock, Carver Co. one light red cow, the owner will please come forward prove property, pay charges and take the same away.

ANDREW NILSON.

Proposal,

TO WHOM IT MAY CONCERN.

In pursuance of authority in me vested, by the Board of Commissioners for the County of Carver, I will receive proposals to board, cloth and support, the paupers of Carver County, by the week, for the term of one year, from and after the acceptance of such proposal. Compensation to be made by the County, to the person whose bid is accepted. The right is reserved to reject any and all bids.

Proposals to be made within two months from the date of this notice.

Dated Chaska Sept. 26th 1869.

PETER WEEGO, County Auditor

Insurance.

For reliable indemnity against loss by Fire apply to Fred E. Du Toit, Agent of the following old and reliable companies at Chaska, Minn.

Aetna, Hartford, capital	$5.052,000
Underwriters; New York,	4.000,000
Western Buffalo,	700,000
Charter Oak, Hartford Life	5,000,000

All of the above companies insure property at reasonable rates and pay their losses promptly.

Poetry.

INFLUENCE SOMEWHERE.

No stream from its source
Flows seaward, how lonely soever its course,
But what some land is gladden'd. No star ever rose
And set, without influence somewhere. Who knows
What earth needs from earth's lowest creatures? No life
Can be pure in its purpose, and strong in its strife,
And all life not be purer and stronger thereby.
The spirits of just men made perfect on high,
The army of martyrs who stand by the Throne
And gaze into the face that makes glorious their own,
Know this surely, at last. Honest love, honest sorrow,
Honest work for the day, honest hope for the morrow,
Are these worth nothing more than the hand they make weary,
The heart they have sadden'd, the life they leave dreary?
Hush! the sevenfold heavens to the voice of the Spirit
Echo: He that overcometh shall all things inherit.

The True Story of How the Medical Students Hooted the Ladies, from an Eye-Witness.

Philadelphia (Nov. 6) Correspondence New York Tribune.

The lecture room of the old Pennsylvania Hospital was the scene of a novel exhibition on Saturday morning last. The managers, having opened the doors for the admission of female medical students to the clinical lectures delivered there, had the pleasure of seeing, for the first time in the history of the institution, about thirty students from the Women's Medical College seated in the little theatre where the "clinics" are held. Three or four hundred male students from the other medical colleges of the city were likewise present, as it was the regular lecture morning. From one of the upper benches I observed that the circular form of the apartment and the rising tiers of seats placed the women in full view as they sat in a body on one side. Two or three of the managers, members of the Society of Friends, were seated on the little stage awaiting the entrance of the lecturer. They were "weighty" [illegible]

"Can't You Have Those Sheets Changed?"

[illegible]

A Favorable Notoriety.—[illegible]

HUMAN BODIES TURNED TO STONE.

The Corpse of Mrs. Willis Cowling after Fifteen Years' Interment—The Petrifaction of Capt. Cady.

To the Editor of the Sun:

Sir: The recent affirmation of Professor H. A. Ward, of the Rochester (N. Y.) University, "that there is no single instance on record of fossil or petrified flesh," is strangely subversive of the truth in many well authenticated cases, recorded in the newspaper presses, and well remembered to this day by hundreds of the most intelligent and reputable citizens resident where the discovery of those phenomena took place.

The instance recently furnished you from Canastota, N. Y., of the petrifaction of the body of Capt. Cady, "an old and well known resident of the town of Sullivan," revives and reclothes with all the freshness and vigor of a yesterday's incident, the exhumation of the body of Mrs. Willis Cowling for re-interment in the new cemetery just erected and completed in the city of Richmond, Va., thirty-five years ago.

The deceased lady, the wife of one of the largest manufacturers of that city, was buried in the grounds attached to the Methodist Episcopal Church. After the lapse of several years Mr. Cowling, in the interim having married again and the second wife dying, determined to bury both wives in the new cemetery, and had the body of the first wife exhumed. The unusual weight of the coffin, exacting the force and power of several men to remove it, and the extraordinary preservation of the wood of which it was manufactured, induced the friends present to investigate the astounding phenomenon, and with that sole object in view, opened the coffin, when, to the utter amazement of every beholder, the body was found to be petrified in it entirely daguerreotyping not only the general contour of the face, but lining each individual feature with such perfect accuracy as to be easily and distinctly recognizable by every friend present, notwithstanding the intervention of fifteen years between the burial of the body and its exhumation.

[illegible]

writes:

On the night of the 10th of October, owing to the extraordinarily sudden rise in the Nile, an inundation occurred, which, for the celerity with which it rose, is, perhaps, without parallel. On this night I happened to be staying in one of the doomed villages. I had therefore opportunities which rarely fall to the lot of an European of witnessing intimately the immediate effect of the calamity on the poor villagers, and I am induced to send you this brief account of what came under my own experience and observation as a tribute to the remarkable patience and fortitude of the Arabs under very trying and perilous circumstances.

About 2 o'clock in the morning our Bedouin servant awoke us, saying that the water was rising rapidly. Every inhabitant of the village—man, woman or child—was working with an energy seldom witnessed here, making banks to stem the encroaching water, or carrying their bread and winter supply of grain to spots which had hitherto proved sufficiently high for safety. But it was of no avail. The banks were washed down and the bread floated away. Now, indeed, the scene began to get dismal enough—the darkness, the uncertainty, the wailing of the Arab women; and then came the fall of the first house. This was an occasion for universal shrieking and lamentation, but the water soon had it all its own way, monopolizing even the noise, and nothing was now heard but house after house surging and coming down with a dull souse into the water.

Our house being higher and stronger than the others, we went to the top and began to construct a raft there, intending to launch it from the roof. We were soon compelled to relinquish our task, and were scarcely clear when the walls gave way, at water level and the whole came down. All made their way, with the water breast high, to the highest spot, fortunately still several feet above the water level. Here was soon collected every inhabitant of the village, but how changed!—the women no longer wailing, and the men no longer discontented, for the last house was gone; it was no longer possible to save anything, and the water was still rising. There was, therefore nothing for them but to await their destiny, which they set about doing with every appearance of contentment, the village beauties (never seen except at such a time) even seeming, as it seemed to me, to enjoy the state of things as a relief to the monotony of their existence.

It now became necessary to think of our raft again, so, after making several excursions from our present comfortable standing place to the site of our late residence, we had collected sufficient wood for the purpose; over this we placed dried cornstalks and bound the whole together with ropes from the camel-packs. So quickly did the water still rise that our raft, commenced on dry land, was finished floating on over a foot of water. We now joined the villagers on the little mound and awaited the sunrise. A conspicuous figure was the dignified old "sheikh" of the village, as he passed from one family group to another, evidently imparting confidence to all. To him we proposed to take off with us as many women and children as our raft would bear, but he replied that 'Allah was great and would send boats in time if it was His will to save His people; that our bark was frail, our poles short, and the current strong, and if any went with us he washed his hands of any responsibility.' His arguments were backed by the sight of a sail in the distance, so we had to put off by ourselves to the base of the hills between two and three miles distant. Arrived there, we sent the raft back by two Bedouins, and made our way to where some boats were employed in carrying stone. One of these we procured for the assistance of our late neighbors, and we had the satisfaction before leaving of seeing them all encamped under the hills."

A Court Scene.

From the New Orleans Picayune.

It is not often that one sees a penitent in court, but an unfortunate prisoner, yesterday, cried lugubriously over his arrest. He begged the recorder, piteously, to turn him loose, and promised never to sin so again.

"I'll do so on one condition."

"What is it, sir."

"That you go home and tell your wife what kind of company you were caught in."

"Oh, sir, I can't!"

"Then I'll have to fine you!"

"Oh, sir, I have no money!"

"I can't help that!"

"But, sir, if you knew my wife!"

"But I don't!"

"Oh, sir, she's awful!"

"Will she whip you?"

"Lord, sir, she'll kill me!"

"Serve you right, too!"

"Judge, let me say I was caught stealing!"

"No, sir!"

"Fighting?"

"No, sir!"

"Murder?"

"No!"

"Drunk?"

"No!"

"Arson?"

"No!"

"You'll have to send me to prison, then," and the man again indulged in a copious flood of tears.

His offence was a common one. He was arrested for disturbing the peace of a concert saloon—*behind the curtain*.

—Burbank's new hotel at Pittsfield, Mass., six stories high, was blown down on the 20th.

See "The Little Corporal" among advertisements.

A CAPITAL JOKE.

A Secretary of State in an Embarrassing Situation.

An Elyria (Ohio) paper tells the following:

A capital joke has just leaked out on the good-natured and affable gentleman, Gen. I. R. Sherwood, Secretary of State. During the late canvass this prince of good fellows, who, by the way, enjoys a good joke, even at his own expense, had occasion to stop at Oberlin. He was provided with a comfortable room at the hotel, and immediately set about the task of doffing his apparel and rigging himself with an entire change of dress. After removing from his person every stitch of clothing, even to the shirt (the General is always very neat and tasty in his dress), he stepped forward and opened a door, as he supposed, of a closet, for the purpose of placing therein the doffed garments. But behold his astonishment, when, instead of opening the way to a closet, he opened a door leading into a commodious sitting room, which was occupied by a number of ladies. A full developed manhood, as barren of clothing as in the moment he made his *debut* in the world, standing unobscured before the ladies, and the illustration of the modest General at the mistake he had made, caused a consternation among the parties that can more easily be judged than related. The General, however, notwithstanding his shocked modesty, retreated in good order, and soon reinvested himself with that of which he had been divested, but fully convinced of the fact that all doors opening out of rooms do not lead the way to clothes closets.

[illegible] the following:

Prof. William Stimson, connected with the Chicago Academy of Science, a short time since, while passing Mr. Thatcher's farm, just beyond the town of Harlem, and adjoining Haas' Park, discovered hillocks which he suspected might belong to the mound-building period, and might contain valuable mementoes of a past age. A few days afterward he obtained permission of the owner of the farm to make an examination of the mounds, and last week he, together with Charles Kennicott, made a personal examination of the premises, and uncovered the earth to the depth of about three feet. They had dug but a short time, when human bones were discovered, which, upon examination, proved to be of a race at present extinct upon the continent of North America. Persevering efforts of several days were rewarded with the finding of several other similar mounds, and the remains of twenty human beings. Two entire skeletons were found, with the exception that one of them lacked two cervical bones, and the other a few of the bones of the hands and feet. The bones themselves were very friable, and required the most careful handling to prevent their falling into dust again.

The bones which mark the peculiar characters of the beings who once possessed them are those of the cranium. It is well known that the heads of Europeans and all descendants of the Caucasian race are usually much greater in length and breadth. They have what is technically called the *dolicho-cephalic* skull which the Iroquois Indians who inhabited America at the landing of Columbus, possessed square heads, or skulls which archæologists call *brachy-cephalic*. The skulls found at Thatcher's farm are of the *brachy-cephalic* type, and this fact stamps them as being at least as old as the first discovery of America. It is said that the influences of civilization have entirely changed the shape of the Indians' skull, so that the present tribes, no matter how much isolated from the white man, present no cases of the antique Indian head.

Another evidence of the antiquity of these remains is the position in which they were found. Prof. Stimson was obliged to remove a large tree which grew on one of the mounds to reach the skeletons. A cross section of tree disclosed 87 rings, and since botanists claim that the evidence of the first 15 years' growth of old trees has been obliterated, it follows that this tree was at least 100 years' old.

The mounds were about two feet above the surface of the prairie, were oval in shape, and were about four or five feet wide, and from 10 to 20 feet in length. They were each surrounded by a well defined trench. Before reaching the remains a layer of hard blue clay was penetrated, and the bones were found reposing in a bed of gravel. The remains were found three feet below the surface.

The tombs of the "mound builders," as they are called are supposed to have been constructed by the ancestors of the ancient Aztecs, or by the Aztecs themselves. The remains are usually found arranged in regular order, and accompanied with tools, weapons, and implements, by which their great antiquity is inferred and, to some extent, measured. The mounds discovered last week by Prof. Stimson contained no tools or weapons, or at least none have yet been discovered, although, as the researches have not terminated, it is impossible that these objects may yet be found. The remains were apparently thrown together promiscuously, as if the rites of sepulture had been hurried—perhaps at the close of a battle.

From all the circumstances, it is believed that when the beings were buried there, the place was the margin of the lake, and thus the phenomena are closely connected with another interesting series of questions relating to the lake and its physical condition and boundaries before the shores were discovered by Europeans.

On yesterday, another mound was discovered, circular in its form, and larger and higher than the others. It has not yet been investigated so as to determine what is the character of its contents.

The subject will be laid before the Academy of Sciences this evening, when, it may be expected, some new light will be thrown upon the matter.

Thrilling Incident.—During the late flood two men near Long Eddy, took a rope and went upon some low land near the Delaware river to fasten a stack of hay, and before they could make it fast and return, the sudden rise of the water cut off their communication with the high lands. They were compelled to seek refuge on the stack, and despite ropes and ties it soon floated off. In a moment more they were floating down the raging tide. No help for them, and no paddle or pole to guide their tender and tottering craft. Down, down the overflowing and surging torrent, they floated and rolled along. No boat could reach them, for the water was too rough and rapid. Soon they passed Callicoon, twelve miles distant, and in a short time was approaching the Cochecton bridge, five miles further down. Three miles more and the Falls would shake their hay raft to atoms and their hopes ended. Near Milanville they were discovered far up the river, and a boat was made ready in time to reach them before they floated by. Just in time, only a short distance above the rapids they were rescued and safely landed on shore, after a most fearful ride of twenty miles upon a stack of hay. Many thanks to the brave and skillful men who snatched them, as it were, from a watery grave.—*Alegdon Press*.

A Dreadful Accident occurred a few miles below Toledo, Ohio, last week. There has been a skiff-ferry running between Manhattan and the iron works on the opposite side of the river. At about 4 o'clock on Monday afternoon four women, three men and a boy started from Manhattan, across the river. The boat also contained meat, flour, and groceries. It was loaded down to within a few inches of the dipping point, yet it was not deemed unsafe. When the boat reached the east channel of the river, the waves were running high, and it filled with water. The man having charge of the boat, Mr. R. Tennant, of Manhattan, Ellen L. Nims and Jeannette Allen, of Toledo, were drowned. Mr. C. W. Allen, the uncle of Jeannette, was standing on the shore, about 15 rods distant, when the boat swamped, and Tennant shouted to him for assistance. Jeannette clung to Mr. Tennant, and Mr. Allen heard him tell her to let go and he could save her, but in her fright she would not let go her grasp, and the two went down together.

THE LAW OF MARRIAGE.

The Wife who was not Married, and Who Was Declared Dead, Still a Wife.

In the suit of Mary Durand against Joseph Durand, in which Mrs. Durand alleges that she went to live with him as his wife sixteen years ago, on his promise to marry her; that they cohabited until a year ago, she bearing him five children, and he recognizing her as his wife until about a year ago, when he treated her cruelly and sent her to France, afterwards publishing notices of her death, Judge Fithian yesterday granted the motion made on behalf of Joseph Durand to vacate the order of his arrest. His Honor holds that the facts set forth by Mrs. Durand constitutes several causes of action in which an order of arrest might be granted; but the difficulty was that upon her showing Mr. Durand was her husband, and neither husband nor wife could maintain a personal action at law against the other for damages for personal injury from either.—The only remedy was a suit for separation, or a criminal prosecution. Though according to Mrs. Durand's statement there was never a formal ceremony of marriage, either religious or civil, yet there was a promise of marriage, consummated by living and cohabiting together as husband and wife for sixteen years. This Judge Fithian holds to be, according to all the authorities, sufficient to constitute the couple husband and wife, and both are estopped as against each other and all the world from denying the relationship. Though Mr. Durand had repudiated the contract of marriage, yet she could not take him at his word, and rescind it on her part, because marital ties could not be annulled by mutual consent.—*N. Y. Sun*.

The Story of a Boy who was Lost for Seven Years.

The following appears in the St. Louis Republican:

About seven years ago Henry Muller, a farmer of Madison county, Ill., who lives only three miles from St. Louis, returned home from the fields, when he was informed that his son a boy of scarcely eight years, could not be found about the premises. Mr. Muller made diligent researches for the discovery of his lost boy, but they were in vain. His house being on the road, he fancied that movers from the interior had stolen the boy and taken him across the river, perhaps to a great distance from his home.

Day before yesterday, more than seven years after the child was lost, he found him, now fifteen years old, in good health and in excellent spirits, at the Orphans' Home, on Eleventh street, between Monroe and Market streets, in St. Louis, and was permitted by the lady patronesses of the institution to take him home, after having proved to their satisfaction that he was the boy's father. A former neighbor of Muller, a farmer by the name of A. B. Evans, who now lives six miles south of Columbia, had discovered him. He passed about three years ago by the Orphans' Home, when he saw among the children playing on the street a boy whom he recognized at once as Muller's son. Evans had left his old place sometime before the child was missing, and thought that Muller himself might have brought him to the asylum. Accordingly time passed on without his advising his friend. Last week, however, three years after he had first discovered little Henry, he met the father here in the city, where both farmers had come to sell their products.

Evans desired to know everything that had happened since his removal from Madison county, and when Muller told him that his boy was stolen, Evans expressed his belief that he knew where the child was. They went together to the asylum. All the children were called into the parlor, and the father at once recognized the boy by his great resemblance to his mother, who had died. The boy, however, did not recognize his father, though he showed great satisfaction at finding that he was not an orphan. His father described the size and location of a mole on the boy's body, which, together with a comparison of the dates, and especially the unmistakable parental sentiment of Evans, completely convinced the ladies of his claims. The child, it appears, was brought to the asylum by an old woman, who found him in the street, sometime in 1862, and he was recorded in the books as Henry Wiston.

Though the boy is not very advanced in literary studies, he received a simple but good moral education, and was regarded as one of the most honest, faithful and laborious boys in the asylum.

Chinese Religion.

I returned to Sacramento in time to witness the great annual "devil-drive" by the Chinese, which was performed yesterday and last night with imposing ceremonies. All the Chinese of this city reside on I street, which for about five blocks is as foreign as a town in China. There were at least three thousand in town yesterday, from the various railroads, and with the blowing of horns, beating gongs, talking and yelling, open-air theatres and bands, they made the evening lively. Nearly all the Chinese in America are Buddhists, there being very few of the followers of Confucius, who constitute the fashionable infidels or philosophers of China, while the Buddhists are the High Church party.

They reason the matter thus: "If God is good, why pray? All right nohow—tend to the Devil." Hence this ceremony of driving out the latter. In company with a few whites I crowded through the mass of Mongolians to where a tobacco factory had been converted into a temporary "Joss-house." We found the Devil "out in the cold," a hideous black figure, easily recognizable as the Evil One, set upon a pedestal just outside the door. Within were two enormous "Josses," ten feet high, one in each corner, over them a shelf filled with little household gods, two feet in length, while behind the altar the Buddhist and attendant boys were going through a ceremony very similar to High Mass. The Buddhists, like the Mormons, believe in a plurality of Gods, rising in regular succession to the great Head God, whom the Mormons call Elohim, and the Chinese "Top-side Joss." Watching the uncouth scene till I was tired, I passed out, and seeing a Chinese acquaintance at the door who understood a little English, I sought information, and received it thus:

Myself—"Hallo, John, do you believe in him?"

Ah Ching—"Oh, velly, Melica man, me believe him."

Myself—"All Chinamen believe in him."

Ah Ching—"Oh, China like Melica man. Some believe him sabvey; some tink he all gosh dumn."

And I felt that I was answered.

A Dying Man in a Difficulty—His Coffin Too Small.

[From the Mountain Gazette, Sept. 28.]

A certain native living in Keelan has been sick, and, apprehending that his end was near at hand, sent into town for a coffin, so that his friends might be prepared to give him proper burial. In due time the coffin arrived, upon seeing which grave doubts arose in the sick man's mind as to whether it would fit. No means to decide the question appearing so conclusive to him as a "personal test," he tried himself and could not get in—the thing was too narrow! He soundly berated his messenger for his stupidity in not getting a coffin suitable for the purpose, and lost no time in saving the capital invested, as far as possible. Knowing of another man sick like himself, who also expected to die, he entered into negotiations with him at once, and succeeded in disposing of the useless (to him) article, at a loss of only four dollars. Our readers will appreciate the above when we state that this provident gentleman is the honorable member from Keelan, who in years past has caused no little mirth on account of his eccentricities. We sincerely hope that the venerable and eccentric gentleman's fears will not be realized, but that he may, instead, long live and make us all laugh many more times.

—Flowers, rocks and rivulets have been introduced in the Prince of Wales Theatre, London, occupying the place of the orchestra.

Personal Items.

—Josepa is a cousin of Eugenie.

—Reverdy Johnson celebrates his golden wedding next week.

—"Sut Lovengood," a southern humorist, has married.

—Wilkie Collins is to spend the winter in Paris.

—Duke Ernst, of Saxe-Coburg-Gotha, is coming to the United States next spring.

—De Cordova has been offered $5,000 to deliver six lectures at San Francisco.

—Sam. Hildebrand has named his youngest son George Washington.

—Laura Keene has taken Wall's Opera House, in Washington, for the winter.

—Father Hyacinthe attended a spiritualist meeting in New York, the other evening.

—Kitjoo Thackersey and Tooleldas Jidaljee, two Hindoo merchants, are in Chicago.

—Mrs. General Custar goes with her husband on Indian campaigns, and is a good shot with the rifle.

—Cassius M. Clay has returned from Europe and will establish himself in business in New York.

—There is a 57-year-old-farmer in New Hampshire who owns a large orchard, but has never tasted a raw apple.

—Col. Sam Hatch, of St. Louis, has contracted with Louisiana to build 1,900 miles of Levee along the Mississippi river.

—Nelaton, the famous French physician, lately charged the Mayor of Paris $600 for a single visit.

—Mr. S. A. Hitchcock, of Brookfield, Mass., has given $40,000 to endow a Hebrew Professorship at Andover.

—John Swanson, a Swede, has bought twelve thousand acres of land in Missouri, intending to found a cotton raising colony.

—Charles Reade, novelist and dramatist, contemplates building a theatre on his own land, in Sloane street, Belgravia.

—The Spanish General Prim, it is affirmed, sleeps in a different place every night, to avoid the possibility of assassination.

—The New York Mail says: "A real, live, two-legged, ten-fingered Duke is residing at an up-town hotel. Matchmaking mammas will regret to learn that he is married.

—A Norfolk man has presented Gen. Lee with a cane made of a piece of the Merrimac, and inscribed: "To Robert E. Lee, from a profound admirer of his character. October, 1869."

—A Paris paper announces the arrival of Madame Ristori at Nice, where she is to give some representations with Signor Rossi. Madame Ristori was last reported at Buenos Ayres.

—King George, of Greece, is devoted to the velocipede, and spends more time on it than in attending to the affairs of his nation. Imagine an ancient Greek dashing around the Acropolis on a bicycle!

—The Prince Imperial of France is to receive the title of Duke of Corsica, according to the precedent established by the first Napoleon, who called his son King of Rome.

—Young Iturbide of the Montezuma dynasty lives in Georgetown, D. C., with his wife, nee Green and with the child that was for some time adopted by the late Maximilian.

—Mark Twain says—"It is a darling country to live in that Hayti. Board two hundred and eleven thousand dollars a month in the best hotels, and ice cream three hundred dollars a saucer."

—Andrew Miller died in Knoxville, Adair county, Mo., on the 18th ult., at the advanced age of 99 years and five months. He had been blind for nearly 25 years, but just before he died he exclaimed: "I shall soon see! I shall soon see!" For 65 years he had been a member of the Methodist Episcopal Church.

—When General Wool was seized with illness he remarked that this would be his last sickness. "Oh, no, General," exclaimed one of his attendants, "you will recover and be with us many years yet."—"No," said the General, "this is the last flickering of a lamp that has long been burning."

—A New York paper publishes a biography of Jim Fisk, in which, among other things, it is said that when, years ago, the inchoate Prince of Erie hired his father at a salary of $3,000, he said to him, "I want you to distinctly understand that you are my clerk, and I don't want you to put on any of your d—d airs," and that the aforesaid father is now in an insane asylum.

—The hand of one of the richest American heiresses in Paris, whose wealth is valued at ten million francs, has been asked by a Spanish Count, on condition of her disposing of her property in excess of his own, which amounts to 1,500,000 francs, in favor of the poor; but at last accounts the American beauty declined to see the matter in that light.

Foreign Specks.

—At Amsterdam diamond cutting is a speciality, and gives employment to 10,000 persons.

—A hat-makers' journal has recently been established in Berlin, and is published by O. Hasse.

—The Great Eastern is getting ready in England to take out and lay a cable between Bombay, India, and Aden on the Red Sea.

—After forty years' labor the Japanese novelist, Kiong de Bakin, has furnished a novel consisting of 106 volumes.

—The barbarious old-fashioned uniform of the British army, it has just been discovered, has induced fatal heart disease in thousands of soldiers.

—It is proposed in France to procure the passage of a law classing debts contracted at a bar or drinking room in the same category as gambling debts.

—There is an establishment in Bristol, England, where a butt of sherry wine can be manufactured from the raw material in half an hour without using a drop of sherry.

—Victor Hugo's dog wears a collar on which is inscribed: "I wish some one would send me home. My state?—Dog. My master?—Hugo. My name?—Senat."

—A French photographer claims to produce pictures in color by a new method, of which he only describes the general method, which is to illuminate the object successively with the different parts of the spectrum.

—Australia consumes twelve pounds of tea per person per year; England three and a half pounds a head in a twelvemonth; America one pound to each individual of some kind of leaves in which there is understood to be an admixture of tea.

—When the military fired upon the riotous striking miners of Aubin, France, a woman, who had her child in her arms, turned to fly, pressing the baby to her breast; the child was struck by several bullets in the head, and the furious mother, turning back and meeting an officer, hurled her child in his face, exclaiming:—"Take it, ruffian! You want our blood; Take it, then—drink it!"

—The Emperor of China is fifteen years old, and is to be married this year with tremendous pomp to his first and chief wife, the Empress. He will be simultaneously provided with second and third wives, and in all parts of the empire victims are being collected to swell the list of his harem. Every Tartar family is obliged to furnish its quota. Local selections are first made, and the holocaust is sent to Pekin, where a fresh selection takes place, and a "chosen" number are condemned to a life-long seclusion. They are not allowed to see their relations, may never see their lord and master, and in the event of his death they are still condemned to perpetual celibacy and isolation.

—A Virginia calf is given to turkey-eating, and has made away with thirteen of them.

THE BROKEN HOME.

"Truth Stranger than Fiction."

In San Francisco, on the north side of Folsom street, overlooking Mission Bay, stands a palatial residence.

The interior of this house is even more beautiful than its exterior, every apartment being in its way a gem of magnificence and refinement.

The library especially realizes the most perfect ideal of an elegant and cultured home.

And yet, at the moment we look in upon him—one August afternoon, as he occupied his library—the proprietor of all this wealth appeared of all men the most miserable.

He was Mr. Morton Preble, for many years a leading banker of San Francisco.

It was in vain that the broad bay-window at the south end of the room had been opened, giving ingress to the sunshine and fragrance of rare flowers—in vain that the walls were lined with richly carved book cases, and paintings—in vain that the couches and luxurious chairs had been gathered around him.

He was wretched.

He lay on a sofa, in the depths of the bay-window, the wreck of a once powerful man. His figure was thin and gaunt; his face white as marble; his eyes having an expression of woful apprehension; of harrowing anxiety, of dreadful expectancy.

It was evident at a glance that no merely physical ailment made him what he was.

By what withering secret, by what destroying affliction, had he been thus agonized? thus haunted? thus haunted? he so noble and good! he so wealthy and distinguished!

As he moved restlessly upon his luxurious cushions the pretty clock on the mantel-piece struck five, every stroke seeming to fall like a hammer upon the heart of the nervous invalid. He aroused himself, struggling feebly to a sitting posture.

"O, will this fatal day never, never pass!" he murmured; "nor bring us relief?"

Noticing with a nervous start, that he was alone, he touched a bell upon a table before him, and called:

"Helen, Helen! where are you?"

Before the echoes of his voice had died out, a step was heard, and his wife entered his presence.

"I left you only for a moment, Morton," she said advancing to the banker's side. "You were dozing I think. I wished to send for the doctor.

She was a beautiful woman, of some six and thirty years, graceful, with broad white brows, and loving eyes, in which the brightness and sweetness of a sunshiny nature were still perceptible, under a grief no less poignant than that evinced by her husband.

"The doctor?" he echoed, half reproachfully.

"Yes, dear," she said in a calm and cheerful voice, as she drew a chair to the side of the sofa, and sat down, stroking the corrugated forehead of the invalid with a magnetic touch. "He will be here immediately. Your last nervous crisis alarmed me. You may become seriously ill."

Mr. Preble bestowed an affectionate look upon his wife, but said despondingly:

"The doctor! He cannot 'minister to a mind diseased!' Oh, if these long hours would only pass! If I only knew what the day has yet in store for us!"

"Look up, Morton," enjoined Mrs. Preble, with a reverently trustful glance upward through the open window at the blue sky, and as if looking beyond the azure clouds therein. "Let us appeal from the injustice and wickedness of earth to the goodness and mercy of Heaven!"

The banker gave a low, sobbing sigh.

"I cannot look up, Helen," he answered, with a passionate tremor in his voice—"only down, down, at the grave that is opening before me!"

"Look up, Morton, always look up!" she again enjoined upon the invalid. "During all these fourteen years of agony I have not once doubted either the goodness or the justice of Heaven. 'Blessed are they that mourn, for they shall be comforted.' I believe that we shall yet rejoice more keenly than we have mourned, and that we shall come to a glorious day beyond all this long night of sorrow!"

The face of the invalid lighted up with an answering glow, and he murmured:

"Glorious faith! My wife, you are indeed a blessed comforter! Perhaps you are right after all!"

A knock resounded on a side door at this juncture, and the next moment Dr. Hutton, the family physician, for whom Mrs. Preble had sent, entered the room.

He was an old man, portly in figure, with white hair and beard, but with a fresh and ruddy complexion, a pair of shrewd blue eyes, and with an exuberant boyishness of manner that sat well upon him. He had a kind heart and a clear head. He approached the sofa, after greeting the husband and wife, and lifted the thin, restless hand of the invalid, feeling his pulse.

"Quite a high fever," he said, after a brief pause. "Worrying again, eh, Mr. Preble? You are wearing yourself out. Medicine will do you no good so long as your mind is in its present condition. I must give you an opiate"——

"Not now, doctor," interposed the banker. "I cannot—must not sleep to-day! I need to be broad awake, now, for I cannot tell at any moment what the next may bring forth. I am looking for the culmination of all my years of anguish—for the crowning agony of the whole. Perhaps, even now—. Ah, what was that!"

He started up wildly, and then, as the sound that disturbed him was not repeated, he sank again upon his cushions, pallid and panting.

The doctor looked at Mrs. Preble with an anxious, inquiring glance.

"It is the anniversary," she replied to his unspoken question—"the anniversary of our loss."

"Ah, yes," said the doctor. "I remember."

"Yes, it's another of those terrible days," said the banker, in a hollow whisper. "Sit down, doctor, and I will tell you the whole story. I can't think of anything else to-day, and am almost wild with apprehension and anxiety. Sit down.

Dr. Hutton drew up a chair and seated himself, his face expressing the double solitude of a friend and physician.

"You knew us fourteen years ago, doctor," said Mr. Preble. "We lived then where we do now, in a cottage on the site of this great mansion. There were but three of us—Helen and I, and our three-year old Jessie. And it was fourteen years ago to-day that our little Jessie was stolen from us."

"I remember it," said the doctor, softly. "Yet she might not have been lost, Mr. Preble? She went out to play in the garden, if I remember rightly, and was never seen by you again. She might have strayed away"—

"So we thought for a whole year, doctor," interrupted the banker. "We never dreamed that she had been stolen. We searched everywhere for her, and offered immense rewards for her recovery. I employed detectives, but all to no purpose. When our little Jessie ran down the steps into that flower-garden," and he pointed to the front of the house, "as if the earth had opened and swallowed her up, we never saw her again."

"She must have found the gate open and wandered out," suggested Dr. Hutton. "She might have strolled down to the waters and been drowned."

The banker fixed his burning eyes upon the physician's face, and whispered:

"I said we never saw the poor child again. I did not say we had not heard of her. She was lost on the 9th of August, 1854. For a year we thought her dead. But on the anniversary of our loss we received a written message concerning her."

"A message!" cried Dr. Hutton, starting.

"A mere scrawl—a single line in a hand evidently disguised," said the banker. "Here it is."

He produced a dingy scrap of paper from a drawer in the table, and held it up to the view of the physician, who read as follows:

"August 9, 1855. *Jessie, ha, ha! Jessie!*"

Dr. Hutton looked, with a puzzled air, from the scrap of paper, which he turned over and over, to the countenance of the banker.

"I can make nothing of this," he declared. "It is merely a date, with the name of your lost daughter. It tells me nothing."

"Nor did it us, at first," said Mr. Preble. "Then that name and that date, with the demon laugh connecting them, set us to thinking. A whole year we agonized over the dreadful problem, and then we received another message, which you shall see."

He thrust a second slip of paper, identical in shape and appearance with the first, before the gaze of Dr. Hutton, who read it aloud:

"August 9, 1856. *Your Jessie still lives.*"

The physician started, as if electrified.

"Ah! this is something definite—something decisive," he muttered. "It convinced you that your daughter was still living."

"Yes, doctor," said Mr. Preble, "and every anniversary of that day has brought us some message. The disappearance of the child, mysterious as it is, does not seem to me half so strange as that the villian who took her away could contrive to communicate with us every year since, and always on a particular day—the anniversary of that on which she was stolen—without our being able to discover who he is. And a still greater wonder to me is what can be his motive. It seems incredible. If it was stated in a novel many people would not believe it. But 'truth is stranger than fiction!'"

Mrs. Preble drew from her husband's breast pocket his note-book, opened it to the proper page; and presented it to the physician.

Dr. Hutton adjusted his spectacles, glanced over the page, and then slowly read the group of entries aloud. The entry the first year was as follows:

"August 9, 1855. *Jessie, ha, ha! Jessie!*"

And the next year it is—

"August 9, 1856. *Your Jessie still lives!*"

And the next—

"August 9, 1857. *She is in good hands!*"

And the next—

"August 9, 1858. *She is well as ever!*"

And the next—

"August 9, 1859. *I saw her yesterday!*"

And the next—

"August 9, 1861. *She continues to do well!*"

And the next—

"August 9, 1862. *I've seen her again!*"

And the next—

"August 9, 1863. *She's becoming a woman!*"

And the next—

"August 9, 1865. *She's lovelier than ever!*"

And the next—

"August 9, 1866. *She's really charming!*"

The physician looked up and fixed his thoughtful gaze upon the bereaved husband and wife.

"How did these messages come to you?" he demanded.

"Invariably by post," replied Mr. Preble. "Usually to the house, but sometimes to the office."

"And you have never seen their author?"

"Never."

"The last of them is dated, I see, a year ago to-day."

"Yes, yes," faltered the banker, "and the time has come for another message. This is the 9th of August, 1868."

"I see," said Dr. Hutton. "And this is the secret of your terrible excitement! You are expecting to receive to-day another of these strange messages."

There was a brief silence. Mrs. Preble's hand fluttered in its task, and her face grew very pale. The banker breathed gaspingly. The physician regarded them both in friendly sympathy.

"We shall hear of her again to-day," said Mr. Preble; "and what will the message be?"

The mother averted her face. Her brave heart faltered as the question echoed in her soul.

"The writer of these letters is unquestionably the abductor of your child!" said Dr. Hutton. "Have you any suspicion as to his identity?"

"Not the slightest," said Mr. Preble. "We have puzzled over the problem for many years, but we cannot guess who he is."

"Think," said the doctor. "Have you no enemy? I do not mean people with whom you are not friendly—every stirring man has plenty of these—but a downright enemy! Is there no man whom you knew in the East who hated you? No one against whom you were called upon to testify—no one whom you possibly injured!"

The banker shook his head. He had asked himself all these questions repeatedly.

"I have no such an enemy, doctor," he answered, with sincerity of voice and manner.

"And Mrs. Preble?" suggested the doctor, turning to her. "Have you no rejected suitor who might be revengeful enough to desolate your home?"

"No," said the lady. "I was married early. Morton was my first lover."

"This is strange—very strange!" muttered the doctor. "You are not conscious of having an enemy in the world, and yet you have an enemy—a hidden foe—a fiend in human form—who is working out against you a fearful hatred! And you have not the slightest suspicion as to whom he is?"

"Not the slightest," declared the banker.

"Not the slightest," echoed Mrs. Preble. "My husband had a step-brother who might have been capable of this infamy—but he is dead!"

"The handwriting is not familiar?"

"No. It is merely a rude scrawl, as you see," said the banker. "It suggests nothing—except that it is evidently disguised!"

Again there was a profound silence.

"Our child is seventeen years old now," at length murmured Mrs. Preble, her voice trembling. "She is in the threshold of womanhood. No doubt, during all these years, she has yearned for us, wherever she may be, as we have yearned for her!"

"But where is she?" asked the physician—and now his voice was broken by his deep sympathy with the agonized parents. "Where can she be?"

"Heaven only knows" answered the mother. "Perhaps in San Francisco—perhaps in some rude hut in the interior, with some obscure farmer, and under a name that is not hers! I think her abductor would have carried her to some lonely region of the interior, among the valleys and mountains. Yet I never see a young girl in the streets without turning to look at her. I never hear a girlish voice without listening eagerly, half fancying that it may prove the voice of my lost Jessie!"

"Oh, pitying heaven!" sighed Dr. Hutton, dashing a flood of tears from his eyes; "will this long agony never be over?"

"We hope so, and even believe so," answered Mrs. Preble, with the firmness of an unfaltering trust in God's mercy. "The last message we received from our enemy seems to point to some kind of a change."

"True," assented Dr. Hutton, looking at the message in question. "It is unlike the others. It says that his 'reward is at hand.' He means either that he intends to marry your daughter, or that he intends to demand money of you for bringing her back—or both."

"We shall soon know," said Mrs. Preble, with forced calmness. "To-day we shall have another message, no doubt. What will it be?"

The banker turned restlessly on his sofa, and his face grew even paler.

"Whatever it is, let it come," he murmured. "Anything can be borne better than this suspense. Let it come."

As if his impatient words had precipitated a crisis, a step was heard on the walk at this moment, and a ring at the front door followed.

"Another message!" breathed the banker.

A servant soon entered, bearing a letter, which he extended to Mr. Preble:

"The bearer is in the hall."

With an eager, anxious gaze, the banker glanced at the superscription of the missive.

It is from *him*," he faltered.

He tore the envelope open.

It contained a slip of paper, of well-known shape and appearance, upon which was scrawled a single line, in an equally well-known hand-writing, which the-banker exhibited to his wife and the physician.

This line was as follows:

"August 8, 18—. At six I will call."

A shock of wonder and horror shook the three simultaneously.

"Will call!" cried Mr. Preble, starting to his feet and glaring wildly around.

"Is coming here!" cried Mrs. Preble, also arising.

"It seems so," said Dr. Hutton, his eyes again reverting to the message. "He will be here at six o'clock, and see! it is six already!"

Even as he spoke, the clock on the mantel-piece commenced striking the appointed hour, and at that instant heavy footsteps resounded in the hall, approaching the library.

"It is he!" cried the doctor, also arising.

As the last stroke of the hour resounded, the door leading from the hall again opened.

One long and horrified glance cast the banker and his wife in that direction, and then she fell heavily to the floor.

Her senses had left her. The above we publish as a specimen chapter; but the continuation of this story will be found only in the N. Y. Ledger. Ask for the number dated December 4th, which can be had at any news office or bookstore. If you are not within reach of a news office, you can have the Ledger mailed to you for one year by sending three dollars to Robert Bonner, publisher, 182 William street, New York. The Ledger pays more for original contributions than any other periodical in the world. It will publish none but the very, very best. Its moral tone is the purest, and its circulation the largest. Everybody who takes it is happier for having it. Leon Lewis, Mrs. Harriet Lewis, Mrs. Southworth, Mr. Cobb, Professor Peck, Mary Kyle Dallas, Fanny Fern and Miss Dupuy will write only for the Ledger hereafter.

Mr. Bonner, like other leading publishers, might issue three or five papers and magazines; but he prefers to concentrate all his energies upon one, and in that way to make it the best. One Dexter is worth more than three or five ordinary horses.

What science only can one genius fit,
So vast is art, so narrow human wit.

An Excellent Medicine.—The leading paper of the Northwest, the Wisconsin, Milwaukee, gets off some very good things, among the latest of which we extract the following:

One of the most popular medicines of the day is Hoofland's German Bitters, which is designed to keep the stomach and liver in a healthy condition. The Bitters is prepared without the use of intoxicating Liquors, and if a person desires to drink liquor under the fashionable name of Bitters, he had best apply for something else than Hoofland's. Druggists tell us that the sale of this article is large, and is continually on the increase,—that all who use it are pleased with its excellent qualities, and that they could not think of keeping store without it. In case of debility or prostration of the system, Hoofland's German Bitters will be found an excellent article, as well as for Dyspepsia.

Hoofland's German Tonic is a combination of all the ingredients of the Bitters, with *pure* Santa Cruz Rum, orange, anise, &c. It is used for the same diseases as the Bitters, in cases where an Alcoholic Stimulant is required. It is a preparation of rare medical value, and most agreeable to the palate.

Wines and Liquors.—H. G. Kuhlman, Importer and Dealer in Foreign and Domestic Wines and Liquors, Old Brandies, Gins, Bourbons, &c., 87 Dearborn street, Masonic Temple, Chicago, Ill., has on hand, and is constantly receiving, the largest stock to be found in the Northwest. The proprietor is a gentleman who thoroughly understands the wants of his customers, and those dealing with him will find first-class goods and low prices.

To those who are afflicted with Chills and Fever, Dumb Chills, or Malarious Diseases of any kind, we would recommend Dr. F. Wilhoft's "Anti-periodic, or Fever and Ague Tonic," which is sold under a guarantee. It has never yet failed, in a single instance, to effect a speedy and permanent cure. Made in New Orleans by Wheelock, Finlay & Co. Sold at wholesale by Fuller, Finch & Fuller, Chicago.

Appleton's Journal, which has only been in existence a few months, has attained a circulation which is unprecedented in the annals of journalism. It only exemplifies the fact that extraordinary liberality of expenditure will always meet with success. Good literature is the crying need of the day, and the Appletons know how to furnish it. See advertisement in another column.

Will Hall's Vegetable Sicilian Hair Renewer change gray hair to its original color and not dye the skin? It will! and is a preparation of acknowledged superior merit.

Read the Following Letter.

(From one of the oldest and most reliable grocery merchants in the city of Davenport.)

Friend Walton: Agreeable to my promise to you when here, I write you (for publication if you see proper,) a true statement of the good effects of Roback's Stomach Bitters upon myself. I had been troubled with indigestion for a long time, attended with severe headache, particularly after eating, when, fortunately, an old soldier friend came into the store and recommended me to use Roback's Bitters. I did so by taking a small wineglass full just before each meal, and to my great joy I was relieved at once, and am now well by their use. I would not be without them at any price. I have not taken any other medicine since I commenced using the Bitters. And I can say with a clear conscience, try Roback's Bitters—they will do all they are recommended to do—if taken according to directions. Yours truly,

Frank H. Miller,
Of the firm of Rudderbeck & Miller, wholesale grocers, Davenport, Iowa.

The Best and Original Tonic of Iron Phosphorus and Calisaya, known as Caswell Mack & Co.'s Ferro Phosphorated Elixir of Calisaya Bark. The Iron restores color to the blood the Phosphorus renews waste of the nerve tissue, and the Calisaya gives a natural healthful tone to the digestive organs thereby curing Dyspepsia in its various forms, Wakefulness, General Debility, and Depression of Spirits. Manufactured only by Caswell, Hazard & Co., successors to Caswell, Mack & Co., New York. Sold by all Druggists.

The Youth's Companion.—This is one of the most promising and readable youth's publications with which we are acquainted. It is issued from Boston, is most judiciously conducted, and has among its contributors such writers as Mrs. Stowe, Rev. Mr. Hale, Elizabeth Stuart Phelps, and others equally acceptable to the young people. Its announcements for 1870 are more than ordinarily attractive.

Benjamin Franklin, 1769.—It is time our people understood and practiced more generally Life Assurance. Many a widow and orphan have had great reason to be grateful that the advantage of Life Assurance was understood and embraced by the husband and father. A large amount has been paid by Life Assurance Companies to widows and orphans when it formed almost their only resource.

Edward F. Jones, 1869.—I have made sufficient examination of the condition of the Washington Life Insurance Company of New York to warrant me in taking a policy of Twenty Thousand Dollars.

Severe lingering coughs are cured by the use of Dr. Pierce's Alterative Extract or Golden Medical Discovery in less than one-half the time necessary to cure them with any other medicine. For hoarseness, laryngitis, or ministers' sore throat, bronchitis, and the early stages of consumption, it surpasses everything before discovered. Sold by druggists, or send three and a quarter dollars to Dr. R. V. Pierce, Buffalo, N.Y., and get three bottles free of express charges.

The Secret of Beauty lies in the use of Hagan's Magnolia Balm for the Complexion. Roughness, Redness, Blotches, Sunburn, Freckles and Tan disappear where it is applied, and a beautiful Complexion of pure, satin-like texture is obtained. The plainest features are made to glow with Healthful Bloom and Youthful Beauty.

Remember, Hagan's Magnolia Balm is the thing that produces these effects, and any Lady can secure it for 75 cents at any of our stores.

To Preserve and Dress the Hair, use Lyon's Kathairon.

Persons in want of Trusses, Supporters, Artificial Limbs, or Surgical Instruments, can be supplied at maker's prices, by addressing L. H. MORTON, Druggist, next to Custom House, Milwaukee. [illegible]

THE MARKETS.

NEW YORK.

[illegible]

CHICAGO.

[illegible]

CINCINNATI.

[illegible]

ST. LOUIS.

[illegible]

MILWAUKEE.

[illegible]

Prince Humbert, who will succeed Victor Emmanuel as King of Italy, is a young man of about twenty-four years of age. He had the misfortune to lose his mother during his early childhood, and has since been brought up by the ladies of King Victor's harem. As might have been expected, he has shown in his conduct, since his arrival at years of indiscretion, the influence of his early associates and of his father's peculiar example. Since his marriage, which took place not many months ago, he has been somewhat more discreet in the pursuit of his pleasures, but he is by no means a nice young man. Indeed, were it not for the fact that he has proved his courage on the field of battle, he might be truthfully called an Italian Albert Edward. Like his father, he has never shown any indication of talent, and, unlike him, he does not appear to possess the bluff, soldierly honesty that won for the King his once popular sobriquet of the *Re Galantuomo*. The Italian people will not find it easy to keep alive the fiction of admiration and respect for so worthless a prince as Humbert is understood to be; and the Mazzinians will doubtless endeavor to make the monarchy share the unpopularity of the monarch. There is, however, a peculiar feature in the relations of Prince Humbert with the Italian radical, which may not be without its influence upon his future as King of Italy. In common with his younger brother, Prince Amadeo, he has always professed a warm personal affection for Garibaldi. If his relations with the great democratic soldier still remain as cordial as they formerly were, Garibaldi may be able to rally his followers to the support of the monarchy. The fate of King Humbert may yet be decided by the rheumatic and feeble old guerrilla captain.

A scene on the Arkansas river is described by a correspondent as follows:

Still farther back, and there rises to a height that seems to almost pierce the clouds a majestic mountain, known far and wide as the greatest of all curiosities upon the Arkansas. Immediately upon its river front it presents the appearance of a monstrous sugar-loaf, the almost perfect proportions of which, aside from all other attractions, form a wonderful curiosity of itself. It is from an up-river view, however, that this mountain takes on the wonderful appearance from which it derives its name. Looking down stream from a standpoint a few miles above, and the former appearance of a sugar-loaf is found to have disappeared. What before seemed to be but one crowning peak is found divided in twain, and the appropriateness of the name "Mammelle," (Woman's Breasts) is acknowledged at a glance. Strange as it may seem the resemblance is perfectly wonderful. Not a line seemingly is wanting to make up the graceful contour, the symmetrical proportions and the matchless beauty of the perfect physical woman. So perfectly wonderful is the resemblance that we can but continue to gaze, in spell bound admiration until the increasing distance and the growing darkness caused by a waning moon slowly hides the seemingly cloud capped tips of "Mammelle" from view.

A Family Puzzle.—Alluding to the report that M. Lesseps and his son—who are referred to as "MM. X. pere et fils"—are about to marry two sisters, the Rappel suggests the following complications as likely to arise from these double espousals: To begin with, X., the son, will be the brother-in-law of his father, and the wife will become the sister-in-law of her own sister. If M. X. senior has a son, and M. X. junior a daughter, and they should marry, the daughter of X. junior will become the sister-in-law of her father; and the son of X. senior will be the son-in-law of his brother and of his sister-in-law. If there should be a child of this second marriage, it will have two grandfathers, MM. X. senior and junior, whence it follows that X. senior will become the brother of his own son. More than that, if a boy, he will be the brother of his own mother, since he and his mother are alike grandchildren of X. senior; and as a mother's brother is an uncle, he will be in the anomalous position of being his own uncle.

A Canadian Pacific Railway to be built from Ottawa to Puget Sound, a distance of over 2500 miles, is now exciting great attention in the Dominion, and a charter will be asked for at the coming meeting of the Legislature. The line, it is asserted, would be shorter than any other route between the Atlantic and the Pacific, and the harbor at Puget Sound is the best on the Pacific coast. The domestic advantages of the road would be very great, the remote part of the British Dominions would be connected; employment would be given to vast armies of laborers; emigrants would be attracted in great numbers, and the capital, $100,000,000, to be raised in England, would be expended in Canada. On the other hand, it is contended that Mr. J. Palliser, who was sent out in 1857 by the English Government to survey the boundary line between the United States and the British Possessions, was also entrusted with the task of finding a suitable route for a railroad to to the Pacific. Mr. Palliser's report, now on file in the Government offices in London, it is asserted, states that such a line does not exist north of the boundaries of the United States.

"Sam," said a guest to his host at dinner, "this is a capital sirloin, please tell me what is the name of your purveyor?" "Addison," was the reply. "Any relation to the Spectator?" added the gentleman. "Probably," said the other; "I have often seen steel by his side."

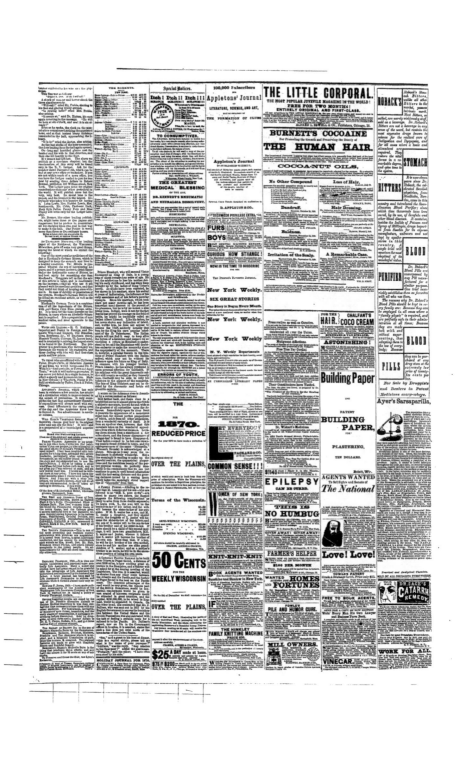

The Chaska Herald.

RATES OF ADVERTISING

1 Square one time ... each subsequent insertion ... One column one year ... Half " " ... Fourth " " ... Business cards not over 5 lines ... over 5 lines and under 10 ... over 10 lines and under 15 ...

Legal Advertisements per square, first insertion, [illegible] each subsequent insertion [illegible]. Local notices 10 cents per line 1st insertion, each subsequent insertion 5 cents per line. All notices less than five lines, 50 cents.

New Store.

At the Post Office in Carver you can get Dry Goods, Hats, Caps, Boots & Shoes, Ready made clothing and all styles of Dress Goods from Sixty to one hundred per cent cheaper than at any other store in Carver Co. We would call special attention to our stock of Glass Ware, Lamps and Looking Glasses

Groceries can be had Twenty per cent cheaper than at any other place in the County. Produce taken in exchange for Goods.

AUCTION EVERY FAIR DAY.

C. E. ROGERS & CO.

MINNESOTA IRON WORKS.

Cor. First and Marshall Streets.
Minneapolis, Minn.
SUPPLIES MILL MEN

With Steam Engines and Boilers, [illegible], complete, Saw Mill Machinery complete, Flouring Mill Machinery complete, Water Wheels, Gears, Bolts, Hangings, Shaftings, Pulleys, &c.

Farmers.

With Horse Powers, Hay Presses, Sorghum Mills, Wind Mills, Force Pumps, Reaper and Mower Castings, Jack Screws, Iron Kettles, from 15 to 50 gallons, Sleigh Runners, &c.

Builders.

With Architectural Castings, as Iron Columns, Fluted and Plain, Iron Caps, ornamental and plain, Iron Store Fronts and Railings, Iron Grates and Doors, Iron Pans and Fire Shutters, Iron Roofing, Iron [illegible], Iron Conductor Shields, Sash Weights, &c.

Pittsburg, Youghiogheny and Lehigh Coal

[illegible] OF ALL KINDS.

All communications, letters of inquiry or orders, must be addressed in full.

"MINNESOTA IRON WORKS"
Minneapolis.

FRANK WARNER

Attorney at Law, Chaska Minn., Office at Court House, opposite Auditors Office.

THE ST. PAUL PIONEER.

Established in 1849.

The Oldest and Best Newspaper in the State

DEMOCRATIC IN POLITICS.

Daily, Tri-Weekly, Weekly.

The St. Paul Pioneer has already entered upon the twenty-first year of its existence, with a larger list of subscribers and more extensive patronage than it ever before enjoyed.

It is reliable democratic, progressive in its ideas, and the organ of the people.

It advocates honesty and economy in the administration of the government.

The reduction of taxation.

The repeal of great modification of the existing oppressive tariff.

The prompt payment of the debt.

The taxation of government bonds the same as other property is taxed.

The banishment of corruption from all the [illegible].

The defence of the national honor at all times.

That the government shall be administered solely for the good of the people.

All the columns of the Pioneer will contain the latest telegraphic dispatches from all parts of the world, the latest news of all kinds; reliable and full market reports; official documents and [illegible]; practical and general editorial; correspondence from all parts of our own State and [illegible], the local news from the various localities in the state; interesting tales, and general reading for the fireside.

TERMS BY MAIL.

DAILY.

One year	$10 00
Six months	5 00
Three months	2 50
One month	1 00

TRI-WEEKLY.

One year	$6 00
Six months	3 00
In clubs of six or more, each copy one year	5 00

WEEKLY.

One copy, one year	$2 00
One copy, six months	1 00
In clubs of [illegible], each copy one year	1 50

A copy of the Weekly will be sent gratis to every person who gets up a club of ten, and of the [illegible] weekly to any person who gets up a club of [illegible].

PIONEER PRINTING Co.,
St. Paul, Minn.

[illegible]

INSURANCE

F. E. DU TOIT.
AGENT

of the following Insurance Co's,

ÆTNA

Hartford, Conn.—Assets 5,052,000,00

UNDERWRITER'S AGENCY

New York City,—Assets 3,555,000,00

CHARTER OAK LIFE INS CO
OF
Hartford, Conn.—Assets, 4,000,000.00

Policies of Insurance issued against loss or damage by fire and perils of inland transportation.

Losses Adjusted and Paid promptly at the place where the *Policy is Issued.*

Will attend promptly, to collections. Paying of Taxes, &c.

OFFICE, AT THE "HERALD" OFFICE.
CHASKA MINNESOTA

JOHN BLOEDEL'S

Brick Wagon and Black-Smith Shop.
Near Zangers Store
CARVER - - - - - - MINN.

This is the oldest, largest and best Shop in the County.

The Celebrated Milwaukee, Wisconsin Wagons are always kept for sale at this shop. They are brought up from Milwaukee and ironed here. They are sold as cheap as Minnesota wagons.—Bob-sleds &c. kept for sale and made to order.

Shoeing Oxen, Horses, and all other blacksmith work done to order.

All those wishing good and durable work and at reasonable prices should call at

BLOEDEL'S SHOP.

Commissioners Notice.

Notice is hereby given, that by order of the Probate Court for Carver County, Minn., the undersigned have been appointed commissioners to receive, examine and adjust claims against the estate of Peter Thompson late of said County deceased, and will meet for that purpose on the first Monday of each month, at the Court House in Chaska in said County, at 2 o'clock P. M., for six months from August 14th 1869, and said period of six months is the time limited by said order for creditors to present their claims.

Chaska, Aug. 14th 1869.

PETER WEBBO,
G. KRAYENBUHL,
F. E. DU TOIT,

PROBATE NOTICE.

State of Minnesota, County of Carver. } S. S.

On reading and filing the oath and petition of Amelia Brandt praying for reasons therein set forth that letters of administration may issue to John Brodmaurer on the estate of August Brandt late of said county deceased.

It is ordered that the 13th day of December A. D. 1869 at 11 o'clock A. M. at the office of the Judge of Probate in Chaska in said County be assigned for the hearing of said petition, and all persons interested in said estate are required to appear at a session of the Probate then and there to be holden to show cause if any there be why the prayer of said petitioner should not be granted. And it is further ordered that said petitioner give public notice of the pendency of said petition by causing a copy of this order to be published in the "Valley Herald" a weekly newspaper published at Chaska in said County for three successive weeks previous to the day of said hearing.

Dated Chaska Nov. 6 1869.

J. A. SARGENT,
Judge of Probate.

PROBATE NOTICE.

State of Minnesota, County of Carver. } S. S.

On reading and filing the oath and petition of Anna Carlson praying for reasons therein set forth that letters of administration may issue to herself on estate of said Johanna Carlson late of said county deceased. It is ordered that December the 13th 1869 at 11 o'clock A. M. at the court house in Chaska in said county be assigned for the hearing of said petition. And all persons interested in the said estate are requested to be and appear before said Court at the time and place aforesaid and show cause if any they have why said petition should not be granted. And it is further ordered that said petitioner give public notice of the pendency of said petition by causing a notice of this order to be published in the Valley Herald a weekly newspaper printed in said county for four weeks previous to said day of hearing.

Chaska Nov. 6th 1869.

J. A. SARGENT,
Judge of Probate.

Manhood: How Lost, How Restored.

Just published, a new edition of Dr. Culverwell's Celebrated Essay on the radical cure (without medicine) of Spermatorrhoea, or Seminal Weakness, Mental and Physical Incapacity, Impediments to Marriage, etc.; also, Consumption, Epilepsy, and Fits, induced by self-indulgence or sexual extravagance.

Price, in a sealed envelope, only 6 cents.

The celebrated author, in this admirable essay clearly demonstrates from a thirty years' successful practice, that the alarming consequences of self-abuse may be radically cured without the dangerous use of internal medicine or the application of the knife; pointing out a mode of cure at once simple, certain, and effectual, by means of which every sufferer, no matter what his condition may be, may cure himself cheaply, privately, and radically.

This Lecture should be in the hands of every youth and every man in the land.

Sent, under seal, in a plain envelope, to any address, post paid, on receipt of six cents, or two post stamps. Also, Dr. Culverwell's "Marriage Guide," price 25 cents. Address the Publishers, CHAS. J. C. KLINE & CO., 127 Bowery, N. Y., Post-Office Box 4,586.

HO! !H Ho!

JUST RECEIVED
BY
HENRY YOUNG,
A Fine and Large Stock of
FURNITURE,
FOR THE
Parlor, Dinging Room, and Chamber
consisting o
Rockers, Chairs, Tables, Bureaus, Stands, Bedsteads, Lounges, Looking Glasses, Picture Frames and Mouldings furnished, &c. &c.

Sales room at my old store on 2d Street.
Chaska Minn.

LEGAL NOTICES.

Mortgage Sale.

Names of Mortgagors, Jacob Haas and Elisabeth Haas of Chaska in the County of Carver and State of Minnesota.

Name of Mortgagee, Henry Young of Chaska aforesaid.

Date of Mortgage, May 1st A. D. 1869.

When recorded, May 11th A. D. 1869 at 10 o'clock in the forenoon of that day in Book "D" of mortgages on page 147 in the office of the Register of Deeds of said County of Carver.

Amount claimed to be due at the date of this notice, one hundred and seventy five dollars & ninety seven cents.

Description of mortgaged premises. The east [½] half of the south east [¼] quarter of section [34] thirty four in township [116] one hundred and sixteen, Range [23] twenty three west, excepting fifteen [15] acres described as follows: Beginning at the south east corner of section [34] thirty four and running thence westerly along the south line of said section [29] twenty chains to a post in the south west corner of the south east [¼] quarter of the south east [¼] quarter of said section; thence northly along the west line of said south east quarter [¼] of the south east quarter [¼] of said section [34] thirty four two [2] chains and [70] seventy links to the center of the Yorkville and Bloomington State road; thence north [43] forty three degrees east along the center of said road [22] twenty two chains and [50] links to a point on the east line of said section thirty four; thence south twelve chains and thirty links to the place of beginning.

Default having been made in the payment of the said sum due on said mortgage as aforesaid and no proceedings at law or otherwise having been instituted to recover the same or any part thereof; now therefore notice is hereby given that by virtue of the power of sale contained in said mortgage and of the statute in such case made and provided the said mortgage will be foreclosed by a sale of said mortgaged premises at public vendue to the highest bidder for cash at the front door of the Court House in Chaska in said county of Carver on the 8th day of January A. D. 1870 at eleven o'clock in the forenoon of that day for the purpose of satisfying the sum then due thereon and secured by said mortgage together with the costs and disbursements of sale and additional sum of twenty five dollars attorneys fees according to the terms of said mortgage.

Chaska, Nov. 22d 1869.

HENRY YOUNG, Mortgagee.
BAXTER & SARGENT, Atty's for Mortgagee.

SHERIFF SALE.

By virtue of an execution issued out of the second Judicial district in and for the County of Ramsey and State of Minnesota in which Frances W. Hutchens is plaintiff and the Board of County Commissioners of the County of Carver defendants to me directed and delivered, I have levied on all of the following described real property as the property of said defendants situated and lying in said County of Carver and described as follows, to-wit: Lots (3, 4, 5, 6, 7 & 8) three, four, five, six, seven and eight, in Block (37) twenty seven in the town site of Chaska according to the plat thereof on record in the office of the Register of Deeds of said County of Carver. Now therefore notice is hereby given that I will sell the aforesaid premises to satisfy said execution and costs, at the front door of the Court House in Chaska in said County of Carver at public auction to the highest bidder for cash on Saturday the 20th day of November A. D. 1869 at one o'clock in the afternoon of that day.

Dated Chaska, Oct. 7th 1869.

F. HECKLIN, Sheriff of Carver County.

Mortgage Sale.

Mortgagors, George E. Bingham and Caroline E. Bingham his wife.

Mortgagee, David Brown.

Date of mortgage, February 10th 1868.

Mortgage recorded in the office for the Registry of Deeds of the County of Carver Minn. on the 29th day of Feb. 1868 at 10 o'clock A. M. in Book "D" of mortgages on pages 265, 266 & 267.

Description of mortgaged premises—the north west quarter of the north east quarter (nw qr of the ne qr) of section twenty seven (27) in township one hundred and sixteen (116) of Range twenty three (23) west, according to government survey; in the County of Carver and State of Minnesota.

Amount claimed to be due at the date of this notice is one hundred and thirty four dollars and sixty two cents ($134,62) and no proceedings at law or otherwise for the collection of said debt or any part thereof having been had or commenced,

Therefore, notice is hereby given, that by virtue of a power of sale contained in said mortgage and recorded therewith, and pursuant to the Statute in such cases made and provided, the said mortgage will be foreclosed, by a sale of said mortgaged premises, to be made at Public Auction or vendue by the Sheriff of said County, at the front door of the Court House in Chaska in said County, on Monday the 13th day of December 1869, at 10 o'clock in the forenoon, to satisfy said debt together with the further sum of twenty five dollars ($25) solicitors fees, according to the terms of said mortgage, and costs and disbursements of sale.

Dated Oct. 26th 1869.

H. J. PECK,
Atty's. for mortgagee.

GUARDIANS SALE.

State of Minnesota, In Probate Court County of Hennepin }

In the matter of the Guardianship of James R. Cummins, Jr. minor.

Notice is hereby given, that by virtue and in pursuance of an order of license made in said matter on the 27th day of August, A. D. 1869, by the Probate Court of said County, the undersigned, guardian of the above named minor, will, on the 6th day of December A. D, 1869, at eleven o'clock A. M. at the front door of the Court House, in the town of Chaska, in Carver County, Minnesota, offer for sale at public vendue all the right and title of the above named James R. Cummins Jr, in and to the above described real estate, situate and being in the aforesaid County of Carver, to wit: north half of the south west quarter; and the south east quarter of the south west quarter of section fourteen, (14) and the north east quarter of the north west quarter of section twenty three (23) town one hundred and fifteen, (115) range twenty six (26)

Terms of sale:—one half cash, and the remainder in one year with interest; the payment to be secured by note and mortgage on the premises.

Dated this 3d day of November, A. D. 1869.

JAMES R. CUMMINS SR.
Guardian of said minor.

SHERIFF'S SALE,

By virtue of an execution issued out of and under the seal of the district Court of the second Judicial district in and for the County of Ramsey and State of Minnesota in which Frances W. Hutchens administrator of John Bassett deceased. Plaintiff and the Board of County Commissioners of the County of Carver defendants to me directed and delivered I have levied on all of the following described real property as the property of said defendants situated and lying in said County of Carver and described as follows to-wit: Lots (3, 4, 5, 6, 7 & 8.) three, four, five, six, seven and eight, in block (27) twenty-seven in the town site of Chaska according to the plat thereof on record in the office of the Register of Deeds of said County of Carver. Now therefore notice is hereby given that I will sell the aforesaid premises to satisfy said execution and costs, at the front door of the Court House in chaska in said county of carver at public auction to the highest bidder for cash on Saturday the 13th day of November A. D. 1869 at one o'clock in the afternoon of that day.

Dated Chaska Sept. 29th 1869.

F. HECKLIN, Sheriff of Carver Co.

The above sale is postponed to Saturday the 20th day of November 1869 at the same hour and place.

Chaska, Nov. 13th 1869.

F. HECKLIN, Sheriff of Car. Co.

FALL & WINTER GOODS
Just Received From
Chicago
And Milwaukee.
AT THE
The New Store
OF
HENRY YOUNG

DOMESTIC AND FANCY
DRY GOODS
CLOTHING
Hats, Caps, Furs, Boots, and Shoes, &
Groceries. Cash paid for farmers produce.

Call At

"THE OLD POST OFFICE STAND"

G. A. DUTOIT.

Wholesale and retail dealer in

Drugs, Paints, Oils,
Perfumery, patent Medicines Etc. Window Glass, Fancy Articles, toys and Notios, Pure Wines and Catawba Brandy for medical purposes.

CARVER MINN.

JOHN DUNN,
Real Estate Agent.
CHASKA .... MINN.

Has large tracts of land for sale in Carver, McLeod and Hennepin Counties.

SALOON!

CARVER - - - MINN.

The best of Liquors, Segars and Beer constantly kept on hand. Farmers call on me.

PETER BUTTENHOFF.

Plow And Wagon Factory AT WACCNA

FRED LUTZ PROPRIETOR.

I would respectfully inform the citizens of Carver County that I now manufacture as good and durable plows as are made in the Union, and offer them as cheap as can be purchased at St. Paul. Also Wagons. Blacksmithing done to order on short notice.

J. R. BARRETT & CO., Proprietors,
MANCHESTER, N. H.
LORD & SMITH,
CHICAGO.
General Agents for the Northwestern States.

[illegible], State Agent, St. Paul, Minn.

WALTHAM WATCHES

For a few months past we have advertised the above Watches at extremely low prices, and the result has been most satisfactory. Our plan has been to sell the genuine Waltham Watch, in Solid Gold or Silver Cases only, and at a very small profit; giving the purchaser every opportunity of examination and comparison, and with [illegible] that if the Watch does not prove satisfactory, it can be exchanged or the money refunded.

These Watches are, without exception, the most perfect specimens of fine [illegible] ever produced [illegible]. Each and every part is made by machinery [illegible] the most accurate and [illegible].

Compared with foreign watches, they possess many advantages, [illegible].

Silver Hunting Watches, [illegible]
Silver Hunting Watches, 18 karat [illegible]
Gold Hunting Watches, [illegible]

[illegible]

Every Watch [illegible] by special certificate from the American Watch [illegible].

We send them by express [illegible] to the purchaser to open the package and examine the Watch before paying, and if afterwards it does not prove satisfactory it can be exchanged or the money will be cheerfully refunded.

Please state that you saw this in the Chaska Herald.

Address, in full, HOWARD & CO.,
No. 619 Broadway, N. Y.

THE CONSTITUTIONAL UNION.

The above is the title of the only Democratic newspaper published at the National Capital, and which is one of the most able expounders of Democratic doctrine there is in the world.—We would say to our Democratic, as well as Republican friends, if you want the best Democratic weekly journal published, send for this. The following unexampled terms are offered to subscribers:

Single copy,	$2 00
Two copies,	3 75
Five copies,	9 00
Ten copies,	17 50
Twenty copies,	33 00
Fifty copies one year to one address	75 00
One hundred copies, to one address	150 00

Terms of subscription invariably in advance.

Any person who will send a club of twenty subscribers, with thirty dollars, will be sent an extra copy of the paper.

Subscribers had better, for their own security, obtain post office orders, where such are procurable, in preference to all other kinds of [illegible].

Address, THOMAS B. FLORENCE
Editor Constitutional Union,
Box 34, Washington City Postoffice.

[illegible]

[illegible] New York Evening Post.

Harper's Weekly may be unreservedly declared the best newspaper in America.—New York Independent.

The articles upon public questions which appear in Harper's Weekly from week to week form a remarkable series of brief political essays. They are distinguished by clear and pointed statement, by good common sense, by independence and breadth of view. They are the expression of mature conviction, high principle and strong feeling, and take their place among the best newspaper writing of the times.—North American Review, Boston, Mass.

SUBSCRIPTIONS. 1870.

TERMS:

Harper's Weekly, one year, $4 00

An extra copy of either the Magazine, Weekly, or Bazar will be supplied gratis for every club of five subscribers at $4 each, in one remittance; or, six copies for $20, without extra copy.

Subscriptions to Harper's Magazine, Weekly, and Bazar, to one address for one year, $10; or, two of Harper's Periodicals, to one address for one year, $7.

Back numbers can be supplied at any time.

[illegible]

The postage on Harper's Weekly is 20 cents a year, which must be paid at the subscriber's post-office.

Address HARPER & BROTHERS, N. Y.

INSURANCE.

We would respectfully notify our friends and patrons that the

UNDERWRITER'S AGENCY
OF NEW YORK.

(Composed of the oldest German Insurance Co. in the U. S. and three other Companies,) is now represented by F. E. Du Toit, who will be prepared to insure Farm property and Stocks of Goods in this and the surrounding Counties at the LOWEST RATES.

Cash Assets, $3,555 000

Losses promptly paid.

Germania, Hanover, Niagara, and Republic Ins. Co., of New York.

A. STODDARD, Gen'l. Agt.

F. E. De TOIT, Local Agent, Chaska.

Estray—Reward

Strayed from the premises of the subscriber in the village of Chaska, one yearling horse colt, of iron grey color; with double main. Said colt is of unusual size. A liberal reward will be given for his return or information leading to his recovery.

Chaska July 21st 1869.

PHILIP HENK.

W. S. COMBS. J. E. WHITNEY.

WEINMANN & LOSSEN.

GENERAL

Fire and Life Insurance Agents.

Also Collection Agents.

Carver, Minn.

Bride And Bridegroom.

Essays for Young Men on the interesting relation of Bridegroom to Bride, in the institution of Marriage.—A Guide to matrimonial felicity, and true happiness. Sent by mail in sealed letter envelopes free of charge. Address, Howard Association, Box P, Philadelphia, Pa.

THE LADY'S FRIEND.

Two Months Gratis!!

The Lady's Friend announces the following Novelets for 1870: Did he Forget Her?" by Louise Chandler Moulton; "The Cameron Aunt by Elizabeth Prescott author of "Between Two," &c.; "Solid Silver; or, Christie Dean's Bridal Gifts." by Amanda M. Douglas, author of "The Debarry Fortune," &c., with numerous shorter stories by a brilliant galaxy of lady writers.

A finely executed steel engraving, a handsome double-page, finely colored fashion plate, and a large assortment of wood-cuts illustrating the fashions, fancy-work, &c., are given in every number.

It will give a popular piece of Music in every number.

Portraits of Distinguished Authors.

The January number will contain portraits engraved on steel; of Mrs. Henry Wood, Florence Percy, Louise Chandler Prescott, Amanda M. Douglas, Mrs. Margaret Hosmer, and August Bell.

New subscribers who send in their names for 1870 before the first of November shall receive the November and December numbers of this year in addition, making 14 months in all. And new subscribers sending in their names by the first of December shall receive the magnificent December holiday number, making 13 months in all.

TERMS.—$2 50 a year, two copies, $4; four copies $6; five copies (and one gratis) $8. One copy of the Lady's Friend and The Saturday Evening Post, $4.

A copy of the large and beautiful Premium Steel Engraving—"Taking the Measure of the Wedding Ring,"—engraved in England at a cost of $2,000, will be sent to every full ($2 50) subscriber, and to every person sending a club. This engraving is a gem of art. Address

DEACON & PETERSON,
319 Walnut street, Phila.

—Specimen copies sent for ten cents.—

Dr. C. B. AMES

PHYSICIAN AND SURGEON.

WATERTOWN . . . MINN.

Office at Lewis Drug Store. Offers his service to the citizens of Watertown and vicinity, and can always be found day or night ready to attend calls.

Court House Saloon.

JOHN ROSS .... Proprietor.

Brick Saloon near Court House. Best of Liquors and Cigars always kept on hand.

The celebrated Shakopee Lager Beer always "fresh tapped."

St. Paul and Sioux City Railroad.

UPWARD TRAINS.

Leaves.		Leaves.
Leave St. Paul	7:45 a. m.	and 3:45 p. m.
Arrive Mendota	8:10 a. m.	and 4:10 p. m.
Ar. Shakopee	10:10 a. m.	and 5:30 p. m.
Ar. Merriam	10:30 a. m.	and 5:50 p. m.
Ar. Brentwood	11:10 a. m.	and 6:01 p. m.
Ar. Belle Plaine	11:35 a. m.	and 6:12 p. m.
Ar. Blakely	12:35 p. m.	and 6:37 p. m.
Ar. Henderson	1:15 p. m.	and 7:08 p. m.
Ar. Lesueur	1:40 p. m.	and 7:18 p. m.
Ar. Ottawa	2:10 p. m.	and 7:35 p. m.
Ar. St. Peter	2:40 p. m.	and 7:55 p. m.
Ar. Mankato	3:40 p. m.	and 8:30 p. m.

DOWNWARD TRAINS.

Leave Mankato	6:30 a. m.	and 9:00 a. m.
Arrive St. Peter	7:05 a. m.	and 9:55 a. m.
Ar. Ottawa	7:22 a. m.	and 10:30 a. m.
Ar. Lesueur	7:40 a. m.	and 11:05 a. m.
Ar. Henderson	7:55 a. m.	and 11:35 a. m.
Ar. Blakely	8:15 a. m.	and 12:15 p. m.
Ar. Belle Plaine	8:35 a. m.	and 12:50 p. m.
Ar. Brentwood	8:51 a. m.	and 1.30 p. m.
Ar. Merriam	9:10 a. m.	and 2:01 p. m.
Ar. Shakopee	9:25 a. m.	and 2:30 p. m.
Ar. Mendota	10:30 a. m.	and 3:35 p. m.
Ar. St. Paul	11.10 a. m.	and 4:30 p. m.

Trains on this road make close connection at Mendota with trains on Milwaukee and Saint Paul Railroad for Minneapolis, Owatonna, Winona, and all points South and East; and at Saint Peter with Minnesota Stage Company's Line of stages for New Ulm, and at Mankato for all points West and Southwest.

Tickets can be procured at the Union Ticket Office, Corner Third and Jackson Streets, and at the Depot, West St. Paul.

JOHN F. LINCOLN,
Superintendent

COMBS & WHITNEY

WHOLESALE & RETAIL
Booksellers and Stationers
AND THE

Emporium for views of Minnesota and other Scenery, Brackets, Engravings, Frames, Chromos, &c. &c.

174 Third, Corner Cedar Street
Saint Paul. Minn.

UNION HOTL.

CHASKA. - - - - - - MINN

A good bar in connection with the house. Also good Stabling.

WM. OCHS, Propr.

For Ladies Only.

For an article having a remarkable sale, address Mrs. MORGAN, 120 Fulton St., N. Y.

Fresh Arrival
AT
LINENFELSER & FAB'R
OF
DRY GOODS
Clothing, Hats, Caps, Boots and Shoes &c.
GROCERIES & PROVISIONS
AT
"At the Brick Store."

Valley Herald.

F. E. DU TOIT Proprietor. TERMS, $1 50, Per Annum.

VOLUME 8 CHASKA, MINNESOTA, FRIDAY, DEC. 10, 1869. NUMBER 16

The Valley Herald

Official County Paper.

BY F. E. DU TOIT.

CHASKA FRIDAY DECEMBER 10 1869.

PRESIDENTS MESSAGE.

The annual Message of the President was transmitted over the wires in due time. It is a fair document and was probably written by Secretary Fish. We shall publish a synopsis of the same next week. The reports of the head of departments were also transmitted as usual and are unusually attractive.

THE MESSAGE.

Opinions of the New York Newspapers,

NEW YORK, Dec. 7.—The Times says the Message is one of good news throughout.

The World says this is the weakest Message ever sent to Congress by an American President. It considers that the Message settles the Cuban insurrection against the patriots, and on financial affairs is too quixotic and chimerical for [illegible] consideration.

The Tribune regards the Message as one of the wisest and most judicious ever transmitted to Congress, and predicts its hearty approval by the American people.

The Herald says that Grant's message is that of an honest, clear-headed, practical man. In the reconstruction business he simply looks to the execution of the laws. His plea for the funding of the debt and gradual return to specie payment, will meet with the general approbation of this country. It considers the Message noncommittal on Cuban affairs.

ST. LOUIS.

Work on the Mississippi Bridge—Festival of Immaculate Conception.

ST. LOUIS, Dec. 8.—Work on the eastern pier of the bridge across the river at this place is progressing rapidly. Two hundred and one hundred cubic yards of masonry have been laid in the past five days. The pier has reached the bottom of the river, and to-day hand pumps were put to work, and the sand and water beneath the pier is being rapidly pumped out; the caison has now only about 39 feet to sink before reaching the bed rock.

A festival of Immaculate Conception has been celebrated to-day, in the Catholic churches. The most solemn exposition of the scene has been continued all day. Altars were ornamented with the most beautiful and costly ornaments, and churches have been thronged with devout worshippers.

Woman's Suffrage—Railroad Compromise.

NEWARK, Dec. 8.—The Woman's State Suffrage Association commenced its annual meeting this evening. A large audience was present. Lucy Stone presided, and addresses were made by Cella Burleigh, Mr. Blackwell and Phoebe Hanford.

The New Jersey Railroad Company have compromised with Mrs. Lane, whose husband was put off the cars on Aackensack bridge and drowned, by paying damages.

The Civil War in Hayti.

NEW YORK, Dec. 7.—The Herald's dispatches from Hayti says Salnave is making vigorous preparations to stand against the combined forces of the Revolutionary leaders. The steamer purchased by the minister for the Haytien government, engaged and sunk the steamer Arubonel, belonging to the Revolutionist. The Insurance are still in possession of Cape Haytien, where they also hold captive the Steamer Petion and Salnave. The pickets had again attacked the garrison, but were repulsed.

During the year ending December 1st, the Milwaukee & St. Paul R. R. has carried from LaCrosse to Milwaukee, four million, six hundred and seventy-five thousand, eight hundred and forty four (4,675,844) bushels of wheat, and one hundred and forty-four thousand, two hundred and thirteen (144,213) barrels of flour! Of this over two-thirds has been handled since the 1st day of September. Nearly all of this was produced in Minnesota.

—The report of the Public Printer for the year ending September 30, 1869, shows that the whole expenditures of the printing office in that year were $1,507,204, which is about $200,000 more than the expense of last year.

HOME ITEMS.

HERALD AGENT CARVER—G. A. DuToit.

Time Table of M. V. R. R.

The following indicates the time for the arrival of trains at Merriam Station:

Up Trains.........10:00 A. M.........3:30 P. M.
Down Trains.....9:00 A. M.........2:05 P. M.

J. F. Lincoln, Supt.

MARRIED.

By Judge of Probate Dec. 4th, Peter Peterson to Mrs. Caroline Thompson both of Carver County.

MARRIED.

By Justice Chas. Johnson, at Carver, Tuesday Evening, Dec. 7th 1869, Mr. Thos. Newmann, to Miss. Josie Weinmann, daughter of Jos. Weinmann.

The wedding was a brilliant one and was attended by the many friends of both Mr. Weinmann and Newman. After the conclusion of the ceremony the happy couple were congratulated by their many friends, who wished them joy and a long life of happiness. The supper prepared under the supervision of Mrs. Weinmann was well worthy the occasion and its merit were well tested by those present. We wish the happy couple a long life and all the blessings vouchsafed to mankind.

NOTICE.—Dr. C. E. Rogers of Carver, is duly authorized to receive subscriptions for the HERALD and to receipt for the same.

WEATHER.—We have been enjoying remarkably mild weather the past week. The snow has entirely disappeared and the ground is once more cleared of her snowy mantle.

COUNTY COMMISSIONERS.—The board of County Commissioners were in session from Tuesday morning until Thursday evening, three days. During that time a large amount of business was transacted that will appear in our columns next week. This is the last session of Commissioners Du Toit and Gothelf, who are succeeded by Commissioners Barthel and Weisbecker, gentleman that will undoubtedly give good satisfaction. With our able board of Commissioners we expect that our county affairs will be administered honestly and with economy.

TAX NOTICE.—We call attention to the tax notice of the Treasurer in another column. It will be seen that he will call "around" and see you soon.—Have your "gelt" ready.

NEW YEAR BALL.—We are informed that Peter Iltis will give a grand new year ball at his place, the National Hotel. Be prepared to attend and dance the new year into existence.

PERSONAL.—With pleasure we welcome Hon. C. H. Lienau as a fellow citizen of our County, From a notice elsewhere it will be seen that he has gone into business with his brother at Watertown. We hope he will find his present business more profitable than journalism. Mr. Lienau was the founder of the "Volksblatt" and its able editor.

Commissioners Griffin, Kelly, Reusse and Gothelf were in town during the week on duty.

Supt. Peck of Watertown also made our city a short visit.

J. H. Brown of Shakopee swung around on Tuesday. Also Mr De ville of Watertown.

As the legislature will convene in about one month we would advise those of our readers who desire any special or general laws passed by the "assembled wisdom of the State" to make known the fact to our Senator Col. Baxter or our Representative J. E. Cullen Esq. whom we presume will do all in their power for the enactment of such laws as may be for the interest of their constituents and the public generally.

IN Justice Court before J. A. Sargent, Swan Bengtson, J. H. Johnson and Niels Thompson were complained of by Ferdinand Strocker for assault and Battery. The two first were fined, Thompson discharged. We understand Johnson paid, Bengtson appealed to Dist. Court.

—The Probate Judge sent to the Hospital for the Insane at St. Peters. Mrs. Caroline Conrad of Watertown.

APPOLOGY.—Our time was taken up on the County Board during the greater part of the week; which is our excuse for the scarcity of local news. Our time being up as a member of that honorable body, we can pledge better behaviour hereafter.

WATERTOWN MILL.

By reference to our advertising column, it will be seen that Wm. Dressler, well and favorably known as one of the former owners and managers of Union Mill, Watertown, has disposed of his interest to Chas. H. Lienau, brother of the former joint owner.

The mill enjoyed a good reputation under the former management and from our acquaintance with Mr. C. H. Lienau we are confident that the Union Mill will run on in the even tenor of its way and if anything enjoy greater confidence.

We cheerfully recommend the firm to the public and wish the new firm unlimited success.

PACKARD'S MONTHLY.—The December number of this popular young men's magazine is upon our table. It has a choice number of articles contributed by some of the best writers of the country. Its editorial department also contain some valuable and interesting articles. Address, S. S. Packard, Pub. 937 Broadway New York.

CHRISTMAS BALL.—We are informed that Mr. Ochs, of the Union Hotel designs giving a Ball on Christmas evening. Govern yourselves accordingly.

PRICE OF GRAIN.—Wheat commands 55 cents per bushel and barley from 55 to 60 per bushel.

Carver Items.

Correspondence.

MISSING.—There is a case of "mysterious disappearance" in McLeod County, near the Carver County Line. The particulars are as follows; for which we are indebted to Mr. Weinmann, who was there a few days ago,

Christian Bigler, an old settler, and well known in McLeod County, and who formerly resided in Saint Paul left his house at day light, on Friday four weeks ago, for the purpose of going to Glencoe to get a Doctor to come and visit some number of his family who were sick, and has not been seen or heard from since.

There has been some 30 or 40 men (friends and neighbors) hunting for him, but as yet no trace of him has been discovered. We understand some suspicious of foul play are entertained by his family.

There is quite an excitement in the neighborhood and every effort possible will be made to ferrit out the mystery.

RECOVERING.—We are glad to hear that our old friend Geo. Slocum, who was so badly injured by a thrashing machine a few weeks ago is getting along finely. We hope Geo. will be around as usual soon,

PERSONAL.—Our friend Jas. Slocum of Young America was in town on Tuesday,

Julius Ackerman of the same place was also here during the week.

Isaac Porter an "old time boy" of Shakopee made us a call on Wednesday.

J Q Spaulding of St. Paul was around on his "30 day trip" as usual

AN ACCOMMODATING AGT.—"Merriam Station" on the Minn. V. R. R. can boast of having one of the best and most accommodating agent on the whole route. We mean Jas. Long Esq. always at his post, pleasant and agreeable, (which is something unusual for those important chaps.) We hope the "powers that be" will see fit to leave Mr. Long at the above named place, as a better man for the position cannot be found.

A CALL.—Col. C. W. Griggs, of St. Paul was in town one day last week.—It seems natural to see the Col. about again.

WHEAT.—This article is bringing 55 and 60 cents per bushel. Barley 50 cents and Potatoes 75 and 80. Corn 50 cents. Pork 7 to 9.

LINIMENT.—That celebrated "Rheumatic Liniment" of Chas. Steizers, is kept for sale by G. A. Du Toit, who is agent for Carver County.

CONTRACT LET.—The Board of Town Supervisors, have let the contract for building the Bridge across Carver Creek on the Glencoe Road, to Peter Michels, for $275.

This is a much needed improvement, and Mr. Michels is just the man to undertake the job.

—McFarland has retained John Graham, the eminent criminal lawyer as his counsel. The letters intercepted by McFarland have been placed in Mr. Graham's hands, but no one is permitted to see them. It is asserted, however, by persons who have seen these letters that there were a number of persons interested in what they call a plot to alienate the affections of Mrs. McFarland from her husband. Several of these persons are said to occupy high positions in social life, and to be well known in the journalistic and literary circles of the city. Two of the participators it is said, married women, and both are referred to by name in Richardson's own handwriting as "capital intriguers, who are helping me."

TAX NOTICE.

The Tax duplicate for the year A. D. 1869, is now placed into my hands for collection. And I will attend at the following times and places for the purpose of collecting said taxes for the year 1869.

In Hollywood Town at M. Kellys on Tuesday 4th of January 1870.
In Watertown at the Drug Store on Wednesday and Thursday the 5th and 6th days of Jany. 1870.
In Waconia, on Friday the 7th of Jany. 1870.
In Laketown, at M. Walk, on Saturday the 8th of Jany. 1870.
In Camden, at J. Morrills on Tuesday the 11th of Jany. 1870.
In Young America, at H. Fabels on Wednesdy and Thursday the 12th and 13th day of Jany 1870.
In Benton, at H. Borghards on Friday the 14th of Jany. 1870.
In Benton, at George Bleichners on Saturday the 15th of Jany. 1870.
In Hancock, at the Saw Mill, Monday the 17th of Jany. 1870
In San Francisco, at J. A. Hillstrom, Tuesday the 18th day of Jany. 1870.
In Dahlgreen at P. Seigels on Wednesday the 19th of Jany. 1870.
In Chanhassen, at Wm. Sarver on Thursday the 20th of Jany. 1870.
In Carver, at the Hotel on Friday the 21st of Jany. 1870.

Afterwards I will attend at the County Seat to receive taxes from those wishing to pay the same.

A Penalty of 5 per cent will be charged according to law after the 1st day of February 1870, on personal property tax.

The amount of taxes levied on the dollar valuation are as follows:

State Taxes,	3	Mills.
Common School Tax,	2	"
Co. Revenue Tax.	6½	"
Co. Special Tax.	2	"
Co. Poor Tax.	2	"
Co. Interest and Sinking Fund.	3	"

TOWN TAXES.

Benton Town, Road and Bridge	4	mills.
Camden Town, Road and Bridge,	5½	"
Carver Town, Road and Bridge,	10	"
Chaska Town, Road and Bridge,	21	"
Chanhassen Town, Road and Bridge	2	"
Hollywood, Town tax,	2	mills.
Laketown, Town Tax, Road and Bridge.	8	"
Hancock, Town Tax,	4	"
San Francisco, Road and Bridge, Town Tax,	5½	"
Watertown, Town Tax, Town & Bounty,	6½	"
Waconia, Town Tax.	4	"
Dahlgreen Town, Road and Bridge.	15	"
Young America, Road and Bridge, Town Tax,	7	mills.

SPECIAL SCHOOL DISTRICT TAX

No.		mills.	No.		mills.
1	4	mills.	30	11	mills.
2	10	"	31	8	"
3	4	"	32	10	"
5	9½	"	33	10	"
6	6½	"	34	8	"
7	6½	"	36	10	"
8	3½	"	39	4	"
10	10	"	40	13	"
11	3	"	41	20	"
12	7½	"	42	7½	"
13	7	"	43	5	"
14	6½	"	44	10	"
15	3	"	45	5	"
17	6½	"	46	3	"
18	4	"	47	3	"
19	11	"	48	4½	"
20	4	"	49	3	"
22	2½	"	50	4	"
24	4	"	51	20	"
26	4	"	52	7½	"
27	10	"	53	14	"
28	10	"	54	4	"
29	1	"	55	14	"
			56	11	"

Chaska, Dec. 4th, 1869.

JOHN DUNN. Treasurer of Carver County

Proposal,

TO WHOM IT MAY CONCERN.

In pursuance of authority in me vested, by the Board of Commissioners for the County of Carver, I will receive proposals to board, cloth and support, the paupers of Carver County, by the week, for the term of one year, from and after the acceptance of such proposal. Compensation to be made by the County, to the person whose bid is accepted. The right is reserved to reject any and all bids.

Proposals to be made within two months from the date of this notice.

Dated Chaska Sept. 28th 1869.

PETER WEBOG, County Auditor

Estray.

Came into my enclosure in the town of Hancock, Carver Co. one light red cow, the owner will please come forward prove property, pay charges and take the same away.

ANDREW NILSON.

Ohaska Jn 28.

TYPOGRAPHICAL.

Selected Miscellany.

ENTOMBED ALIVE.

...me should fall and block me up? I seized my rifle and sprang toward the outlet. The storm was preferable to my place of shelter.

"Heaven have mercy!" I cried, as I felt the movements of the cliff above me; and then, to my horror and despair, the great boulder, loosened by the torrents of rain, slipped from its resting place, and ere I could escape hemmed me in in perfect darkness.

I was entombed alive!

The horror of my situation came upon me with such force that I did what I never did before nor since—I fainted away.

How long I remained insensible I know not; but when at last I came to myself again I thought it was a terrible dream. But the illusion soon wore off, and the stern reality was before me, and I began calmly to think of what chance I had of escaping from my living tomb.

Very little indeed was there to hope in the prospect before me. No prison bars were as strong as those that held me back from the outer world, that I had never prized so highly as I now began to do.—There seemed no possible hope; for man, with his unaided strength, could never move the huge rock that sealed up the entrance to my sepulchre.

A faint ray of light came in one side of my prison door, and through the crevice came the sound of the roaring water, swollen to double its usual volume, down in the bed of the ravine. The crevice would give me air, and would tell me when night would come and go, so long as life might remain to me. My companions would doubtless search long for me, and could I not make myself heard should they chance to pass near? This gave me a ray of hope that I hugged to my heart as drowning men will, they say, clutch at straws; but my heart again sank within me as the roar of the torrent filled my ears. No human...

[illegible]

A KLEPTOMANIAC.

The Propensity to Steal Inherent.

[illegible]

NORTHWEST IRON-MINERS.

Society Around Lake Superior—Outlook of the Future.

[illegible]

THE FUTURE.

[illegible]

False Hair.

[illegible]

It Plunges His Family into Ruin.

[illegible]

Special Notices.

NEW YORK.

[illegible market quotations]

CHICAGO.

[illegible market quotations]

ST. LOUIS.

[illegible market quotations]

MILWAUKEE.

[illegible market quotations]

—A Peoria, Ill., policeman, the other day, noticing a person that looked ... suspicion ... Tell... and in the ... pulled off four coats, two vests, four pairs of pants, and eleven shirts.

U. S.

[illegible] ... NATIONAL PUBLISHING CO., Publishers, St. Louis, Mo.

AGENTS WANTED FOR

Paris BY Sunlight and Gaslight

A WORK descriptive of the MYSTERIES, VIRTUES, VICES, SPLENDORS and CRIMES of the CITY OF PARIS.

It tells how Paris has become the finest and most Beautiful City in the world ... [illegible] ... Circulars sent free. Address NATIONAL PUBLISHING CO., Chicago, Ill. or St. Louis, Mo.

BEST SEWING MACHINE EXTANT. ... Address WHITNEY MANUFACTURING CO., East Hampton, N. H.

The DOLLAR Sun.

CHAS. A. DANA, Editor.

The cheapest, smartest, and best New York newspaper. ... [illegible] ... I. W. ENGLAND, Publisher Sun, New York.

PEIRCE AND WHALING

STEEL, NAILS, HEAVY HARDWARE AND RAILWAY SUPPLIES

133, 135, 137 & 139 West Water St.

MILWAUKEE.

Goods shipped PROMPTLY, and at LOWEST MARKET RATES, whether ordered PERSONALLY or BY MAIL. We keep in stock SUPERIOR BRANDS of goods only, and guarantee satisfaction to our customers as to QUALITY. PRICE LIST containing valuable tables, and also weekly quotations, mailed to THE TRADE when requested.

$10. WATCHES. $10.

[illegible] ... Broadway, corner Fulton street, New York.

Chicago Business Directory.

The following are among the prominent leading business houses in their several departments:

CARPETINGS.

S. NICKERSON, 215 Lake street, Carpetings, Oil Cloths, and Mattings, Wholesale and Retail. Orders promptly filled.

MILLINERY GOODS.

FISK, D. B. & CO., 53 and 55 Lake st., wholesale dealers in Straw Goods, Millinery, White Goods, Hosiery, Gloves and Fancy Goods, ... Lake street, Chicago.

PAPER AND RAGS.

LAFLIN, BUTLER & CO., Dealers in Paper, Printers' Stock, &c. Cash paid for Rags. ... State street, Chicago.

SHIP CHANDLERY.

GILBERT, HUBBARD & CO., Manilla, tarred, ... steel, and iron wire rope, tar, pitch and oakum, tackle blocks, anchors and chains, 205 S. Water st., Chi.

TWINES AND CORDAGE.

GILBERT, HUBBARD & CO., cotton and flax twines of all kinds, wool sacks and burlaps, nets & seines, tents, covers and flags, 205 S. Water st., Chicago.

Milwaukee Business Directory

The following are among the prominent leading business houses in their several departments:

ARCHITECTS.

E. TOWNSEND MIX, Designs for church and school architecture. Established since 1856.

BOOKS AND STATIONERY.

STRICKLAND & CO., Wholesale Dealers in Books, Stationery, School Books, Paper and Fancy Goods, 242 East Water street, Milwaukee.

BOOTS AND SHOES.

ATKINS, STEELE & WHITE, Exclusive Wholesale Dealers in Boots and Shoes, 304 East Water street, Milwaukee.

COFFEE, SPICES, &C.

W. & J. G. FLINT, Teas, Ground Coffees, Spices, Mustard, Cream Tartar, Blacking, &c., Star Mills, 130 West Water street, Milwaukee.

CROCKERY.

BLAIR & PERSONS, Crockery and Cutlery, Looking Glasses, Lamps, and Curtain Papers, ... East Water street.

DRUGGISTS.

J. H. TESCH & CO., Wholesale and Retail Manufacturing and Analytical Chemists. Keep Photographic Stock, ... Spring street.

ENGRAVERS.

C. H. CLARKE, Fine Brands, Seals, Stencil Dies and Tools, Key Check Dies, Gold Pens ... Box 1006, Milwaukee.

FRUITS AND NUTS.

A. B. BLANCHARD & CO., General Dealers and Commission Merchants in Foreign and Domestic, Green and Dried Fruits, Can Goods, Nuts, &c., ... East Water street, Milwaukee.

FURNITURE.

YANKEE FURNITURE STORE, Matthews Bros., Manufacturers and Dealers in Furniture and Upholstered Goods, ... East Water street.

GROCERIES.

LEDYARD & WOOD, fine Groceries, Wines, Liquors, Cigars and Canned Fruits. Agents for Powell's Ale and Royal Baking Powder. ... Milwaukee street.

DUTCHER, BALL & GOODRICH, Wholesale Grocers, 214 & 216 East Water st., Milwaukee.

GOODRICH & TERRY, Wholesale Grocers, ... East Water street, Milwaukee.

HARDWARE.

R. HANEY, Importer and Wholesale Dealer in Shelf Hardware, iron, Steel, Nails, &c., ... East Water street, Milwaukee.

JEWELRY.

C. H. PREUSSER & BRO., Wholesale and Retail Dealers in Watches, Clocks, Jewelry, &c. Established in 1851. ... East Water street.

LUMBER.

R. W. PIERCE & CO., Wholesale and Retail Dealers in Lumber, Lath, Shingles, Pickets, Cedar Posts, &c. Office ... West Water street, corner Sycamore, Milwaukee.

MARBLE WORKS.

N. MERRILL & CO., ... Spring street, wholesale Dealers and Manufacturers of all kinds of Marble Work, Granite Burial Plots, &c.

NOTIONS.

H. S. MANVILLE, Notions and White Goods, ... Milwaukee.

PHOTOGRAPHERS.

H. S. BROWN, ... Photographer, ... Milwaukee.

STATIONERY.

NOONAN & McNAB, Dealers in all kinds of Papers, Cards, ... Stationery, ... Milwaukee.

TOBACCO & CIGARS.

F. ADAMS & CO., Manufacturers and Wholesale Dealers in Tobacco, Snuff and Cigars, ... Milwaukee.

$25 A DAY made at home.

... entirely new articles for Agents. ... Address ... Alfred, Me.

LET EVERYBODY ...

... PACKARD & CO., ... Cleveland, Ohio.

For Sale by most Druggists Everywhere. ...

TOWLE'S PATENT

Grade & Drainage Level, Price only $15.

... Broadway, New York.

CURIOUS HOW STRANGE!

... Hanover, Pa.

THE HINKLEY FAMILY KNITTING MACHINE

PRICE $30.

... 176 Broadway, New York.

The celebrated Imitation

GOLD WATCHES! AND JEWELRY.

Collins Metal

... C. E. COLLINS & CO., ... New York.

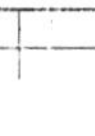

NERVOUS AND MIXED ... Attention paid to diseases of WOMEN.

J. B. LIPPINCOTT & CO.'S MAGAZINES for 1870.

Now is the Time to Subscribe. Send for Specimen Copies before selecting your periodicals for the new year.

Lippincott's Magazine.

An Illustrated Monthly of Literature, Science and Education.

Yearly Subscription, $4.00.

"Lippincott well maintains its hold upon the public favor. It is one of the most sprightly, varied, and interesting monthlies."—*Charleston Courier.* Liberal arrangements have been made for the forthcoming volume.

The Sunday Magazine.

A Monthly of Recreation and Instruction. Profusely Illustrated.

Yearly Subscription, $4.00.

"A perusal of this single number (Oct.) will satisfy everybody that this is exactly the sort of periodical, instructive and serious, but free from sectional prejudice, to introduce into the family, particularly where there are young people."—*Philadelphia Press.*

Good Words.

Yearly Subscription only $2.75.

"Good Words is in every respect a first-class monthly, its contributions being from the pens of the most able writers of England. It is now by far the most popular magazine issued in that country, and is already favorably known here.

Good Words for the Young

A Monthly Magazine for Young People. Profusely Illustrated.

Yearly Subscription only $2.50.

We pronounce it undoubtedly the first of juvenile periodicals. We have seen nothing of its class that can compare with it in the beauty, variety, and good taste of the reading matter, nor that approaches it in the number and excellence of its illustrations."—*Balt. Statesman.*

The FOUR MAGAZINES to one address, $12.25 per annum. SPECIMEN NUMBER of any one of the above mailed on receipt of 35 cents, or one each for 1.35 cents.

A FULL PROSPECTUS of the above, with CLUB RATES and PREMIUM LISTS mailed on application.

Address J. B. LIPPINCOTT & CO., Publishers, 715 and 717 Market street, Philadelphia.

BURNETT'S COCOAINE

THE HUMAN HAIR.

The Inventors of COCOAINE—knowing that, when loss of hair occurs, it is generally from that part of the head where the greatest heat is necessarily generated, and that animal fats by their nature induce heat rather than alleviate it—turning their attention and pharmaceutical science towards Vegetable Oils as the basis of a medicament to promote the growth and preserve the beauty of the Hair. The Olive, Cocoa, or

COCOA-NUT OILS,

presented itself most strongly as possessing many properties peculiarly adapted for the purpose. By a scientific selection of other ingredients, ... [illegible]

No Other Compound

possesses the peculiar properties which so exactly suit the various conditions of the human hair. ... [illegible]

Dandruff.

[illegible] ... A. A. FULLER.

Baldness.

[illegible] ... M. T. BALDWIN.

[illegible] ... JOSEPH HILL, JR.

Loss of Hair.

[illegible] ... SUSAN R. POPE.

Hair Dressing.

[illegible] ... FRANK LESLIE.

[illegible] ... J. O. MITCHELL.

A Remarkable Case.

[illegible] ... WM. S. EDDY.

BURNETT'S COCOAINE is the BEST and CHEAPEST Hair-Dressing in the world. It promotes the GROWTH OF THE HAIR, and is entirely free from all Irritating matter. ... All unauthorized use of this Trade-Mark will be promptly prosecuted.

Manufacturers and Proprietors, - - No. 27 Central St., Boston, Mass.

FOR SALE BY DRUGGISTS EVERYWHERE.

Agents Wanted

We offer a new practical work needed by all business men. ... WESTERN PUBLICATION CO., 37 Clark St., Chicago, Ill.

DR. LANGLEY'S

A very superior regulating Tonic, imparting vigor and strength to the constitution—A thorough

PURIFIER OF THE BLOOD,

a regulator of nervous force, and a powerful sustainer of health against the encroachments of disease. ... [illegible]

DYSPEPSIA OR INDIGESTION,

[illegible]

FEVER AND AGUE,

[illegible]

PLANTATION AGUE CURE.

[illegible] ... Langley's Cathartic Pills, $1 a bottle.

PULMONIC REMEDY,

[illegible]

MANUFACTURED ONLY BY

The Rocky Mountain Bitters Company,

... Fulton Street, N. Y.

Sold by all Druggists and Grocers throughout the country.

COMMON SENSE!!!

WANTED—AGENTS, ... to sell the only GENUINE IMPROVED COMMON SENSE FAMILY SEWING MACHINE. Price only $18. ... [illegible]

WOMEN OF NEW YORK;

or, the Under-world of the Great City. ... [illegible] ... N. Y. BOOK CO., ... Nassau street, N. Y.

TO THE WORKING CLASS.—We are now prepared to furnish all classes with constant employment at home, ... [illegible] ... E. C. ALLEN & CO., Augusta, Maine.

KNIT-KNIT-KNIT

AGENTS WANTED everywhere to sell the AMERICAN KNITTING MACHINE, the only practical Family Knitting Machine ever invented. ... AMERICAN KNITTING MACHINE CO., Boston, Mass., or St. Louis, Mo.

WORDS OF WISDOM to Young Men on the Ruling Passion in Youth and Early Manhood, ... HOWARD ASSOCIATION, Box P, Philadelphia, Pa.

FOR THE HAIR. CHALFANT'S COCO CREAM

It is purely vegetable, contains no alcohol, sulphur, lead or mineral ingredient; is clean, highly perfumed and different from any other article. ... BURNHAMS & VAN SCHAACK, CHICAGO, Wholesale Agents. Sold by all druggists.

ASTONISHING!

MADAME LA RUE can produce, by means of the horoscope, a true picture of your future husband or wife, ... [illegible] ... Address, in confidence, M. LE RUE, Drawer 2082, Chicago, Ill.

AGENTS

Five Dollars will buy the Fairy Sewing Machine ... [illegible] ... Fairy Sewing Machine Co., Chicago, Illinois.

WANTED.

Building Paper

THE

PATENT

BUILDING PAPER,

FOR

PLASTERING.

Its cost is so trifling that an ordinary house can be covered on all sides for less than

TEN DOLLARS.

Beloit, Wis.

AGENTS WANTED

To Sell Sights and Secrets of

The National

A work descriptive of Washington City; Inside and Outside Unmasked and Exposed. ... JONES, JUNKIN & CO., Publishers.

MILL OWNERS.

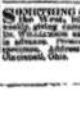

WILL RECEIVE, on application, descriptive ... NORDYKE, MARMON & CO., Richmond, Ind. Dealers in ... Genuine Dutch Anchor Bolting Cloths, &c.

SOMETHING in the Hour for Everybody. ... WILLIAMSON & CANTWELL, Cincinnati, Ohio.

CHICAGO TRIBUNE,

THE GREAT

Radical Republican Organ, and the Leading Newspaper of the West. The Cheapest and Best Family Newspaper in the Land.

Rates of Subscription for the Year 1870.

Daily, one copy, one year ... $12.00

[illegible rates]

On all clubs to the Weekly, in addition to a commission of ... per cent., we offer for the thirteen largest clubs received on or before the 15th day of January, 1870, the following

For the 1st largest Club ... [illegible premium list]

There are thirteen premiums, and they will be mailed to the thirteen parties entitled to them ... [illegible] ...

Address TRIBUNE COMPANY, Chicago, Illinois.

AGENTS WANTED!

TO SELL

Mr. George Ticknor Curtis'

[illegible] ... MOSES WARREN, Gen. Agent, 30 Dearborn St., CHICAGO, ILL.

The Youth's Companion

A WEEKLY PAPER FOR YOUNG PEOPLE AND THE FAMILY.

The Companion is an eight-page weekly Paper, Practical in its character, wide-awake and entertaining.

It gives a great variety of reading, interesting alike to young and old, and has for contributors such writers as

Together with many other well known and popular authors.

... copy.

Publishers Youths' Companion,

151 Washington Street, Boston, Mass.

NOW IS THE TIME TO SUBSCRIBE

FOR THE

THE PEOPLE'S FAVORITE JOURNAL.

New York Weekly.

At present there are

SIX GREAT STORIES

One Story is Begun Every Month.

New subscribers are thus sure of having the commencement of a new continued story, no matter when they subscribe for the

New York Weekly.

Each number of the NEW YORK WEEKLY contains several Beautiful Illustrations, Double the amount of Reading Matter of any paper of its class, and the Sketches, Short Stories, Poems, &c., are by the ablest writers of America and Europe. The

New York Weekly

does not confine its usefulness to amusements, but publishes a great quantity of really Instructive Matter, in the most condensed form. The

N. Y. Weekly Departments

have attained a high reputation for their brevity, excellence, and correctness.

THE PLEASANT PARAGRAPHS are made up of the concentrated wit and humor of many minds.

THE KNOWLEDGE BOX is confined to useful information on all manner of subjects.

THE NEWS ITEMS give in the fewest words the most notable doings all over the world.

THE GOSSIP WITH CORRESPONDENTS contains answers to inquiries upon all imaginable subjects.

AN UNRIVALLED LITERARY PAPER

Each issue contains from EIGHT to TEN STORIES and SKETCHES, and HALF A DOZEN POEMS, in ADDITION to the SIX SERIAL STORIES and the VARIED DEPARTMENTS.

The Terms to Subscribers:

One Year—single copy ... Three Dollars.

" Four copies ($2.50 each) ... Ten Dollars.

" Eight copies ... Twenty Dollars.

Those sending $20 for a club of Eight, all sent at one time, will be entitled to a copy FREE. Getters-up of clubs can afterwards add single copies at $2.50 each.

STREET & SMITH, Proprietors, No. 55 Fulton Street, New York.

DR. WHITTIER.

A REGULAR GRADUATE OF MEDICINE, as diploma at office will show, has been longer engaged in the treatment of Venereal, Sexual and Private Diseases than any other physician in St. Louis. ... [illegible]

The Writings of a Physician whose reputation is Union-wide should be worth reading.

[illegible] ... St. Louis, Mo.

Love! Love!

FULL INSTRUCTIONS.

... VENTRILOQUISM, ... J. F. JAGGERS & CO., Box ..., St. Louis, Mo.

WORK FOR ALL.

A Watch or Sewing Machine Free. ... [illegible] ... Address J. H. BEATON & CO., Waterville, Maine.

TO PRINTERS AND BOOK BINDERS.

SANBORN'S PATENT

PAPER AND BOOK CUTTING MACHINES.

THE LATEST AND THE BEST!

Wherever used, these machines are pronounced in both Principle and Quality, superior to any in the market, without exception.

All are delighted with them.

They cut easy, true, smooth and rapidly, and are strong in every part.

30 inch Lever Cutting Machine	...	$275
30 " Power " "	...	400
32 " Lever " "	...	[illegible]
32 " Hand or Power "	...	[illegible]
34 " Power, (very heavy and strong)	...	[illegible]

We have very many endorsements of all the machines speaking of them with unqualified praise.

Send for Catalogues and Full Descriptions.

SANBORN BROTHERS, 78 Duane Street, N. Y.

American Patent Co.

For Introducing and Negotiating Valuable Patents. Office: 164 Lake Street, Chicago, Ill.

L. J. FARWELL. E. A. ELLSWORTH. D. J. POWERS.

CHEAPEST PAPER IN THE WORLD.— ... UNION BANNER, Belfast, Maine.

LORILLARD'S

YACHT CLUB SMOKING TOBACCO is everywhere pronounced by competent judges to be superior to others for the following reasons: ... [illegible]

EUREKA SMOKING TOBACCO is also a very good article, ... [illegible]

LORILLARD'S SNUFFS "the best" wherever used. ... have now been in general use in the United States over 110 years, and still acknowledged

LORILLARD'S CENTURY Chewing Tobacco. ... [illegible]

SEND FOR CIRCULAR.

$290 ... [illegible] ... New York.

EPILEPSY

CAN BE CURED.

[illegible] ... New York City.

THIS IS NO HUMBUG

BY SENDING 35 CENTS, with age, height, color of eyes and hair, you will receive, by return mail, a correct picture of your future husband or wife, with name and date of marriage. Address W. FOX, P. O. Drawer No. 8, Fultonville, New York.

GIVEN AWAY! GIVEN AWAY!

The Excelsior Package, ... [illegible] ... APHAR & CO., 39 Grand St., N. Y. City.

FARMER'S HELPER

SHOWS HOW TO DOUBLE THE PROFITS OF THE FARM, and how farmers and their sons can each make

$100 PER MONTH

In Winter. 10,000 copies will be mailed free to farmers. Send name and address to ZEIGLER, McCURDY & CO., Chicago, Ill.

WANTED AGENTS FOR HOMES AND FORTUNES

In the Boundless West and Sunny South. ... PEOPLE'S PUBLISHING CO., ... State street, Chicago, Ill.

FOWLE'S

PILE AND HUMOR CURE.

THE only perfect cure for PILES of all kinds. ... [illegible] ... H. D. FOWLE, Chemist, Boston, Mass. $1 a bottle. Sold everywhere. Send for Circulars free.

THE MAGIC COMB will change any colored hair or beard to a permanent Black or Brown. One Comb sent by mail for $1. For sale by Merchants and Druggists generally. Address MAGIC COMB CO., Springfield, Mass.

A Book for the Million. MARRIAGE GUIDE.

A Private Counselor to the Married or those about to marry, on the physiological mysteries and revelations of the sexual system, ... [illegible] ... Send to any one (free of postage) for Fifty Cents. Address Dr. Butts' Dispensary, N. W. corner Fifth and Market streets, St. Louis, Mo.

Notice to the Afflicted and Unfortunate. ... [illegible] ... St. Louis, Mo.

LOOK TO YOUR CHILDREN.

Mrs. Whitcomb's Syrup.	Cures Colic and Griping in the Bowels, and facilitates the process of Teething.	Price 25 Cents.
Mrs. Whitcomb's Syrup.	Subdues Convulsions and overcomes all diseases incident to Infants and Children.	Price 25 Cents.
Mrs. Whitcomb's Syrup.	Cures Diarrhea, Dysentery, Summer Complaint in Children of all ages.	Price 25 Cents.

It is the Great Infant's and Children's Soothing Remedy in all disorders brought on by Teething or any other cause. Prepared by the Grafton Medicine Co., St. Louis, Mo.

Sold by druggists and dealers in medicines everywhere.

Possesses peculiar qualities as an equalizer of the circulation and as a support—a sort of extra skin—in all muscular and nervous pains, whether of the side, head kidneys, or back; and in sciatica they should be applied at once. They are now widely used in hospitals, both in America and Europe, and approved by all physicians. They give immediate relief in Lumbago, as well as in pains of the side and back, whether they proceed from weakness, fatigue, or other causes.

Seaside House, Rockaway Beach, Sept. 1, 1869.

Messrs. ALLCOCK & CO., Sing Sing:

GENTLEMEN—Your Plasters have wonderful qualities, and every traveler should have them by him. My guests give great accounts of their efficacy. Some cured of coughs; some of rheumatic pains; some of severe pains in the breast, side and back. In sciatica and kidney affections their application is equally successful. I myself was attacked with a severe pain in my left kidney. I was in agony for twenty-four hours. At length I applied one of your Plasters. The pain soon began to abate, and in the course of a few hours was entirely removed. I send you this that you may publish it if you think well. I am yours, A. D. FAILING, Proprietor of the Seaside House.

New York, August 15, 1869.

THOMAS ALLCOCK & CO., Sing Sing:

For years I have suffered from inflammation of the kidneys, my physicians gave me but little relief, and I moved about like an old man, bent down by years of suffering. At length your Porous Plasters were recommended to me. I applied one to each kidney, and the relief was immediate: I wore them for thirty days, when my back and kidneys were perfectly well and I was once more able to walk erect. I think the half of the virtues of your Plasters yet remain to be told, but should any one wish to hear thereof, I shall be pleased to tell of my experience. I am yours, respectfully,

THOMAS H. JACKSON, 126 East Thirty-second street.

PRINCIPAL AGENCY, BRANDRETH HOUSE, NEW YORK, and sold by all Druggists.

Why

Is it that Dr. Roback's Stomach Bitters increase in sale every year?

Because

They are the best combination ever made.

Why

Do the Druggists recommend Dr. Roback's Bitters

Because

After years of experience and trial they have been proven to be a sure cure for Dyspepsia and Indigestion.

Why

Is it that Physicians use and recommend Dr. Roback's Sugar-coated Blood Pills?

Because

They know the ingredients of which they are made.

Why

Are Dr. Roback's Blood

Because

The Blood Purifier is the

costly Drugs imported expressly from Sweden for its manufacture, and the Pills contain the active principle of Podophyllum (Mandrake Root,) and is a substitute for Mercury.

Stomach Bitters, Blood Purifier and Blood Pills the three greatest remedies the world has ever known?

Because

After eleven years' experience and trial the sales have increased each and every year, and thousands of letters (unsolicited) of the remarkable cures they have performed bear witness. Read the letters in Local Column of cures by these

Ayer's Hair Vigor,

Its natural Vitality and Color.

A dressing which is at once agreeable, healthy, and effectual for preserving the hair. *Faded or gray hair is soon restored to its original color, with the gloss and freshness of youth.* Thin hair is thickened, falling hair checked, and baldness often, though not always, cured by its use. Nothing can restore the hair where the follicles are destroyed, or the glands atrophied and decayed. But such as remain can be saved for usefulness by this application. Instead of fouling the hair with a pasty sediment, it will keep it clean and vigorous. Its occasional use will prevent the hair from turning gray or falling off, and consequently prevent baldness. Free from those deleterious substances which make some preparations dangerous, and injurious to the hair, the Vigor can only benefit but not harm it. If wanted merely for a

nothing else can be found so desirable. Containing neither oil nor dye, it does not soil white cambric, and yet lasts long on the hair, giving it a rich, glossy lustre and a grateful perfume.

PRACTICAL AND ANALYTICAL CHEMISTS,

LOWELL, MASS.

PRICE $1.00.

DECEMBER PRIVILEGE EXTRA. A first-class Magazine for 1870, and a Standard Steel Engraving ... for ONE DOLLAR. ... HOME ECLECTIC, Chicago, Ill.

FURS A fine set of Siberian Squirrel Furs can be got in any village ... Address, for sample page and terms, HOME ECLECTIC, Chicago, Ill.

BOYS We have a new Premium for you. ... HOME ECLECTIC, Chicago, Ill.

SEND FOR A COPY OF NEW EDITION

Wells' Every Man His Own Lawyer and Business Form Book.

A complete and reliable guide to all matters of law and business transactions for every State in the Union. ... [illegible] ... Address JOHN G. WELLS, Publisher, No. 432 Broome street, New York.

VINEGAR. HOW MADE FROM CIDER, WINE, MOLASSES, OR SORGHUM, in 10 hours, without using drugs. For circulars, address F. I. SAGE, Vinegar Maker, Cromwell, Conn.

$75 to $200 per Month paid to agents ... [illegible]

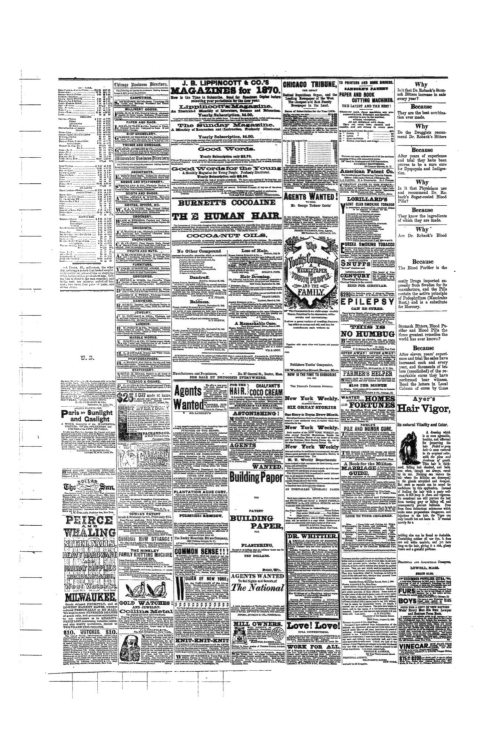

The Chaska Herald.

RATES OF ADVERTISING

1 Square one time	6[illegible]
each subsequent insertion	50
One column one year	60 00
Half " " "	35 00
Fourth " " "	22 00
Business cards not over 5 lines	5 00
over 5 lines and under 10	7 00
over 10 lines and under 15	10 00

Legal Advertisements pr square, first insertion, 75 cents, each subsequent insertion [illegible] cents. Local notices 10 cents per line 1st insertion, each subsequent insertion 5 cents per line. All notices less than five lines, 50 cents.

MINNESOTA IRON WORKS.

Cor. First and Marshall Streets.
Minneapolis, Minn.
SUPPLIES MILL-MEN

With Steam Engines and Boilers, both Portable and Stationary, Flouring Mill Machinery, complete, Saw Mill Machinery complete, Planing Mill Machinery complete, Water Wheels, Grate Bars, Hangings, Shaftings, Pulleys, &c.,

Farmers.

With Horse Powers, Hay Presses, Sorghum Mills, Wind Mills, Force Pumps, Reaper and Mower Castings, Jack Screws, Iron Kettles, from 15 to 300 gallons, Sledge Hammers, &c.,

Builders.

With Architectural Castings, as Iron Columns, Fluted and Plain, Iron Caps, ornamental and plain, Iron Stair Plates and Railings, Iron Grates and Doors, Iron Doors and Fire Shutters, Iron Fencing, Iron Cornices, Iron Conductor Shields, Sash Weights, &c.

Pittsburg, Youghiogheny and Lehigh Coal.

IRON AND BRASS CASTINGS OF ALL KINDS.

All communications, letters of inquiry or orders, must be addressed in full,
"MINNESOTA IRON WORKS"
Minneapolis.

JOHN DUNN,
Real Estate Agent.
CHASKA .... MINN.

Has large tracts of land for sale in Carver, McLeod and Hennepin Counties.

SALOON!
CARVER - - - MINN.

The best of Liquors, Segars and Beer constantly kept on hand. Farmers call on me.
PETER BUTTENDORF.

Plow And Wagon Factory
AT WACONIA
FRED LUTZ PROPRIETOR.

I would respectfully inform the citizens of Carver County that I now manufacture as good and durable plows as are made in the Union, and offer them as cheap as can be purchased at St. Paul. Also Wagons, Blacksmithing done to order on short notice.

J. R. BARRETT & CO., Proprietors,
MANCHESTER, N. H.
LORD & SMITH,
CHICAGO,
General Agents for the Northwestern States.
G. A. DU TOIT, Agent for [illegible] County
E. H. BIDDLE, State Agent, St. Paul, Minn.

WALTHAM WATCHES

For a few months past we have advertised the above Watches at extremely low prices, and the result has been most satisfactory. Our plan has been to sell the genuine Waltham Watch, in Solid Gold or Silver Cases only, and at a very small profit; giving the purchaser every opportunity of examination and comparison, and with the understanding that if the Watch does not prove satisfactory, it can be exchanged or the money refunded.

These Watches are, without exception, the most perfect specimens of fine mechanism ever produced in any country. Each and every part is made by machinery of the most delicate and elaborate construction.

Compared with foreign watches, they possess many advantages, excelling not only in accuracy [illegible], but still more in their reliability as time-keepers. As an indication of the prices we permit the following:

Silver Hunting Watches,	$18 00
Gold Hunting Watches, 18 karat case,	80 00
Gold Hunting Watches, ladies size	70 00

We often receive orders direct from our advertisement, only after that every one should send first for our descriptive price list, which explains all the different kinds, tells the weight and quality of the cases, and gives prices of each. This we will forward to any one on application, and it will be found very useful in making a selection.

Every Watch is warranted by special certificate from the American Watch Co.

We send the Watch by express to any address,— Allow the purchaser to open the package and examine the Watch before paying, and if afterwards it does not prove satisfactory, it can be exchanged or the money will be cheerfully refunded.

Please state that you saw this in the Chaska Herald.

Address, in full, HOWARD & CO.
No. 619 Broadway, N. Y.

THE CONSTITUTIONAL UNION.

The above is the title of the only Democratic newspaper published at the National Capital, and which is one of the most able expounders of Democratic doctrine there is in the world.— We would say to our Democratic, as well as Republican friends, if you want the best Democratic weekly journal published, send for this. The following unexampled terms are offered to sub-scribers:

Single copy,	$2 00
Two copies,	3 75
Five copies,	9 00
Ten copies,	17 50
Twenty copies,	30 00

Fifty copies one year to one address 55 00; one hundred copies, to one address 100 00.

Terms for subscription invariably in advance. Any person who will send a club of twenty subscribers, with thirty dollars, will be sent an extra copy of the paper.

☞ Subscribers had better, for their own security, register their letters [illegible], in preference to all other kinds of funds.

Address, THOMAS P. FLORENCE
Editor Constitutional Union.
Box 44, Washington City Postoffice.

New Store.

At the Post Office in Carver you can get Dry Goods, Hats, Caps, Boots & Shoes, Ready made clothing and all styles of Dress Goods from Sixty to one hundred per cent cheaper than at any other store in Carver Co. We would call special attention to our stock of Glass Ware, Lamps and Looking Glasses

Groceries can be had Twenty per cent cheaper than at any other place in the County. Produce taken in exchange for Goods.

AUCTION EVERY FAIR DAY.

C. E. ROGERS & CO.

FRANK WARNER

ATTORNEY AT LAW, Chaska Minn., Office at Court House, opposite Auditors Office.

THE ST. PAUL PIONEER.

Established in 1849.

The Oldest and Best Newspaper in the State

DEMOCRATIC IN POLITICS.

Daily, Tri-Weekly, Weekly.

The St. Paul Pioneer has already entered upon the twenty-first year of its existence, with a larger list of subscribers and more extensive patronage than it ever before enjoyed.

It is reliable democratic, progressive in its ideas, and the organ of the people.

It advocates honesty and economy in the administration of the government.

The reduction of taxation.

The repeal or great modification of the existing oppressive tariff.

The prompt payment of the debt.

The taxation of government bonds the same as other property is taxed.

The banishment of corruption from all the places where it is lodged.

The defense of the national honor at all times.

That the government shall be administered solely for the good of the people.

All the editions of the Pioneer will contain the latest telegraphic dispatches from all parts of the world, the latest news of all kinds; reliable and full market reports; official documents and the laws; political and general editorial; correspondence from all parts of our own State and from abroad, the local news from the various localities in the state; interesting tales, and general reading for the fireside.

TERMS BY MAIL,

DAILY.

One year	$10 00
Six months	5 00
Three months	2 50
One month	1 00

TRI-WEEKLY.

One year	$4 00
Six months	2 00
In clubs of six or more, each copy one year	3 00

WEEKLY.

One copy, one year	$2 00
One copy, six months	1 00
In clubs of ten or more, each copy one year	1 50

A copy of the weekly will be sent gratis to any person who gets up a club of ten, and of the tri-weekly to any person who gets up a club of twenty weekly subscribers. Address
PIONEER PRINTING Co.,
St. Paul, Minn.

"A Complete Pictorial History of the Times"

The best, cheapest, and most successful Family Paper in the World.

Harper's Weekly.

SPLENDIDLY ILLUSTRATED.

[illegible]

Critical Notices of the Press

The model newspaper of our country. Complete in all the departments of an American Family paper, Harper's Weekly has earned for itself a right to its title, "A Weekly Journal of Civilization."—New York Evening Post.

Harper's Weekly may be unreservedly declared the best newspaper in America.—New York Independent.

The articles upon public questions which appear in Harper's Weekly from week to week form a remarkable series of brief political essays. They are distinguished by clear and pointed statement, by good common sense, by independence and breadth of view. They are the expression of mature conviction, high principle and strong feeling, and take their place among the best newspaper writing of the times.—North American Review, Boston, Mass.

SUBSCRIPTIONS. 1870.

TERMS:

Harper's Weekly, one year, $4 00

An extra copy of either the Magazine, Weekly, or Bazar will be supplied gratis for every club of Five Subscribers at $4 each, in one remittance; or, Six copies for $20, without extra copy.

Subscriptions to Harper's Magazine, Weekly, and Bazar, to one address for one year, $10; or, two of Harper's Periodicals, to one address for one year, $7.

Back Numbers can be supplied at any time.

The annual volumes of Harper's Weekly, in neat cloth binding, will be sent by express, free of expense, for $7 each. A complete set, comprising 13 volumes, freight at expense of purchaser. Volume 13 ready Jan 1, 1870.

The postage on Harper's Weekly is 20 cents a year, which must be paid at the subscriber's post-office.

Address HARPER & BROTHERS, N. Y.

INSURANCE.

We would respectfully notify our friends and patrons that the

UNDERWRITER'S AGENCY
OF NEW YORK.

(Composed of the oldest German Insurance Co. in the U. S. and three other Companies,) is now represented by F. E. Du Toit, who will be prepared to insure Farm property and Stocks of Goods in this and the surrounding Counties at the LOWEST RATES.

Cash Assets, $3, 535 000

Losses promptly paid.

☞ Germania, Hanover, Niagara, and Republic Ins. Co., of New York.

A. STODDARD, Gen'l. Agt.
F. E. Du TOIT, Local Agent, Chaska.

Estray—Reward

Strayed from the premises of the subscriber in the village of Chaska, one yearling horse colt, [illegible]

Chaska July 24 1869.

PHILIP HENK.

INSURANCE

F. E. DU TOIT.
AGENT

of the following Insurance Co's,

ÆTNA

Hartford, Con,—Assets 5,052, 000,00

UNDERWRITER'S AGENCY

New York City,—Assets 3,555,000,00

CHARTER OAK LIFE INS CO
OF
Hartford, Conn.—Assets, 4,000,000.00

Policies of Insurance issued against loss or damage by fire and perils of inland transportation.

Losses Adjusted and Paid promptly at the place where the *Policy is Issued*.

Will attend promptly, to collections. Paying of Taxes, &c.

OFFICE, AT THE "HERALD" OFFICE.
CHASKA MINNESOTA.

JOHN BLOEDEL'S

Brick Wagon and Black-Smith Shop.
Near Zangers Store
CARVER - - - - - - MINN.

This is the oldest, largest and best Shop in the County.

The Celebrated Milwaukee, Wisconsin Wagons are always kept for sale at this shop. They are brought up from Milwaukee and ironed here. They are sold as cheap as Minnesota wagons.— Bob-sleds &c. kept for sale and made to order.

Shoeing Oxen, Horses, and all other Blacksmith work done to order.

All those wishing good and durable work and at reasonable prices should call at

BLOEDEL'S SHOP.

W. S. COMBS. J. E. WEINMANN.

WEINMANN & LOSSEN.

GENERAL

Fire and Life Insurance Agents.

Also Collection Agents.

Carver, Minn.

Bride And Bridegroom.

Essays for Young Men on the interesting relation of Bridegroom to Bride, in the institution of Marriage —a Guide to matrimonial felicity, and true happiness. Sent by mail in sealed letter envelopes free of charge. Address, Howard Association, Box P, Philadelphia, Pa.

THE LADY'S FRIEND.

Two Months Gratis!!

The Lady's Friend announces the following Novelets for 1870: Did he Forget Her? by Louise Chandler Moulton; "The Cassannena Aunt by Elizabeth Prescott author of "Between Two," &c.; "Solid Silver; or, Christie Dean's Bridal Gifts," by Amanda M. Douglas, author of "The Debarry Fortune," &c. with numerous shorter stories by a brilliant galaxy of lady writers.

A finely executed steel engraving, a handsome double-page, finely colored fashion-plate, and a large assortment of wood-cuts illustrating the fashions, fancy work, &c., are given in every number.

It will give a popular piece of Music in every number.

Portraits of Distinguished Authors.

The January number will contain portraits (engraved on steel) of Mrs. Henry Wood, Florence Fanny, Louise Chandler Prescott, Amanda M. Douglas, Mrs. Margaret Hosmer, and August Bell.

New subscribers who send in their names for 1870 before the first of November shall receive the November and December numbers of this year in addition, making 14 months in all. And new subscribers sending in their names by the first of December shall receive the magnificent December holiday number, making 13 months in all.

TERMS.—$2 50 a year, two copies, $4; four copies $6; five copies (and one gratis) $8. One copy of the Lady's Friend and The Saturday Evening Post, $4.

A copy of the large and beautiful Premium Steel Engraving—"Taking the Measure of the Wedding Ring,"—engraved in England at a cost of $2,000, will be sent to every full ($2 50) subscriber, and to every person sending a club. This engraving is a gem of art. Address

DEACON & PETERSON,
319 Walnut street, Phila.

—Specimen copies sent for ten cents.—

Court House Saloon.

JOHN ROSS .... Proprietor.

Brick Saloon near Court House. Best of Liquors and Cigars always kept on hand.
☞ The celebrated Waukegan Lager Beer always "fresh tapped."

Insurance.

For reliable Indemnity against loss by Fire apply to Fred E Du Toit, Agent of the following old and reliable companies at Chaska, Minn.

Aetna, Hartford, capital	$5,052,000
Underwriters, New York,	4,000,000
Western Buffalo,	700,000
Charter Oak, Hartford Life	5,000,000

All of the above companies insure property at reasonable rates and pay their losses promptly.

Commissioners Notice.

Notice is hereby given, that by order of the Probate Court for Carver County, Minn., the undersigned have been appointed commissioners to receive, examine and adjust claims against the estate of Peter Thompson late of said County deceased, and will meet for that purpose on the first Monday of each month, at the Court House in Chaska in said County, at 2 o'clock P. M., for six months from August 14th 1869, and said period of six months is the time limited by said order for creditors to present their claims.

Chaska, Aug. 14th 1869.

PETER WEGGO,
G. KRAYENBUHL,
F. E. DU TOIT,

PROBATE NOTICE.

State of Minnesota, County of Carver. } S. S.

On reading and filing the oath and petition of Amelia Brandt praying for reasons therein set forth that letters of administration may issue to John Bondemirer on the estate of August Brandt late of said county deceased.

It is ordered that the 13th day of December A. D. 1869 at 11 o'clock A. M. at the office of the Judge of Probate in Chaska in said County be assigned for the hearing of said petition, and all persons interested in said estate are required to appear at a session of the Probate then and there to be holden to show cause if any there be why the prayer of said petitioner should not be granted. And it is further ordered that said petitioner give public notice of the pendency of said petition by causing a copy of this order to be published in the "Valley Herald" a weekly newspaper published at Chaska in said County for three successive weeks previous to the day of said hearing.

Dated Chaska Nov. 8 1869.

J. A. SARGENT,
Judge of Probate.

PROBATE NOTICE.

State of Minnesota, County of Carver. } S. S.

On reading and filing the oath and petition of Anna Carlson praying for reasons therein set forth that letters of administration may issue to herself on estate of said Johanes carlson late of said county deceased. It is ordered that December the 13th 1869 at 11 o'clock A. M. at the court house in chaska in said county be assigned for the hearing of said petition. And all persons interested in the said estate are requested to be and appear before said Court at the time and place aforesaid and show cause if any they have why said petition should not be granted. And it is further ordered that said petitioner give public notice of the pendency of said petition by causing a notice of this order to be published in the Valley Herald a weekly newspaper printed in said county for four weeks previous to said day of hearing.

chaska Nov. 6th 1869.

J. A. SARGENT,
Judge of Probate.

St. Paul and Sioux City Railroad.

UPWARD TRAINS.

	Leaves.	Leaves.
Leave St. Paul	7:45 a. m.	and 3:40 p. m.
Arrive Mendota	8:10 a. m.	and 4:10 p. m.
Ar. Shakopee	10:10 a. m.	and 5:20 p. m.
Ar. Merriam	11:20 a. m.	and 5:35 p. m.
Ar. Brentwood	11:15 a. m.	and 5:51 p. m.
Ar. Belle Plaine	11:45 a. m.	and 6:13 p. m.
Ar. Blakely	12:33 p. m.	and 6:27 p. m.
Ar. Henderson	1:10 p. m.	and 7:03 p. m.
Ar. LeSueur	1:40 p. m.	and 7:18 p. m.
Ar. Ottawa	2:10 p. m.	and 7:35 p. m.
Ar. St. Peter	2:40 p. m.	and 7:58 p. m.
Ar. Mankato	3:40 p. m.	and 8:30 p. m.

DOWNWARD TRAINS.

Leave Mankato	6:30 a. m.	and 9:00 a. m.
Arrive St. Peter	7:00 a. m.	and 9:35 a. m.
Ar. Ottawa	7:20 a. m.	and 10:30 a. m.
Ar. LeSueur	7:40 a. m.	and 11:05 a. m.
Ar. Henderson	7:50 a. m.	and 11:35 a. m.
Ar. Blakely	8:10 a. m.	and 12:15 p. m.
Ar. Belle Plaine	8:30 a. m.	and 12:50 p. m.
Ar. Brentwood	8:51 a. m.	and 1.20 p. m.
Ar. Merriam	9:15 a. m.	and 2:05 p. m.
Ar Shakopee	9:23 a. m.	and 2:30 p. m.
Ar. Mendota	10:00 a. m.	and 3:35 p. m.
Ar. St. Paul	11:10 a. m.	and 4:30 p. m.

Trains on this road make close connection at Mendota with trains on Milwaukee and Saint Paul Railroad for Minneapolis, Owatonna, Winona, and all points South and East; and at Saint Peter with Minnesota Stage Company's Line of stages for New Ulm, and at Mankato for all points West and Southwest.

Tickets can be procured at the Union Ticket Office, Corner Third and Jackson Streets, and at the Depot, West St. Paul.

JOHN F. LINCOLN,
Superintendent.

"A Repository of Fashion, Pleasure, And Instruction."

HARPER'S BAZAR.

A supplement containing numerous full sized patterns of useful articles accompanies the paper every fortnight, and occasionally an elegant colored Fashion Plate.

Harper's Bazar contains 16 folio pages of the size of Harper's Weekly, printed on superfine calendered paper, and is published weekly.

CRITICAL NOTICES OF THE PRESS.

Harper's Bazar contains, besides pictures, patterns, etc., a variety of matter of special use and interest to the family; articles on health, dress and housekeeping in all its branches; its editorial matter is specially adapted to the circle it is intended to interest and instruct; and it has besides, good stories and literary matter of merit. It is not surprising that the journal, with such features, has achieved in a short time an immense success; for something of its kind was desired in thousands of families, and its publishers have filled the demand. The young lady who buys a single number of Harper's Bazar is made a subscriber for life.—New York Evening Post.

The Bazar is excellent. Like all the periodicals which the Harper's publish, it is almost ideally well edited, and the class of readers for whom it is intended—the mothers and daughters in average families—can not but profit by its good sense and good taste, which we have no doubt, are to-day making very many homes happier than they may have been before the women began taking lessons in personal and household and social management from this good natured mentor.—The Nation.

It has the merit of being sensible, of conveying instruction, of giving excellent patterns in every department, and of being well stocked with reading matter.—Watchman and Reflector.

Subscriptions—1870.

TERMS:

Harper's Bazar, one year, $4 00.

An Extra copy of either the Magazine, Weekly or Bazar, will be supplied gratis for every Club of Five subscribers at $4 00 each, in one remittance; or Six Copies for $20 00, without extra copy.

Subscriptions to Harper's Magazine, Weekly, and Bazar, to one address, one year, $10 00; or two of Harper's Periodicals, to one address, one year, $7 00.

Back numbers supplied at any time.

Vols. I, and II. of Harper's Bazar, for the years 1868-9, elegantly bound in green morocco cloth, will be sent by express, freight prepaid, for 7 00 each.

The postage on Harper's Bazar is 20 cents a year, which must be paid at the subscriber's post office.

Address HARPER & BROTHERS,
New York.

CHASKA
LUMBER YARD

The undersigned will keep an extensive stock OF

All Kinds of Lumber
AT
LIBERAL PRICES.

FERD. THIES.

LEGAL NOTICES.

Mortgage Sale.

Names of Mortgagors, Jacob Hess and Elizabeth Hess of Chaska in the County of Carver and State of Minnesota.

Name of Mortgagee, Henry Young of Chaska aforesaid.

Date of Mortgage, May 1st A. D. 1868.

When recorded, May 11th A. D. 1868 at 10 o'clock in the forenoon of that day in Book "B" of mortgages on page 147 in the office of the Register of Deeds of said County of Carver.

Amount claimed to be due at the date of this notice, one hundred and seventy five dollars & ninety seven cents.

Description of mortgaged premises. The east [½] half of the south east [¼] quarter of section [34] thirty four in township [116] one hundred and sixteen, Range [23] twenty three west, excepting fifteen [15] acres described as follows: Beginning at the south east corner of section [34] thirty four and running thence westerly along the south line of said section [20] twenty chains to a post in the south west corner of the south east [¼] quarter of the south east [¼] quarter of said section; thence northly along the west line of said south east quarter [¼] of the south east quarter [¼] of said section [34] thirty four two [2] chains and [70] seventy links to the center of the Yorkville and Bloomington State road; thence north [43] forty three degrees east along the center of said road [23] twenty two chains and [50] links to a point on the east line of said section thirty four; thence south twelve chains and thirty links to the place of beginning.

Default having been made in the payment of the said sum due on said mortgage as aforesaid and no proceedings at law or otherwise having been instituted to recover the same or any part thereof; now therefore notice is hereby given that by virtue of the power of sale contained in said mortgage and of the statute in such case made and provided the said mortgage will be foreclosed by a sale of said mortgaged premises at public vendue to the highest bidder for cash at the front door of the Court House in Chaska in said county of Carver on the 8th day of January A. D. 1870 at eleven o'clock in the forenoon of that day for the purpose of satisfying the sum then due thereon and secured by said mortgage together with the costs and disbursements of sale and additional sum of twenty five dollars attorneys fees according to the terms of said mortgage.

Chaska, Nov. 22d 1869.

HENRY YOUNG, Mortgagee.
BAXTER & SARGENT, Atty's for Mortgagee.

SUMMONS.

State of Minnesota, District Court, 4th Judicial Dist. County of Carver. } S. S.

Johannus Anderson, vs. J. F. L. Jetter.

The State of Minnesota, To the above named defendant:

You are hereby summoned and required to answer the complaint in this action which has been filed in the office of the Clerk of the District Court at Chaska in said County, and to serve a copy of your answer to the said complaint on the subscriber, at his office in Watertown in said County within twenty days after the service of this summons upon you, exclusive of the day of such service, and if you fail to answer the said complaint within the time aforesaid, the Plaintiff in this action will apply to the Court for the relief demanded in the Complaint.

Dated Watertown, Dec. 6th A. D. 1869.

H. J. PECK,
Plaintiff's Attorney, Watertown Minn.

Mortgage Sale.

Mortgagors, George E. Bingham and Caroline E. Bingham his wife.

Mortgagee. David Brown.

Date of mortgage, February 18th 1868.

Mortgage recorded in the office for the Registry of Deeds of the County of Carver Minn. on the 25th day of Feb. 1868 at 10 o'clock A. M., in Book "D" of mortgages on pages 355, 356 & 357.

Description of mortgaged premises—the north west quarter of the south east quarter (nw qr of the se qr) of section twenty seven (27) in township one hundred and sixteen (116) of Range twenty three (23) west, according to government survey; in the County of Carver and State of Minnesota.

Amount claimed to be due at the date of this notice is one hundred and thirty four dollars and sixty two cents ($134,62) and no proceedings at law or otherwise for the collection of said debt or any part thereof having been had or commenced.

Therefore, notice is hereby given, that by virtue of a power of sale contained in said mortgage and recorded therewith, and pursuant to the Statute in such cases made and provided, the said mortgage will be foreclosed, by a sale of said mortgaged premises, to be made at Public Auction or vendue by the Sheriff of said County, at the front door of the Court House in Chaska in said County, on Monday the 13th day of December 1869, at 10 o'clock in the forenoon, to satisfy said debt together with the further sum of twenty five dollars ($25) solicitors fees, according to the terms of said mortgage, and costs and disbursements of sale.

Dated Oct. 26th 1869.

H. J. PECK,
Atty's. for mortgagee.

UNION HOTL.

CHASKA. - - - - - - - - MINN

A good bar in connection with the hous. Also good Stabling.

WM. OCHS, Propr.

COMBS & WHITNEY
WHOLESALE & RETAIL
Booksellers and Stationers
AND THE

Emporium for views of Minnesota and other Scenery, Brackets, Engravings, Frames, Chromos, &c. &c.

174 Third, Corner Cedar Street
Saint Paul. Minn.

Dr. C. B. AMES
PHYSICIAN AND SURGEON.

WATERTOWN . . . MINN.

Office at Lewis Drug Store. Offers his service to the citizens of Watertown and vicinity, and can always be found day or night ready to attend calls.

E. D. K. RANDALL,
Wholesale Dealers in School, Miscellaneous & Blank
Books, Stationery,
Writing Paper, Photograph Albums &c.,
☞ Retail Dealers supplied at lowest rates.
Dealer in, Notions, Toys and
Fancy Goods,
of every discription.
WITH D. D. MERRILL AT,
109 3d .St., S. Paul Minn.

Canvassers Wanted, $5 to $10 per day.

To sell the new Immigration letter papers with a compendium of the attractions of Minnesota to immigrants, printed in English, German, Norwegian, and Swedish; two pages blank for writing letters; price, $1.00 per single quire, $3.50 for four quires, to canvassers 50 cents per quire. Note paper cheaper.

Also, canvassers for a 50 cent edition of "Minnesota as it is in 1870." Every county and town included; to be issued in June. A $3.00 edition to follow, with a map of the State, also for advertisements. Send for circulars.

J. W. McCLUNG, St. Paul.

FALL & WINTER GOODS
Just Received From
Chicago
And Milwaukee.
AT THE
The New Store
OF
HENRY YOUNG

DOMESTIC AND FANCY
DRY GOODS
CLOTHING
Hats, Caps, Furs, Boots, and Shoes, &

Groceries. Cash paid for farmers produce.

Call At

"THE OLD POST OFFICE STAND"

G. A. DUTOIT.

Wholesale and retail dealer in

Drugs, Paints, Oils,

Perfumery, patent Medicines Etc. Window Glass, Fancy Articles, toys and Notios,

Pure Wines and Catawba Brandy for medical purposes.

CARVER MINN,

Fresh Arrival
At
LINENFELSER & FAB'R
OF
DRY GOODS
Clothing, Hats, Caps, Boots and Shoes &c.
GROCERIES & PROVISIONS
AT
"At the Brick Store."

Historical Society.

Valley Herald.

F. E. DU TOIT Proprietor. TERMS, $1 50, Per Annum.

VOLUME 8 — CHASKA, MINNESOTA, FRIDAY, DEC. 17, 1869, — NUMBER 17

The Valley Herald

Official County Paper.

BY F. E. DU TOIT.

CHASKA FRIDAY DECEMBER 17 1869.

Proceedings County Board.

AUDITOR'S OFFICE, CARVER COUNTY. Dec. 7th 1869.

10 o'clock, a. m, Board of County Commissioners met pursuant to adjournment—members all present—called to order by F. E. Du Toit Chairman.

Petitions were presented from citizens legal voters of School Districts No. 12 & 15 for nwl sec 20 T 116 R 23 to be set off from School District No 15 and to be attached to school district No 12.

Resolved—That the Auditor is hereby instructed to cause notices to be posted in accordance with law.

On motion board adjourned until one o'clock p. m.

One o'clock p. m Board of County Commissioners met pursuant to adjournment—members all present—called to order by the chairman.

The petition of John G. Souter and others for a change of School Districts Nos. 42, 44 and 46 presented at September session 1869, was taken up, a [illegible] against the [illegible]. It is hereby ordered [illegible] that the above petition [illegible] and that the Territory mentioned in said petition, be known as School District No. fifty seven (57) of Carver County for all purposes whatsoever.

The petition of Jacob Walter, presented at September session 1869, for the [illegible] qr. Sect. 22, T. 116, R. 24 to be set off from School Distr. No. 1[illegible], no remonstrance appearing.

It is hereby ordered and determined that the sw qr of ne qr. Sect 22, T. 116 R. 24 be attached to and made a part of School District No. 19.

Bill of John H. Brown for defending [illegible] by order of the Court allowed, $7.35.

The petition of Gottfried Albers, presented at September session 1869, for the [illegible] qr. Sect. 22 T. 116, R. 24 to be set off from School Distr. No. [illegible] was taken up no remonstrance appearing.

It is hereby ordered and determined that the se qr of ne qr, Sect. 22, Town 116, R. 24 be attached to and made a part of School District No. 19.

Resolved—That one hundred dollars be reduced from 1868, for the valuation upon lot 5 and sw qr of sw qr, Sec. 8, T. 116, R. 23 belonging to Henry Jansel.

Bill of Charles Brandenburgh for conveying Charlotte Conrad an insane person to asylum at St. Peter, allowed, $16.00

Bill of J. A. Sargent Judge of Probate, costs in the matter of Charlotte Conrad an insane person, allowed, $13.70

Bill of Commr Reusse for services on Road Committee, allowed, $10.50.

Bill of Commr Kelly for services as Road Committee, allowed, $18 00

Bill of Commr. Gotheif for services on Road Committee and attendance on poor, $18,00.

On motion Board adjourned until 9 o'clock a. m., to morrow.

Dec. 8th. 1869. 9 o'clock a m.

Board of County Commissioners met pursuant to adjournment, members all present, except Commr. Gothelf.—Board called to order by the Chairman.

Resolved—That fifteen ($15,) dollars be allowed in full as damages for the laying out of a County Road across the land of Bridget Burns in Hollywood.

Resolved—That fifteen $15. dollars be allowed in full as damages for the laying out of a County Road across the land of James Burns in Hollywood.

The petition of Dominicus Wagner, presented at September session 1869, for the wh of nw qr, Sect. 27, T. 116, Range 25, to be set off from School District No 40, no remonstrance appearing, action postponed.

A petition was presented signed by Warner Dudley and others praying for an organization of a new School Distr, to be comprised of the following Territory from School Distr. No. 33, viz: nh sect. 12, se qr sect. 11, nh sect. 13, nh sect. 14, eh sw qr sect. 11 in Town 117, Range 25, and to be attached to School Distr. No. 84 of Hennepin Co.

Resolved—That the Auditor be instructed to cause notices to be given according to law, before next session of this Board.

A petition was presented signed by Michael Brewsworth and others for a new Road commencing near Township line between T 116, R. 25 and T 115, R 25, where the Victoria road crosses said Town line, thence west on said line between sect. 31 and 6 to intersect Chaska and old Waconia road, referred to Commr. Griffin, Reusse and Kelly, to meet on Dec. 10th 1869, at 10 o'clock a. m. at the House of Henry Moser.

Bill of J. M. Troll for furnishing Tamarac timber for Court House Ladders, allowed, $9.00

Resolved—That one hundred and fifty ($150) dollars be reduced from the valuation, for 1868, upon 117 acres in sect 8, belonging to Jacob Ebinger in Chaska Town, and to be refunded accordingly, and that the Auditor reduce in the same proportion for 1869.

On motion County Board adjourned until one o'clock p. m

1 o'clock p. m. Board of County Commissioners met pursuant to adjournment, called to order by the Chairman.

The Report of the Committee upon the petition of Fred. Walter and others heretofore laid over, was taken up and ordered to be laid over until January session 1870.

The report of the Committee upon the petition of John Roe and others for a change of Watertown and Hutchinson road, laid over at last session, taken up and laid over until January session 1870.

Bill of Dr. C. E. Rogers for surgical operations and visits to Andrew Humquist a pauper by order of Commr. Griffin, allowed, $80.00.

Resolved—That the amount of twelve ($12) dollars be allowed from the County Poor Fund to Leonard Van Sloan to procure clothing for Peter Coppe a pauper.

Resolved—That one hundred dollars be appropriated to the Town of Carver, out of the County Revenue fund, for building bridges destroyed by the late rains.

Bill of F. E. Du Toit, for printing tax statements and Receipts, allowed, $22.00.

Bill of F, E. Du Toit, for printing Oct, financial statement, allowed $21.00

Bill of Geo. A. Du Toit for medicine for paupers, allowed, $8.65

Bill of Dr. Griffin for visits and medicine for poor, allowed as amended, $102.00

On motion County Board adjourned until 9 o'clock a. m to-morrow.

Dec. 9th 1869. 9 o'clock a. m.

Board of County Commissioners met pursuant to adjournment, members present except Dr. Gothelf, called to order by the chairman.

A petition was presented by John Haug and others for a lengthening of the Chaska, Benton and Waconia road, referred to Commrs. Reusse, Griffin and Kelly as committee to meet on Saturday December 10th 1869 at 10 o'clock a. m. at the house of Joachim Fick.

The committee on the Road, petitioned for by Anthony Clasgens, recommended that the prayer of petitioners be rejected. Report adopted and committee discharged.

The committee on the Road petition of Ferdinand Zellmann, Christian Hondimer and others, recommended that the prayer of petitioners be rejected.—Report adopted and committee discharged.

A petition was presented signed by Carl Valdvogel and others for a change of the Chaska and Smith Town road, referred to Commrs. Griffin, Kelly and Reusse and to meet on Friday December 10th 1869, at 2 o'clock p. m., at the House of Carl Valdvogel.

Resolved—That the room occupied by the present County Attorney be assigned to the Judge of Probate and that the Room at present occupied by the Judge of Probate be assigned to the County Attorney on and after the 1st of January 1870 as office.

Resolved—That M H Iltis is granted a License as auctioneer, for one year from date by him complying with former Resolutions governing the same.

The Patrons of Husbandry applied to the Board of County Commissioners for the use of the Court House Hall for their meetings, referred to the Chairman with authority to act.

Bill of F. Dolsing for bedsteads, allowed, $6,00

(Concluded next week.)

Presidents Message.

We publish this week the Presidents Message in full on our inside pages... We shall not comment upon the same, but let our readers be their own judges of its merit and importance. It is itself and will well pay perusal.

NOTICE.

Change of Fair Day.

Inasmuch as the last Saturday of the month happens to be Christmas—the regular fair day, the fair will be held on the following Monday, Dec. 27th. The change for this month only.

Carver Fair. THE COMMITTEE.

FRESH OYSTERS...Frank Ess of the chaska House, has just received a large lot of Fresh Oysters, which will be served up in all styles, or sold by the can.

Rufus Chapman of Liberty, Maine, had a stiff leg bent at the knee, limbered and strengthened by the use of Johnson's Anodyne Liniment.

The proprietors of Johnson's Anodyne Liniment, Parsons' Purgative Pills, and Sheridan's cavalry condition Powders, have published a readable and instructive pamphlet, which may be had free at the stores.

CHASKA MARKET PRICE

Wheat 55 to 60 per	bushel,	
Oats 35 to 37	"	
Barley 55 to 60	"	
chickens 8 cts per	lbs,	
Turkeys 12½	"	
Geese 10	"	
Pork 10½ to 11 cts	"	

We believe the chaska Merchants and buyers are paying higher price for Pork than in any other place in the county or Valley.

Mr. Trenwith, the wheat buyer at this place is buying wheat in addition to our merchants and seems to have taken the lead in this branch of business. He pays cash for all purchases.

ATTENTION GIRLS.—Henry Ramsekers and Gerhard Van Sloan, at present engaged chopping wood at the burch house in Laketown, wants a couple of servant cooks female, to keep house &c., and engages to pay good wages. Now this is a fair chance and should be improved.

LATE...We are behind time with our issue this week, owing to a pressure of job work.

LAID OVER...Several communications and an advertisement are crowded out this week. They will appear in our next issue.

TOYS CANDYS &c.—Lucien Warner, Henry Young, Lincenfelser & Faber and John Bennett have a large number of Christmas presents on hand and offer them cheap for cash. Give them a call and prepare for the Holidays.

INSTALLED.—The officers of the Patrons of Husbandry were sworn in last week by deputy Paist of St. Paul.—The Lodge is not yet in working order.

SHOOTING MATCH.—Frank Ess of the chaska House, is making arrangements for a grand shooting match for Turkeys, Watches, and other articles on Dec, 24th 1869. Frank knows how to do the thing up brown. Give him a call and try your luck.

Carver Items.

Correspondence.

PERSONAL.—We were pleased to receive calls last week from Commissioners, Ed, Reusse of Benton, Matthew Kelly of Hollywood, and Griffin of Carver. These gentlemen together with Mr. Weisbecker and Bartel, will make an able board of Commissioners. Call again.

Dr. E, Bray of Young America was in town one day last week. The Dr. report everythings flourishing in that direction.

A GOOD THING.—"Albert Iron Tonic Bitters," for the stomach, loss of appetite &c. Geo. A. Du Toit is sole agent for Carver Co. Try them.

PORK.—This article has been "way up" in price for a week past, bringing 11 cts per pound. It came in quite freely, and finally dropped to 9½ and 10 cts. with plenty of buyers.

ANOTHER CONTRACT.—The Board of Supervisors have let the contract to Peter Michels, to build a bridge across the Carver Creek on the Henderson road. The price being $300. Work has already been commenced. It will be a good substantial one.

SOCIAL REUNION.—A number of the friends of Jos, Weismann were invited to spend the evening at his house one day last week, all present enjoyed themselves hugely, for particulars we refer to H, R, Denny or John Bloedel.

BUSINESS.—Business has been somewhat better than usual for the last two weeks. We hope it will continue so.—Wheat brings 55 cents.

IN TOWN.—We noticed quite a number of strangers in town during the week, and some who were not strangers, among whom was, Jos. Long, the accommodating agent at Merriam, and W. H. McMollum of St, Paul.

TOYS, TOYS!—Go to "Du Toits Drug Store," and get your Toys for the Holidays, a full stock to pick from.

HOLIDAY GOODS.—E, Holmes and H, Zanger have both a cheap and good assortment of Fancy Goods, Cheap for cash.

VELOCIPEDE.—F. Cook has one, which draws an immense crowd. Go and see it.

NURSING CHAIRS.—Go to Du Toits Drug Store and get one, a good thing for children.

FANCY CANDIES.—Wm, Glitschka has a good assortment of assorted candies, for Christmas trees &c. Give him a call.

BIG TIME.—The Christmas trees at the Church. It will be nice, go and see it.

A GOOD JOB.—Chas. Johnsons "play house" done up in shape.

TAX NOTICE.

The Tax duplicate for the year A. D. 1869, is now placed into my hands for collection. And I will attend at the following times and places for the purpose of collecting said taxes for the year 1869.

In Hollywood Town at M. Kellys on Tuesday 4th of January 1870.

In Watertown at the Drug Store on Wednesday and Thursday the 5th and 6th days of Jany. 1870.

In Waconia, on Friday the 7th of Jany. 1870.

In Laketown, at M. Walk, on Saturday the 8th of Jany. 1870.

In Camden, at J. Marrills on Tuesday the 11th of Jany. 1870.

In Young America, at H. Fabels on Wednesdy and Thursday the 12th and 13th day of Jany 1870.

In Benton, at H. Bonghards on Friday the 14th of Jany. 1870.

In Benton, at George Reichners on Saturday the 15th of Jany. 1870.

In Hancock, at the Saw Mill, Monday the 17th of Jany. 1870

In San Francisco, at J. A. Hillstrom, Tuesday the 18th day of Jany. 1870.

In Dahlgreen at P. Seigals on Wednesday the 19th of Jany. 1870.

In Chanhassen, at Wm. Server on Thursday the 20th of Jany. 1870.

In Carver, at the Hotel on Friday the 21st of Jany. 1870.

Afterwards I will attend at the County Seat to receive taxes from those wishing to pay the same.

A Penalty of 5 per cent will be charged according to law after the 1st day of February 1870 on personal property tax.

The amount of taxes levied on the dollar valuation are as follows:

State Taxes,	5	Mills.
Common School Tax,	2	"
Co. Revenue Tax,	6¼	"
Co. Special Tax,	½	"
Co. Poor Tax,	2	"
Co. Interest and Sinking Fund,	3	"

TOWN TAXES.

Benton Town, Road and Bridge	4	mills.
Camden Town, Road and Bridge,	5½	"
Carver Town, Road and Bridge,	10	"
Chaska Town, Road and Bridge,	21	"
Chanhassen Town, Road and Bridge	2	"
Hollywood, Town tax,	2	mills.
Laketown, Town Tax, Road and Bridge,	8	"
Hancock, Town Tax,	4	"
San Francisco, Road and Bridge, Town Tax,	5½	"
Watertown, Town Tax Town & Bounty,	6¼	"
Waconia, Town Tax,	4	"
Dahlgreen Town, Road and Bridge,	15	"
Young America, Road and Bridge, Town Tax,	7	mills.

SPECIAL SCHOOL DISTRICT TAX

No.		mills.	No.		mills.
1	6	mills.	30	1½	mills.
2	10	"	31	8	"
3	3	"	32	3½	"
5	2½	"	33	10	"
6	6½	"	34	5½	"
7	4½	"	35	15	"
8	2½	"	39	6	"
10	10	"	40	1½	"
11	3	"	41	2½	"
12	16	"	42	3½	"
13	7	"	43	5	"
14	6½	"	44	10	"
16	5	"	45	5	"
17	6½	"	46	5	"
18	4	"	47	3	"
19	11	"	48	5½	"
20	3	"	49	5	"
22	3½	"	50	5	"
24	4	"	51	20	"
26	4	"	52	7½	"
27	16	"	53	14	"
29	2	"	54	4	"
28	1	"	55	14	"
			56	31	"

Chaska, Dec. 4th, 1869.

JOHN DUNN. Treasurer of Carver County

Proposal,

TO WHOM IT MAY CONCERN.

In persuance of authority in me vested, by the Board of Commissioners for the County of Carver, I will receive proposals to board, cloth and support, the paupers of Carver County, by the week, for the term of one year, from and after the acceptance of such proposal. Compensation to be made by the County, to the person whose bid is accepted. The right is reserved to reject any and all bids.

Proposals to be made within two months from the date of this notice.

Dated Chaska Sept. 30th 1869.

PETER WEBGO, County Auditor

Estray.

Came into my enclosure in the town of Hancock, Carver Co. one light red sow, the owner will please come forward, prove property, pay charges and take the same away.

ANDREW NILSON.

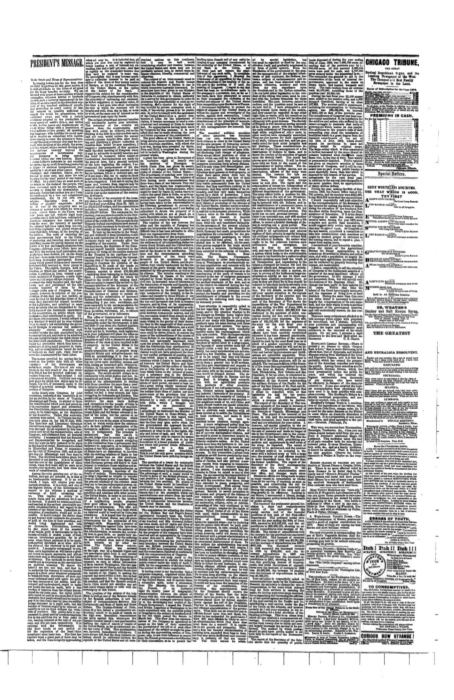

PRESIDENT'S MESSAGE.

To the Senate and House of Representatives:

In coming before you for the first time as Chief Magistrate of this great nation, it is with gratitude to the Giver of all good for the many benefits we enjoy. We are blessed with peace at home, and are without entangling alliances abroad to forebode trouble, with a territory unsurpassed in fertility, of an area equal to the abundant support of five hundred millions of people, and abounding in every variety of useful mineral in quantity sufficient to supply the world for generations, with exuberant crops and with a variety of climate adapted to the production of every species of earth's riches, and suited to the habits, tastes and requirements of every living thing; with a population of forty millions of free people, all speaking one language; with facilities for every mortal to acquire an education; with institutions closing to none the avenues to fame, or any blessing or fortune that may be coveted; with freedom of the pulpit, the press, and the school; with a revenue flowing into the national treasury beyond the requirements of Government. Happily, harmony is being rapidly restored within our own borders. Manufactures hitherto unknown in our country are springing up in all directions, producing a degree of national independence unequaled by that of any other power. These blessings, and countless others, are intrusted to your care, and mine for safe keeping for the brief period of our tenure of office. In a short time we must each of us return to the ranks of the people, who

[illegible]

NEW YORK.

CHICAGO.

CINCINNATI.

ST. LOUIS.

MILWAUKEE.

Sixty Dakotas Burned Alive.

Your readers are more or less familiar with the name of Two Bear, the greatest Indian chief in this portion of the country, of the Pankton band of Dakotas. His party met with a great disaster a short time since. They were out on a hunt and were camped at the head of Knife River. All day preceding the night on which misfortune came upon them, they say the air was full of smoke, but, being a calm day, could not tell the direction from which it came. About midnight a brisk breeze sprung up, and before they could get out of their tepees, the fire was down upon them. It is scarcely possible to describe the scene of confusion that followed, or the suffering endured.

The fire consumed sixty tepees, and burned over sixty of the Indians, besides many of the ponies. Nine Indians have died, and there is a band of forty tepees out on the prairie that have not been heard from since the fire. Most of the badly burned, also the ponies, were left with this band. Their provisions and blankets, in many cases, were entirely consumed, and their sufferings in consequence are great.

Two Bear says the fire was worse than his fight with General Sully out at the White Hill. If the suffering was confined to the warriors alone it would not be so bad, but it extends to women and children. I saw one baby with its left hand nearly burned to a crisp, the fingers were burned off to the second joints, and the stubs of fingers were drawn back. The little thing could not have been more than eight months old; his knees and head were also badly burned. It was crying bitterly, the mother mourning most pitifully. The sight was truly distressing.

Two Bear has gone to the Grand river agency to see if he cannot get something for tepees, as the weather is quite cold, having frozen to the depth of an inch on barrels of water standing out doors.—*Yankton Dakotaian.*

No Humbug.—We do not wish to inform you, reader, that Dr. Wonderful or any other man has discovered a remedy that cures all disease; of mind, body or estate, and is designed to make our sublunary sphere a blissful paradise, to which Heaven itself shall be but a side show, but we do wish to inform [illegible]

[illegible]

The Chaska Herald.

RATES OF ADVERTISING
1 Square one time [illegible]
each subsequent insertion [illegible]
One column one year [illegible]
Half " " [illegible]
Fourth " " [illegible]
[illegible]
Legal Advertisements per square. First insertion, [illegible] cents each subsequent insertion [illegible] cents.
[illegible] notices [illegible] per line. 1st insertion, each subsequent insertion [illegible] per line. All notices less than five lines, [illegible] cents.

MINNESOTA IRON WORKS.

Cor. First and Marshall Streets. Minneapolis, Minn.

SUPPLIES MILL MEN

With Steam Engines and Boilers, both Portable and Stationary, Flouring Mill Machinery, [illegible], Saw Mill Machinery complete, [illegible] Mill Machinery complete, Water Wheels, [illegible], Hangings, [illegible], Pulleys, &c.

Farmers.

With Horse Powers, Hay Presses, Sorghum Mills, Wind Mills, Force Pumps, [illegible] and Mower Castings, Jack Screws, Iron Kettles, from 15 to 100 gallons, Sledge Hammers, &c.

Builders.

With Architectural Castings, as Iron Columns, Fluted and Plain, Iron Caps, ornamental and plain, Iron Stair Plates and Railings, Iron Grates and Doors, Iron Doors and Fire Shutters, Iron Fencing, Iron Crestings, Iron Conductor Shields, Sash Weights, &c.

Pittsburg, Youghiogheny and Lehigh Coal.

[illegible] ALL KINDS.

All communications, letters of inquiry or orders, must be addressed in full,

"MINNESOTA IRON WORKS"
Minneapolis.

JOHN DENN,

Real Estate Agent.

CHASKA .... MINN.

Has large tracts of land for sale in Carver, McLeod and Hennepin Counties.

SALOON!

CARVER - - - MINN.

The best of Liquors, Segars and Beer constantly kept on hand. Farmers call on me.

PETER BUTTANDORF.

Plow And Wagon Factory
AT WACCKA
FRED LUTZ PROPRIETOR.

I would respectfully inform the citizens of Carver County that I now manufacture as good and durable plows as are made in the Union, and offer them as cheap as can be purchased at St. Paul. Also Wagons. Blacksmithing done to order on short notice.

J. R. BARRETT & CO., Proprietors,
MANCHESTER, N. H.

LORD & SMITH,
CHICAGO,
General Agents for the Northwestern States.
[illegible]

WALTHAM WATCHES

For a few months past we have advertised the above Watches at extremely low prices, and the result has been most satisfactory. Our plan has been to sell the genuine Waltham Watch, in Solid Gold or Silver Cases only, and at a very small profit; giving the purchaser every opportunity of examination and comparison, and with the understanding that if the Watch does not prove satisfactory, it can be exchanged or the money refunded.

These Watches are, without exception, the most perfect specimens of fine mechanism ever produced in any country. Each and every part is made by machinery of the most delicate and elaborate construction.

Compared with foreign watches, they possess many advantages, excelling not only in principle and finish, but still more in their reliability as time-keepers. As an indication of the prices we subjoin the following:

Silver Hunting Watches, $18 00
Gold Hunting Watches, 18 karat case, 80 00
Gold Hunting Watches, ladies size 70 00

We often receive orders direct from our advertisement, but prefer that every one should send first for our descriptive price list, which explains all the different kinds, tells the weight and quality of the cases, and gives prices of each. This we will forward to any one on application, and it will be found very useful in making a selection.

Every Watch is warranted by special certificate from the American Watch Co.

We send them by express to any address.—Allow the purchaser to open the package and examine the Watch before paying, and if afterwards it does not prove satisfactory, it can be exchanged or the money will be cheerfully refunded.

Please state that you saw this in the Chaska Herald.

Address, in full, HOWARD & CO.,
No. 619 Broadway, N. Y.

THE CONSTITUTIONAL UNION.

The above is the title of the only Democratic newspaper published at the National Capital, and which is one of the most able expounders of Democratic doctrine there is in the world.—We would say to our Democratic, as well as Republican friends, if you want the best Democratic weekly journal published, send for this. The following unexampled terms are offered to subscribers:

Single copy,	$2 00
Two copies,	3 75
Five copies,	9 00
Ten copies,	17 50
Twenty copies,	30 00

Fifty copies one year to one address 75 00
One hundred copies, to one address 100 00
Terms for subscription invariably in advance.
Any person who will send a club of twenty subscribers, with thirty dollars, will be sent an extra copy of the paper.
Subscribers had better, for their own security, procure post office orders, where such are procurable, in preference to all other kinds of [illegible].

Address, THOMAS B. FLORENCE,
Editor Constitutional Union,
Box 56, Washington City Postoffice.

New Store.

At the Post Office in Carver you can get Dry Goods, Hats, Caps, Boots & Shoes, Ready made clothing and all styles of Dress Goods from Sixty to one hundred per cent cheaper than at any other store in Carver Co. We would call special attention to our stock of Glass Ware, Lamps and Looking Glasses

Groceries can be had Twenty per cent cheaper than at any other place in the County. Produce taken in exchange for Goods.

AUCTION EVERY FAIR DAY.

C. E. ROGERS & CO.

FRANK WARNER

ATTORNEY AT LAW, Chaska Minn., Office at Court House, opposite Auditor's Office.

THE ST. PAUL PIONEER.

Established in 1849.

The Oldest and Best Newspaper in the State.

DEMOCRATIC IN POLITICS.

Daily, Tri-Weekly, Weekly.

The St. Paul Pioneer has already entered upon the twenty-first year of its existence, with a larger list of subscribers and [illegible] than it ever before enjoyed.

It is reliable democratic, progressive in its ideas, and the organ of the people.

It advocates honesty and economy in the administration of the government.

The reduction of taxation.

The repeal of great [illegible] of the existing oppressive tariff.

The prompt payment of the debt.

The taxation of government bonds the same as other property is taxed.

The extermination of corruption from all the places where it is lodged.

The defence of the national honor at all times.

That the government shall be administered solely for the good of the people.

All the editions of the Pioneer will contain the latest telegraphic dispatches from all parts of the world, the latest news of all kinds; reliable and full market reports; [illegible] documents and [illegible]; political and general editorial; correspondence from all parts of our own State and from abroad, the local news from the various localities in the state; interesting tales and general reading for the fireside.

TERMS BY MAIL.

DAILY.

One year	$10 00
Six months	5 00
Three months	3 00
One month	1 00

TRI-WEEKLY.

One year	$6 00
Six months	3 00
In clubs of six or more, each copy one year	5 00

WEEKLY.

One copy, one year	$2 00
One copy, six months	1 00
In clubs of ten or more, each copy one year	1 50

A copy of the weekly will be sent gratis to any person who gets up a club of ten, and of the tri-weekly to any person who gets up a club of twenty weekly subscribers. Address
PIONEER PRINTING Co.,
St. Paul, Minn.

"A Complete Pictorial History of the Times"

"The Best, Cheapest, and Most Successful Family Paper in the World."

Harper's Weekly.
SPLENDIDLY ILLUSTRATED.

In November will be commenced "Man and Wife," a new serial story, splendidly illustrated, by Wilkie Collins, [illegible] "The Woman in White," "No Name," "Armadale," and "The Moonstone." New subscribers will be supplied with Harper's Weekly from the commencement of the story to the end of 1870 for $4.

CRITICAL NOTICES OF THE PRESS

The model newspaper of our country. Complete in all the departments of an American Family paper. Harper's Weekly has earned for itself a right to its title, "A Weekly Journal of Civilization."—New York Evening Post.

Harper's Weekly may be unreservedly declared the best newspaper in America.—New York Independent.

The articles upon public questions which appear in Harper's Weekly from week to week form a remarkable series of brief political essays. They are distinguished by clear and pointed statement, by good common sense, by independence and breadth of view. They are the expression of mature conviction, high principle, and strong feeling, and take their place among the best newspaper writing of the times.—North American Review, Boston, Mass.

SUBSCRIPTIONS. 1870.

TERMS:

HARPER'S WEEKLY, one year, $4 00

An extra copy of either the Magazine Weekly, or Bazar will be supplied gratis for every club of Five Subscribers at $4 each, in one remittance; or, Six copies for $20, without extra copy.

Subscriptions to Harper's Magazine, Weekly, and Bazar, to one address for one year, $10; or, two of Harper's Periodicals, to one address for one year, $7.

Back Numbers can be supplied at any time.

The annual volumes of Harper's Weekly, in neat cloth binding, will be sent by express, free of expense, for $7 each. A complete set, comprising 13 volumes, sent on receipt of cash at the rate of $5.25 per vol., freight at expense of purchaser. Volume 13 ready Jan 1, 1870.

The postage on Harper's Weekly is 20 cents a year, which must be paid at the subscriber's post-office.

Address HARPER & BROTHERS, N. Y.

INSURANCE.

We would respectfully notify our friends and patrons that the

UNDERWRITER'S AGENCY OF NEW YORK.

(Composed of the oldest German Insurance Co. in the U. S. and three other Companies,) is now represented by F. E. Du Toit, who will be prepared to insure Farm property and Stocks of Goods in this and the surrounding Counties at the LOWEST RATES.

Cash Assets, $3,555 000

Losses promptly paid.

Germania, Hanover, Niagara, and Republic Ins. Co., of New York.

A. STODDARD, Gen'l. Agt.
F. E. DU TOIT, Local Agent, Chaska.

Estray—Reward.

Strayed from the premises of the subscriber in the village of Chaska, one yearling horse colt, of iron grey color, with double teats. Said colt is of unusual size. A liberal reward will be given for his return or information leading to his recovery.

Chaska July 21st 1869.

PHILIP HENK.

INSURANCE

F. E. DU TOIT.
AGENT

of the following Insurance Co's,

ÆTNA

Hartford, Con.—Assets 5,052,000,00

UNDERWRITER'S AGENCY

New York City,—Assets 3,555,000,00

CHARTER OAK LIFE INS CO
OF
Hartford, Conn.—Assets, 4,000,000,00

Policies of Insurance issued against loss or damage by fire and perils of Inland transportation.

Losses Adjusted and Paid promptly at the place where the *Policy is Issued.*

Will attend promptly, to collections. Paying of Taxes, &c.

OFFICE, AT THE "HERALD" OFFICE.
CHASKA MINNESOTA

JOHN BLOEDEL'S

Brick Wagon and Black-Smith Shop
Near Zangers Store

CARVER - - - - - - MINN.

This is the oldest, largest and best Shop in the County.

The Celebrated Milwaukee, Wisconsin Wagons are always kept for sale at this shop. They are brought up from Milwaukee and ironed here. They are sold as cheap as Minnesota wagons.—Bob-sleds &c. kept for sale and made to order.

Shoeing Oxen, Horses, and all other Blacksmith work done to order.

All those wishing good and durable work and at reasonable prices should call at

BLOEDEL'S SHOP.

W. S. COMBS. J. S. WEINMANN.

WEINMANN & LOSSEN.

GENERAL

Fire and Life Insurance Agents.

Also Collection Agents.

Carver, Minn.

Bride And Bridegroom.

Essays for Young Men on the interesting relation of Bridegroom to Bride, in the institution of Marriage.—a Guide to matrimonial felicity, and true happiness. Sent by mail in sealed letter envelopes free of charge. Address, Howard Association, box P. Philadelphia, Pa.

THE LADY'S FRIEND.

Two Months Gratis!!

The Lady's Friend announces the following Novelets for 1870: Did he Forget Her? by Louise Chandler Moulton; "The Cameron Aunt" by Elizabeth Prescott author of "Between Two," &c.; "Valid Silver; or, Christie Deen's Bridal Gifts" by Amanda M. Douglas, author of "The Deberry Fortune," &c., with numerous shorter stories by a brilliant galaxy of lady writers.

A finely executed steel engraving, a handsome double-page, finely colored fashion plate, and a large assortment of wood-cuts illustrating the fashions, fancy work, &c., are given in every number.

It will give a popular piece of Music in every number.

Portraits of Distinguished Authors.

The January number will contain portraits (engraved on steel) of Mrs. Henry Wood, Harriet Prescott, Louise Chandler Prescott, Amanda M. Douglas, Mrs. Margaret Hosmer, and August Bell.

New subscribers who send in their names for 1870 before the first of November shall receive the November and December numbers of this year in addition, making 14 months in all. And new subscribers sending in their names by the first of December shall receive the magnificent December holiday number, making 13 months in all.

TERMS—$2 50 a year; two copies, $4; four copies $6; five copies (and one gratis) $8. One copy of the Lady's Friend and The Saturday Evening Post, $4.

A copy of the large and beautiful Premium Steel Engraving—"Taking the Measure of the Wedding Ring"—engraved in England at a cost of $2,000, will be sent to every [illegible] subscriber, and to every person sending a club. This engraving is a gem of art. Address

DEACON & PETERSON,
319 Walnut street, Phila.

—Specimen copies sent for ten cents.—

Court House Saloon.

JOHN BOSS .... Proprietor.

Brick Saloon near Court House. Best of Liquors and Cigars always kept on hand.
The celebrated Shakopee Lager Beer always "fresh tapped."

Insurance.

For reliable indemnity against loss by Fire apply to Fred E Du Toit, Agent of the following old and reliable companies at Chaska, Minn.

Aetna, Hartford, capital $5,052,000
Underwriters, New York, 4,000,000
Western Buffalo, 700,000
Charter Oak, Hartford Life 5,000,000

All of the above companies insure property at reasonable rates and pay their losses promptly.

Commissioners Notice.

Notice is hereby given, that by order of the Probate Court for Carver County, Minn., the undersigned have been appointed commissioners to receive, examine and adjust claims against the estate of Peter Thompson late of said County deceased, and will meet for that purpose on the first Monday of each month, at the Court House in Chaska in said County, at 2 o'clock p. m., for six months from August 14th 1869, and said period of six months is the time limited by said order for creditors to present their claims.

Chaska, Aug. 14th 1869.

PETER WEGGO.
G. KRAYENBUHL.
F. E. DU TOIT.

PROBATE NOTICE.

State of Minnesota, County of Carver. } S. S.

On reading and filing the oath and petition of Amelia Brandt praying for reasons therein set forth that letters of administration may issue to John Bendemeyer on the estate of August Brandt late of said county deceased.

It is ordered that the 13th day of December A. D. 1869 at 11 o'clock A. M. at the office of the Judge of Probate in Chaska in said County be assigned for the hearing of said petition, and all persons interested in said estate are required to appear at a session of the Probate then and there to be holden to show cause if any there be why the prayer of said petitioner should not be granted. And it is further ordered that said petitioner give public notice of the pendency of said petition by causing a copy of this order to be published in the "Valley Herald" a weekly newspaper published at Chaska in said County for three successive weeks previous to the day of said hearing.

Dated Chaska Nov. 8 1869.

J. A. SARGENT,
Judge of Probate.

PROBATE NOTICE.

State of Minnesota, County of Carver. } S. S.

On reading and filing the oath and petition of Anna Carlson praying for reasons therein set forth that letters of administration may issue to herself on estate of said Johannes Carlson late of said county deceased. It is ordered that December the 13th 1869 at 11 o'clock A. M. at the court house in Chaska in said county be assigned for the hearing of said petition. And all persons interested in the said estate are requested to be and appear before said Court at the time and place aforesaid and show cause if any they have why said petition should not be granted. And it is further ordered that said petitioner give public notice of the pendency of said petition by causing a notice of this order to be published in the Valley Herald a weekly newspaper printed in said county for four weeks previous to said day of hearing.

Chaska Nov. 5th 1869.

J. A. SARGENT,
Judge of Probate.

St. Paul and Sioux City Railroad.

UPWARD TRAINS.

Leaves.		Leaves.
Leave St. Paul	7:45 a. m.	and 3:45 p. m.
Arrive Mendota	8:10 a. m.	and 4:10 p. m.
Ar. Shakopee	10:10 a. m.	and 5:20 p. m.
Ar. Merriam	[illegible] a. m.	and 5:50 p. m.
Ar. Brentwood	11:10 a. m.	and 6:01 p. m.
Ar. Belle Plaine	11:35 a. m.	and 6:13 p. m.
Ar. Blakely	12:05 p. m.	and 6:27 p. m.
Ar. Henderson	1:15 p. m.	and 7:05 p. m.
Ar. LeSueur	1:40 p. m.	and 7:15 p. m.
Ar. Ottawa	2:10 p. m.	and 7:35 p. m.
Ar. St. Peter	2:40 p. m.	and 7:50 p. m.
Ar. Mankato	3:45 p. m.	and 8:30 p. m.

DOWNWARD TRAINS.

Leave Mankato	6:00 a. m.	and 9:00 a. m.
Arrive St. Peter	7:00 a. m.	and 9:55 a. m.
Ar. Ottawa	7:25 a. m.	and 10:[illegible] a. m.
Ar. LeSueur	7:45 a. m.	and 11:05 a. m.
Ar. Henderson	7:55 a. m.	and 11:[illegible] a. m.
Ar. Blakely	8:15 a. m.	and 12:15 p. m.
Ar. Belle Plaine	8:25 a. m.	and 12:35 p. m.
Ar. Brentwood	8:45 a. m.	and 1:30 p. m.
Ar. Merriam	9:10 a. m.	and 2:00 p. m.
Ar. Shakopee	9:30 a. m.	and 2:30 p. m.
Ar. Mendota	10:30 a. m.	and 3:50 p. m.
Ar. St. Paul	11:10 a. m.	and 4:30 p. m.

Trains on this road make close connection at Mendota with trains on Milwaukee and Saint Paul Railroad for Minneapolis, Owatonna, Winona and all points South and East; and at Saint Peter with Minnesota Stage Company's Line of Stages for New Ulm, and at Mankato for all points West and Southwest.

Tickets can be procured at the Union Ticket Office, Corner Third and Jackson Streets, and at the Depot, West St. Paul.

JOHN F. LINCOLN,
Superintendent.

"A Repository of Fashion, Pleasure, And Instruction."

HARPER'S BAZAR.

A supplement containing numerous full sized patterns of useful articles accompanies the paper every fortnight, and occasionally an elegant colored Fashion Plate.

Harper's Bazar contains 16 folio pages of the size of Harper's Weekly, printed on superfine calendered paper, and is published weekly.

CRITICAL NOTICES OF THE PRESS.

Harper's Bazar contains, besides pictures, patterns, etc., a variety of matter of especial use and interest to the family; articles on health, dress and housekeeping in all its branches; its editorial matter is specially adapted to the circle it is intended to interest and instruct; and it has besides, good stories and literary matter of merit. It is not surprising that the journal, with such features, has achieved in a short time an immense success; for something of its kind was desired in thousands of families, and its publishers have filled the demand. The young lady who buys a single number of Harper's Bazar is made a subscriber for life.—New York Evening Post.

The Bazar is excellent. Like all the periodicals which the Harper's publish, it is almost ideally well edited, and the class of readers for whom it is intended—the mothers and daughters in average families—can not but profit by its good sense and good taste, which we have no doubt, are to-day making very many homes happier than they may have been before the women began taking lessons in personal and household and social management from this good natured mentor.—The Nation.

It has the merit of being sensible, of conveying instruction, of giving excellent patterns in every department, and of being well stocked with reading matter.—Watchman and Reflector.

Subscriptions—1870,

TERMS:

Harper's Bazar, one year, $4 00.

An Extra copy of either the Magazine, Weekly or Bazar, will be supplied gratis for every Club of Five subscribers at $4 00 each, in one remittance; or Six Copies for $20 00, without extra copy.

Subscriptions to Harper's Magazine, Weekly, and Bazar, to one address, one year, $10 00; or two of Harper's Periodicals, to one address, one year, $7 00.

Back numbers supplied at any time.

Vols. I. and II. of Harper's Bazar, for the years 1868-9, elegantly bound in green morocco cloth, will be sent by express, freight prepaid, for $7 00 each.

The postage on Harper's Bazar is 20 cents a year, which must be paid at the subscriber's post office.

Address HARPER & BROTHERS,
New York.

CHASKA
LUMBER YARD

The undersigned will keep an extensive stock OF

All Kinds of Lumber
AT
LIBERAL PRICES.

FERD. TRIES.

LEGAL NOTICES.

Mortgage Sale.

Names of Mortgagors, Jacob Hase and Elisabeth Hase of Chaska in the County of Carver and State of Minnesota.

Name of Mortgagee, Henry Young of Chaska [illegible].

Date of Mortgage, May 1st A. D. 1868.

When recorded, May 11th A. D. 1869 at 10 o'clock in the forenoon of that day in Book "B" of mortgages on page 147 in the office of the Register of Deeds of said County of Carver.

Amount claimed to be due at the date of this notice, one hundred and seventy five dollars & ninety seven cents.

Description of mortgaged premises. The east [½] half of the south east [¼] quarter of section [34] thirty four in township [116] one hundred and sixteen, Range [23] twenty three west, excepting fifteen [15] acres described as follows: Beginning at the south east corner of section [34] thirty four and running thence westerly along the south line of said section [20] twenty chains to a post in the south west corner of the south east [¼] quarter of the south east [¼] quarter of said section; thence northly along the west line of said south east quarter [¼] of the south east quarter (¼) of said section [34] thirty four two [2] chains and [70] seventy links to the center of the Yorkville and Bloomington State road; thence north [43] forty three degrees east along the center of said road [22] twenty two chains and [50] links to a point on the east line of said section thirty four; thence south twelve chains and thirty links to the place of beginning.

Default having been made in the payment of the said sum due on said mortgage as aforesaid and no proceedings at law or otherwise having been instituted to recover the same or any part thereof; now therefore notice is hereby given that by virtue of the power of sale contained in said mortgage and of the statute in such case made and provided the said mortgage will be foreclosed by a sale of said mortgaged premises at public vendue to the highest bidder for cash at the front door of the Court House in Chaska in said county of Carver on the 8th day of January A. D. 1870 at eleven o'clock in the forenoon of that day for the purpose of satisfying the sum then due thereon and secured by said mortgage together with the costs and disbursements of sale and additional sum of twenty five dollars attorneys fees according to the terms of said mortgage.

Chaska, Nov. 23d 1869.

HENRY YOUNG, Mortgagee.
BAXTER & SARGENT, Atty's for Mortgagee.

SUMMONS.

State of Minnesota, District Court, 4th Judicial Dist. County of Carver. } S. S.

Johannes Anderson, vs. J. F. L. Jetter.

The State of Minnesota, To the above named defendant:

You are hereby summoned and required to answer the complaint in this action which has been filed in the office of the Clerk of the District Court at [illegible] in said County, and to serve a copy of your answer to the said complaint on the subscriber, at his office in Watertown in said County within twenty days after the service of this summons upon you, exclusive of the day of such service, and if you fail to answer the said complaint within the time aforesaid, the Plaintiff in this action will apply to the Court for the relief demanded in the Complaint.

Dated Watertown, Dec. 6th A. D. 1869.

H. J. PECK,
Plaintiff's Attorney, Watertown Minn.

SHERIFF SALE.

By virtue of an execution issued out of and under the seal of the district court of the Fourth Judicial District in and for the County of Carver in the State of Minnesota, to me directed & delivered upon a judgment in an action in which Florian [illegible] was Plaintiff and George Krumbolz and Berthold Herts were defendants. Said execution bearing date December fifteenth A. D. 1869. I have levied on all of the following described land and real estate as the property of the said defendant Berthold Herts and all of the right title interest and estate which the said defendant Berthold Herts had thereof on the fourteenth day of December A. D. 1869, the day of the docketing of said judgment or at any time since have had on the same, to wit: Lots [7, 8, 9, & 10,] seven, eight, nine and ten and the south west [½] half of lot [11] eleven in Block 34 fifty four in the townsite of Carver in the County of Carver aforesaid according to the plat thereof on record in the office of the Register of Deeds of said county carver. Now therefore notice is hereby given that by virtue of the said execution. I will sell the said above described premises at public auction to satisfy said execution and the costs thereon, on the 29th day of January A D 1870 at one o'clock in the afternoon of said day, at the front door of the Court House in Chaska in said County of Carver to the highest bidder for cash.

Chaska, Dec., 15th 1869.

FREDK. HECKLIN, sheriff Carver Co Minn.
Baxter & Sargent, Plff's. Attys.

State of Minnesota, County of Carver, In Probate Court, } S. S.

In the matter of the estate of Hermann Koopmann late of said County deceased.

On reading and filing the oath and petition of Luther L. Baxter whereby it appears to this Court that said Hermann Koopmann died intestate on or about the 1st of August 1866 being at the time of his death an inhabitant of said County of Carver, and being seized in fee of about forty acres of real estate in said county, and it further appearing that said deceased left no relatives in this State entitled to the administration of the estate of said deceased. And it further appearing that none of the creditors of said deceased are willing to accept the trust as administrator of the estate of said deceased. And it further appearing that it is necessary and would be for the interest of all concerned in the estate of said deceased that an administrator be appointed upon the estate of said deceased.

Now therefore it is ordered that Saturday the 5th day of February 1870 at 2 o'clock in the afternoon of said day, at the Probate court room in chaska be assigned as the time and place for hearing said petition.

And it is ordered that notice be given to all persons interested in said estate to appear before the Probate Court of said county on the said 5th day of February 1870, at 2 o'clock in the afternoon in chaska aforesaid, to show cause, if any they have why the said Luther L. Baxter should not be appointed administrator of the estate of Hermann Koopmann deceased.

And it is further ordered that notice be given of the pendency of said petition, by publishing copies of above orders in the Valley Herald a weekly newspaper published in chaska in said county four weeks previous to the said day of hearing.

Dated chaska Dec 11 1869.

J. A. SARGENT,
Judge of Probate carver co., Minn.

UNION HOTL.

CHASKA. - - - - - - - MINN

A good bar in connection with the house. Also good Stabling.

WM. OCHS, Propr.

COMBS & WHITNEY
WHOLESALE & RETAIL

Booksellers and Stationers

AND THE

Emporium for views of Minnesota and other Scenery, Brackets, Engravings, Frames, Chromos, &c. &c.

174 Third, Corner Cedar Street
Saint Paul, Minn.

Dr. C. B. AMES.

PHYSICIAN AND SURGEON.

WATERTOWN . . . MINN.

Office at Lewis Drug Store. Offers his services to the citizens of Watertown and vicinity, and can always be found day or night ready to attend calls.

FALL & WINTER GOODS
Just Received From
Chicago
And Milwaukee.

AT THE

The New Store
OF
HENRY YOUNG

DOMESTIC AND FANCY

DRY GOODS

CLOTHING

Hats, Caps, Furs, Boots, and Shoes, &

Groceries. Cash paid for farmers produce.

Call At

"THE OLD POST OFFICE STAND"

G. A. DUTOIT.

Wholesale and retail dealer in

Drugs, Paints, Oils,

Perfumery, patent Medicines

Etc. Window Glass, Fancy Articles, toys and Notions,

Pure Wines and Catawba Brandy for medical purposes.

CARVER MINN.

Fresh Arrival

At

LINENFELSER & FABER

OF

DRY GOODS

Clothing, Hats, Caps, Boots and Shoes &c.

GROCERIES & PROVISIONS

AT

"At the Brick Store."

F. E. DU TOIT Proprietor. | TERMS, $1 50, Per Annum.

VOLUME 8 | CHASKA, MINNESOTA, FRIDAY, DEC. 24, 1869, | NUMBER 18

The Valley Herald

Official County Paper.

BY F. E. DU TOIT,

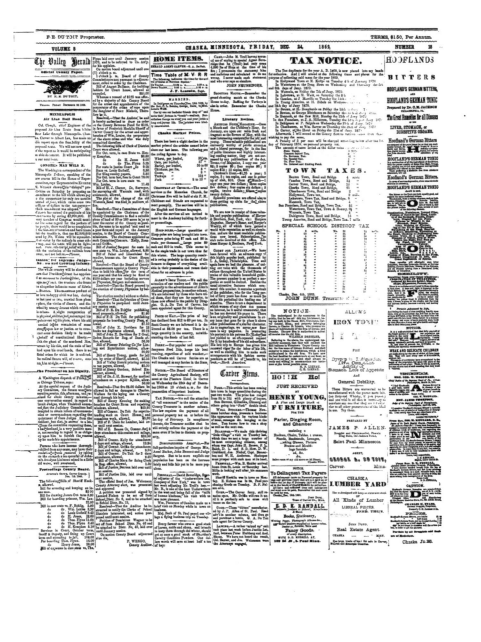

CHASKA FRIDAY DECEMBER 24 1869.

MINNEAPOLIS Air Line Rail Road,

Col. Clough, chief Engineer of the proposed Air Line Route from White Bear Lake through Minneapolis, Chaska, Carver to Albert Lea, has made an able report upon the feasibility of the proposed route. We will not now speak of the report as it would be anticipating an able document. It will be published in our next issue.

CONGRESSMAN WILSON.

The Washington correspondent of the Minneapolis *Tribune*, speaking of the new census bill in the House of Representatives, says "Representative EUGENE M. WILSON showed his "disloyal" proclivities on Saturday by proposing an amendment to the bill which allows pay to the enumerator for only *two* months instead of *four*, which saves some two millions of dollars to the tax-payers—which amendment was adopted." Mr. Wilson has earned the gratitude of his constituents by saving $2,000,000. If every member of Congress would manifest the same regard for the pockets of the people, there would be no complaints of the burdens of taxation and hard times but the trouble is, that the $2,000,000 saved by Mr. Wilson will be squandered or stolen by the radicals in some other way, and the taxes will not be lightened. Sure, substantial relief will come with the exclusion of the radicals from power, and not before.—*Pioneer*.

Stanton for Supreme Judge—The New and Crowning Infamy.

The whole country will be shocked to learn that President Grant has appointed as successor to Justice Grier, of the Supreme Court, the creature who bears the altogether infamous name of Edwin M. Stanton. This monstrous product of our late unhappy civil war has, during the last year or two, crawled from place to place, the victim of disease, and disturbed by uneasy dreams which recalled his crimes. A slight recuperation of his physical abilities had encouraged his appointment to this place, where his aid is needed in the commission of some outrage upon law or justice, or to counteract some decision likely to be made in behalf of constitutional liberty.—With the ghost of the murdered Mrs. Surratt by his side, and the stain of her blood upon his cruel hands, there is no official crime for which he is unfitted. The radical Senate will, of course, confirm him at sight.—*Pioneer*.

The President on his Dignity.

A Washington dispatch of Friday, to the Chicago Tribune, says:

At the special request of the Judiciary Committee, the Senate went into executive session this afternoon, and remained for about twenty minutes.—Some conversation ensued in regard to Circuit Judges, when Trumbull announced that the Judiciary Committee had attempted to obtain letters of recommendation or correspondence regarding the appointment of these Judges from the President, but that, in answer to a letter from the committee requesting these, he had declined in a very positive manner, not seeming to regard it as obligatory upon him to furnish the reasons why he made his appointments.

Persons who have become thoroughly chilled from any cause, may have their circulation at once restored by taking into the stomach a tea spoonful of Johnson's Anodyne Liniment mixed in a little cold water, well sweetened.

Proceedings County Board.

AUDITOR'S OFFICE, Carver County. }
Dec. 7th 1869. }

The following Bills of Sheriff Hecklin, allowed.

Bill for arresting and keeping an insane man.	$2 00
Bill for drawing Jurors Oct term	3.00
Bill for boarding prisoner, Wm. Louise,	21.00
Bill in case state vs. F. Bohlig,	5.00
do do Wm. Louise	3.90
do do Louis Gothelf	8.40
do do H. Jones,	12.00
do do Thos. Flynn	11.00
do do Thos. Flynn	3.40
do do H. Kempkes	5.10
Services in Court, October term, Sheriff & Deputy, and fixing up Court room and attending to jail,	108.00
For boarding Thos. Flynn.	16.00
do Henry Jones,	28.00

Bill of expenses in case state vs. Thos. Flynn laid over until January session 1870, and to be referred to Co. Att'y. for his oppinion.

On motion board adjourned until one (1) o'clock p. m.

1 o'clock p. m. Board of County Commissioners met pursuant to adjournment, called to order by the Chairman.

Bill of August Bullmer, for building ladders for Court house, allowed as amended, $21.00

Whereas a reward of $125 was offered by a majority of this County Board for the arrest and apprehension of the perpetrator of the crime of rape upon the daughter of Peter Michels, Therefore be it,

Resolved,—That the Auditor be and is hereby authorised to draw an order on the County Revenue Fund for $125, in favor of Frederick Hecklin Sheriff of Carver County for the arrest and apprehension of Wm. Louise, the perpetrator of the above crime and who was duly committed therefore.

The following bills of Clerk of District Court were allowed.

For Oct. term, in case State vs. Henry Kemphes,	$3.60
do do H. Jones	9.00
do do Ths. Flynn	5.25
For costs in justice Court do	9.25
State vs. Louis Gothelf,	6,50
For filing sundry papers,	5.85
For Oct. term last, fees in Court	76.00
For Oct. term in case state vs. Wm. Louise,	11.45

Bill of H. J. Chever, Co. Surveyor, for surveying old Waconia road, with assistances, allowed, $16.50

The plat of the change of the old Waconia Road was filed in auditors office.

Resolved.—That a Committee of three be appointed by the Chairman of the County Commissioners to find a suitable piece of land of 80 or 160 acres in or as near the center of the County as possible, the same to be applied and used as a poor farm and report at the January session, to the Board of County Commissioners. The chairman appointed as such Committee Commrs. Kelly, Reasse and Griffin.

Bill of Justice Sergent for costs in case state vs. Wm. Louise, allowed, 8.90

Bill of Faber and Linenfelser for candles, brooms etc. for Court House allowed, $11.70

Resolved—That the Board of County Commissioners appoint a County Physician to hold his office for the term of one year and that his salary be fixed at $300 dollars per year including service as Physician, Surgeon and assistance.

Resolved—That the Board proceed to the election of County Physician by ballot,

The election resulted without a choice.

Resolved—That the election of County Physician be postponed until January session next.

Bill of F. E. Du Toit for publishing wood proposals, allowed, $1.80

Bill of F. E. Du Toit for publishing proposals for boarding County Poor, allowed, $7.10

Bill of John X. Davidson for 12 books tax duplicates allowed, 20.75

Bill of John X. Davidson for 2 Genl. Index Records for Reg. of Deeds office, allowed, 56.00

Bill of Pioneer Printing Co for Listing and Equalization notices, allowed, 20,00

Bill of Henry Young, goods for jail etc. by order of Sheriff, allowed, 25.55

Bill of Valley Herald printing notices to tax payers, allowed, $5.00

Bill of Henry Gerdson, School Examiner, allowed, 4 00

Bill of Dr. J. H. Stewart, for medical attendance on a pauper Kjillis, allowed, 50.00

Resolved—That five $5.00 dollars be allowed in full as damages to Charles Wallace for the laying out a County road through his land.

Bill of Henry Kenning for making benches for Court Room and repairing windows, allowed, $25.90

Bill of Commr. Du Toit for superintending work on Court House, and committee work, allowed, $5,00

Bill of F. Theis for Lumber, laid over until next session.

Bill of E. Reasse Co. Commr. for 3 days attendance this session and milage, allowed, $10.50

Bill of Commr. Kelly for attendance 3 days and milage, allowed, 12.24

Bill of Commr. Griffin for attendance 3 days and milage, allowed, 9.24

Bill of Commr. Du Toit for 3 days attendance, allowed, 9.00

Bill of Charles Marx for fixing Clock in Reg. office, allowed, 1.50

Bill of Justice Berreau laid over until next session.

Bill of Justice Iltis, laid over until next session,

The official Bond of Jos. Weinmann County Attorney elect, was presented and approved

A petition was presented signed by Leonard Finken to be set off from School Distr. No 6, and to be attached to School Distr. No. 19,

Resolved—That the Auditor be instructed to notify the Clerks of School Districts interested, and action postponed until next session.

Petition of Dominicus Wagner to be set off from School Distr. No. 46 and be attached to Distr. No. 45, laid over until January session.

On motion County Board adjourned sine die,

P. WEEGO,
County Auditor.

HOME ITEMS.

HERALD AGENT CARVER—G. A. DuToit.

Time Table of M. V. R. R

The following indicates the time for the arrival of trains at Merriam Station:

Up Trains.........10:38 A. M.......... 5:30 P. M.
Down Trains...... 9:04 A. M............3 06 P. M.

J. F. Lincoln, Supt.

MARRIED.

In Dahlgreen on Thursday Dec. 18th 1869, by the Rev. C. L. Reinke, George Raltz, to Miss. Louisa Wolf.

One by one our bachelor friends drop of and unite their fortune in "bonds"—wedlock. Nevertheless George we wish you and your bride a long and joyous life. The printers were kindly remembered.

Chaska Market Prices.

There has been a slight decline in the market price of the articles named below since our last issue. The following are the ruling figures to day.

Wheat, per bushel,	55 cts.
Oats, per bushel,	37 "
Barley, per bushel,	55 to 60
Chickens, per lbs,	8 "
Geese, "	8 "
Turkeys "	12½ "
Pork "	8 to 10 "

CHRISTMAS AT CHURCH.—The usual services in the Moravian Church, for Christmas Eve will be held at six P. M. Children and friends are requested to meet promptly. The services will be in the English and German languages.

After the services all are invited to meet in the Academy building for further proceedings.

HOOP-POLES.—Large quantities of Hoop-poles are being brought into town. Common poles bring $7 cash and $8 in trade per thousand. Large poles $9 cash and $10 in trade. This seems to be the staple trade in our town thus far this winter. The large quantity received is owing probably to the desire of the farmers to dispose of everything available in their possession and retain their wheat for an advance in price.

ALLEN'S IRON TONIC.—We call the attention of our readers and the public generally to the advertisement of Allen's Medical preparations, in another column. We are informed by those who have tried them, that they are far superior, to those now offered to the public by Druggist. G. A. Du Toit of Carver, has been appointed agent for this County.

PRICE OF HAY.—The price of hay has declined from $12 to $9 per ton. In Scott County we are informed it is delivered at $8.00 per ton. There is a large quantity in the country, notwithstanding the floods of last fall.

FERRY.—Our popular and energetic ferryman Fred Iltis, keeps his boat running, regardless of cold weather.—The Chaska and Carver ferries are as well managed as any ferries in the State.

NOTICE.—The Board of Directors of the County Agricultural Society, will meet at the Planters Hotel in Carver on Wednesday the 29th day of December 1869 at 10 o'clock a. m., for the transaction of important business.

TAX NOTICE.—We call the attention of "all concerned" to the notice of the County Treasurer in another column. The law requires the payment of all personal property tax on or before the 1st day of February. In compliance thereto, the Treasurer notifies that he will strictly enforce the payment of the same even if he has to distrain on property.

DISTINGUISHED ARRIVAL.—For full particulars inquire of George Mix, Ansel Barker, John Bennett and Judge Sargent. But to be more explicit our population has been on the increase lately and bids fair yet to be more populous.

PERSONAL.—David Beveridge, Special adjuster of the "Underwriters Ins. Company of New York," was in town last week adjusting Mr. Troll's loss.—Mr. B., is one of the best Underwriters in the west and being full of the "milk of human kindness," his visit with us was most pleasant.

Wm. Patterson of Camden made us a brief visit on Monday while in town on business.

Maj. Bech of St. Paul payed our village a flying business trip on Tuesday.

Every farmer who owns a good stock of horses, cattle and sheep, and intends to keep them through the winter, should get at once a good stock of Sheridan's Cavalry Condition Powders. One dollar worth will save at least half a ton of hay.

CARD.—John M. Troll having accused me of saying to special Agent Beveridge that he (Troll) had only some 4,000 lbs of Hops at the time of his fire; I pronounce the statement false and malicious and calculated to do me wrong. I never made such statement and who ever says so slanders.

JOHN NEUNSINGER.

SHOOTING MATCH.—Remember the grand shooting match at the Chaska House to-day. Raffling for Turkeys is also in order. Remember the Chaska House.

Literary Notices.

ARTHURS HOME MAGAZINE.—Once a Month and the Children's Hour, for January, are upon our table fresh and fragrant as the flowers of May, with the most interesting contents for the old and young. These valuable publications are eminently worthy of public attention and a liberal patronage, for in the line of polite literature and highly interesting reading matter, they are not surpassed by any publications of the day. Terms.—of Magazine, 1 copy one year $2; 3 copies $5; four copies $6; 8 copies $12; 15 copies, $20.

Children's Hour.—$1,25 a year; 5 copies, 5; ten copies, and one to getter up of club, $10. Once a Month—1 copy one year two dollars; three copies five dollars; four copies six dollars; 8 copies, twelve dollars; fifteen copies twenty dollars.

Splendid premiums are offered also to those getting up clubs for the above publications.

We are now in receipt of those valuable and popular publications of Harper & Brothers, New, York, viz: Harpers Magazine, Harper's Bazar, and Harper's Weekly, all of which have gained a world wide reputation as well as circulation, and are the most readable publications now issued. Subscriptions, at club rates received at this office. Address Harper & Brothers, New York.

GODEY FOR JANUARY.—We have been favored with an advance copy of this highly popular book, published by L. A. Godey, Philadelphia. Time and again have we had the pleasure of uniting our voice with the thousands of editors throughout the United States in praise of this valuable household guide. The present number is as perfect a magazine as could be desired. Besides the usual attractive features which commend this number, it contains a portrait of the publisher, who for the long period of forty years has done so much to make his periodical the leading one of America. There is not a department in which women of any class can possess an interest, be it useful ornamental, that he has not devoted his pages to. There is an originality and gracefulness in every issue that goes far to place it above other publications of a similar character. As to engravings, we never saw finer ones in any magazine. In presenting his portrait to his patrons Mr. Godey has but yielded to an oft-repeated request for it by hundreds of his old subscribers. His late trip to Europe has given him renewed vigor for the labor of his life, as well as enabling him to make such arrangements with his fashion correspondents as will be of benefit to his book.—*North American*.

Carver Items.

Correspondence.

PORK.—This article has been coming into town in large quantities during the past two weeks. The price has ranged from 8½ to 10½ with plenty of buyers.

Sam Stevens, Glitschka, Ohnsorg and others going into "Pork" double shod.

WELL STOCKED.—Thomas Newmans butcher shop, presents a business like appearance with its various kinds of meat, sausages &c. hanging at the door. Tom knows how to run a shop as well as the next one.

SHAKOPEE.—We made this thriving "little village" a visit on Tuesday last, which time we met a large number of its most enterprising citizens, among whom was Capt. John H. Brown, F. L. Balch, D. L. and S. D. How, D. W. Coulthard, Jos. Niehof, Capt. Sencerbox and W. H. Anderson. Shakopee must prosper with such men at its head.

PERSONAL.—Wm. B. Mohler arrived home from St. Louis on Saturday last. Billie is looking well after his summers work.

Sheriff Hecklin was in town on Monday. E. Holmes was in St. Paul purchasing Goods on Tuesday. N. P. Nelson also.

OPEN.—The Carver ferry, still remains open. Mr. Griffin will run it until it is perfectly safe to cross with teams on the ice.

GOOD.—Those "bitters" manufactured by J. P. Allen of St. Paul. Read adv't in another column, and then go and purchase a bottle, G. A. Du Toit sole agent for Carver County.

LAWING.—A rather "mixed up" suit took place last week before Justice Latford, between Peter Hultberg and And. Skone. We have not heard the result, Col. Baxter, and Jos. Weinmann were the Attorneys engaged.

TAX NOTICE.

The Tax duplicate for the year A. D. 1869, is now placed into my hands for collection. And I will attend at the following times and places for the purpose of collecting said taxes for the year 1869.

In Hollywood Town at M. Kelly's on Tuesday 4th of January 1870
In Watertown at the Drug Store on Wednesday and Thursday the 5th and 6th days of Jany. 1870.
In Waconia, on Friday the 7th of Jany. 1870.
In Laketown, at M. Walk, on Saturday the 8th [illegible]
In Camden, at J. Merrills on Tuesday the 11th [illegible]
In Young America, at H. Fabels on Wednesday [illegible] and 13th day of Jany 1870.
In Benton, at H. Bougharde on Friday the 14th [illegible]
In Benton, at George Bleichoers on Saturday the 15th of Jany 1870.
In Hancock, at the Saw Mill, Monday the 17th of Jany 1870
In San Francisco, at J. A. Hillstrom, Tuesday the 18th day of Jany 1870
In Dahlgreen at P. Selgels on Wednesday the 19th of Jany. 1870
In Chanhassen, at Wm. Sarver on Thursday the 20th of Jany 1870
In Carver, at the Hotel on Friday the 21st of Jany. 1870

Afterwards I will attend at the County Seat to receive taxes from those wishing to pay the same,

A Penalty of 5 per cent will be charged according to law after the 1st day of February 1870, on personal property tax.

The amount of taxes levied on the dollar valuation [illegible]

State Taxes,	5 Mills
Common School Tax,	2 "
Co. Revenue Tax.	6½ "
Co. Special Tax.	1 "
Co. Poor Tax.	2 "
Co. Interest and Sinking Fund.	2 "

TOWN TAXES.

Benton Town, Road and Bridge	4	mills
Camden Town, Road and Bridge,	5½	"
Carver Town, Road and Bridge,	10	"
Chaska Town, Road and Bridge,	21	"
Chanhassen Town, Road and Bridge	2	"
Hollywood, Town tax,	2	mills
Laketown, Town Tax, Road and Bridge.	8	"
Hancock, Town Tax,	4	"
San Francisco, Road and Bridge, Town Tax.	5½	"
Watertown, Town Tax, Town & Bounty.	0½	"
Waconia, Town Tax.	4	"
Dahlgreen Town, Road and Bridge,	15	"
Young America, Road and Bridge, Town Tax.	7	mills

SPECIAL SCHOOL DISTRICT TAX

No.			No.		
No. 1	6	mills.	No. 30	11	mills.
" 2	45	"	" 31	8	"
" 3	3	"	" 32	[illegible]	"
" 5	9½	"	" 33	10	"
" 6	6½	"	" 34	[illegible]	"
" 7	4½	"	" 35	[illegible]	"
" 8	3½	"	" 39	[illegible]	"
" 10	20	"	" 40	[illegible]	"
" 11	3	"	" 41	[illegible]	"
" 12	16	"	" 42	[illegible]	"
" 13	7	"	" 43	[illegible]	"
" 14	6½	"	" 44	[illegible]	"
" 16	3	"	" 45	[illegible]	"
" 17	4½	"	" 46	4	"
" 18	4	"	" 47	2	"
" 19	11	"	" 48	3½	"
" 20	3	"	" 49	[illegible]	"
" 22	2½	"	" [illegible]	[illegible]	"
" 24	4	"	" [illegible]	[illegible]	"
" 25	6	"	" [illegible]	[illegible]	"
" 27	15	"	" [illegible]	[illegible]	"
" 28	1	"	" 54	4	"
" 29	1	"	" 55	14	"
			" 56	11	"

Chaska, Dec. 4th, 1869.
JOHN DUNN. Treasurer [illegible]

NOTICE.

The undersigned hereby announces to the public, that he has sold this day his interest, being one half, in the Union Mill, Watertown, Carver County, Minn., and property belonging thereto, to Charles H. Lienau, who assumes his share all indebtedness of the firm of Lienau and Dressler. The new firm is authorized to collect all monies due the old firm.

WILHELM DRESSLER.

Referring to the above, the undersigned respectfully announce, that they will conduct the Mill business in Watertown Carver County under the firm name of Lienau Brothers and shall endeavor to retain the confidence, which a kind public placed in the old firm. We have now the best facilities for custom work at our flour, as well as at our saw mills and shall always be ready and willing to accommodate our customers at the lowest possible rates.

N. F. LIENAU.
C. H. LIENAU.

NOTICE.

To Delinquent Tax Payers

All delinquent taxes on Personal property for 1868 and previous years that are not paid on or before the 1st day of February 1870 will be placed in the hands of Sheriff Hecklin for collection. All have had sufficient time and indulgence and must now be paid. Remember the cost must be paid by you.

Chaska, Dec, 15th 1869.

John Dunn,
Treas of Carver Co., Minn.

Poetry.

What can we bear beyond the unknown portal?
No gold, no gains,
Of all our toiling; in the life immortal
No hoarded wealth remains,
Nor gilds, nor stains.

[illegible]

Yet fearless toward that midnight, black and hollow
Our footsteps fare;
The beckoning of a Father's hand we follow—
His love alone is there,
No curse, no care.

—*From the Liberal Christian.*

Astronomers have been revealing so many wonders in the vast globe which rules the planetary scheme, that we cannot yet hope to see the startling results of their researches co-ordinated into a consistent whole—On every hand new marvels are being brought to light. At one time Mr. Lockyer surprises us by exhibiting the amazing velocities with which the solar storms range across the blazing surface of our luminary. At another, the energetic astronomer who presides over the Roman observatory tells us of water within the fierce tumult of the solar spots. The Kew observers track the strange influences of the planets on the solar atmosphere, watching not only the great tide of spots which sweeps in the ten-year period over the solar storm-zones, and then leaves our sun clear from speck or stain, but also the ripples of spot formation which come in shorter periods, and seem inextricably blended to ordinary observers with the great periodic disturbances. Lastly, Lockyer, Huggins, Zollner, and Secchi describe the magic changes of form which pass over tongues of flame, projecting thousands of miles from the solar surface. We have before us as we write a series of colored prominence-pictures taken by Dr. Zollner, the eminent photometrician. It is impossible to contemplate these strange figures without a sense of the magnificence of the problem which the sun presents to astronomers. Here are vast entities—flames, if we will, but flames unlike all those with which we are familiar. And these vast tongues of fire assume forms which speak to us at once of the action of forces of the utmost violence and intensity. The very aspect of these objects at once teaches this, but it is the rapid changes of place and of figure to which the spots are subjected that are most significant on this point. Here is a vast cone-shaped flame, with a mushroom-shaped head of enormous proportions, the whole object standing 16,000 or 17,000 miles from the sun's surface. In the cone figure we see the uprush of lately imprisoned gases in the outspreading head the sudden diminution of pressure as these gases reach the rarer upper atmosphere. But turn from this object to a series of six pictures placed beside it, and we see the solar forces in action. First, there is a vast flame, some 13,000 miles high, bowed towards the right, as though some fierce wind were blowing upon it. It extends in this direction some four or five thousand miles. The next picture represents the same object ten minutes later. The figure of the prominence has wholly changed. It is now a globe-shaped mass, standing on a narrow stalk of light above a row of flame-hillocks. It is bowed towards the left, so that in those short minutes the whole mass of the flames has swept thousands of miles away from its former position. Only two minutes later, and again a complete change of appearance. The stalk and flame-hillocks have vanished, and the globe-shaped mass has become elongated. Three minutes later, the shape of the prominence has altered so completely that one can hardly recognize it for the same. The stalk is again visible but the upper mass is bowed down on the right so that the whole figure resembles a gigantic A, without the cross-bar, and with the down-stroke abnormally thick. This great A is some 20,000 miles in height, and the whole mass of our earth might be bowled between its legs without touching them! Four minutes pass, and again the figure has changed. The flame-hillocks reappear, the down-stroke of the A begins to raise itself from the sun's surface. Lastly, after yet another interval of four minutes, the figure of the prominence has lost all resemblance to an A, and may now be likened to a camel's head looking towards the right. The whole series of changes has occupied but 23 minutes, yet the flame exceeded our earth in volume tenfold at the least. But Mr. Lockyer has recorded an instance of a yet more marvellous nature. A vast prominence extending 70,000 or 80,000 miles from the sun's surface vanished altogether in ten minutes.—The very way in which Zollner's drawings were taken savors of the marvellous. We have spoken of them as colored. They are ruby-red, and so the prominence appeared to the astronomer. The real light of the prominence is not ruby-red, however, but rose-colored, with faint indications of pink, or even bluish tints. The fact is, that by the new method of observation the image of a prominence is formed by only a certain part of its light. We may say that out of the several colored images of the same prominence the astronomer selects one only for examination. The explanation of this is worth consideration, as it involves the essence of the method by which the prominences are seen at all.—When we analyze light with a simple prism as Newton did, we get instead of a round spot of white—that is, mixed light—a row of overlapping spots of different color. It was only when, instead of a round spot, a fine line of white light was analyzed, that one could detect the absence of images of this line along certain parts of the rainbow colored streak—in other words, it was thus only that the dark lines of the spectrum could be seen. And it was to see these lines more clearly that the slit of the spectroscope was made so narrow and the rainbow-spectrum made so long by spectroscopists. But the observers of the prominences go back to the old method. If they used a narrow slit, a narrow strip of the prominence would alone form its spectrum, which would consist of a few bright lines. But by having a wide slit the whole prominence form its spectrum, which consists of a few bright pictures of the prominence. There is a green picture corresponding to the bright spectral line called F, a red picture corresponding to the bright spectral line called C, and so on. If the whole set of pictures were formed at once we could see none of them, for there would be side by side with them the blazing solar spectrum which would obliterate them altogether, just as in ordinary telescopic observation the bright sunlight blots out the prominences from the view. But if the observer uses such a battery of prisms that the solar spectrum would be very long indeed, and if he admits to view only that part of the spectrum opposite which one of the prominence-images exists, he can then see that image quite distinctly, for the neighboring part of the solar spectrum is so reduced in splendor that it no longer obliterates the prominence-figure. In this way, then, the observer selects one or other of the pictures of a prominence, either the red or the green picture, to examine. And strangely enough, it is by no means certain that the two pictures are alike.—Rather it is highly probable that they are different, though we have not space here either to indicate reasons for believing this, or to explain the significance of the circumstance should it eventually be established.

It seems to us that when we consider the real dimensions of the solar globe, we appreciate more fully the wonderful nature of those processes of action indicated by recent researches, than when we regard these without direct reference to the sun's magnitude. How many of us really appreciate the enormous volume of the sun? We read certain figures in books of astronomy, but do we grasp their full significance? There is, however, a simple way of viewing the matter which at once opens our eyes to the vastness of the solar globe.

Bridal Costumes a Century Ago.

To begin with the lady:—Her locks were strained upward over an immense cushion, and sat like an incubus on her head, and plastered over with pomatum, and then sprinkled over with a shower of white powder. The height of this tower was somewhat over a foot. One single white rosebud lay on its top, like an eagle on a haystack. Over her neck and bosom was folded a lace handkerchief, fastened in in front by a bosom pin, rather larger than a copper cent, containing her grandfather's miniature set in virgin gold. Her airy form was braced up in a satin dress, the sleeves as tight as the natural skin of the arm, with a waist formed by a bodice, worn outside, whence the skirt flowed off and was distended at the top of an ample hoop. Shoes of white kid, with peaked toes, and heels of two or three inches elevation, enclosed her feet, and glittered with spangles, as her little pedal members peeped curiously out. Now for the swain. His hair was slicked back and plentifully bepowdered, while his queue projected like the handle of a skillet. His coat was a sky-blue silk, lined with yellow; his long vest of white satin embroidered with gold lace; his breeches of the same material, and tied at the knee with pink ribbon. White silk stockings and pumps with laces, and ties of the same hue, completed the habiliments of his nether limbs. Lace ruffles clustered around his wrist, and a portentous frill, worked in correspondence and bearing the miniature of his beloved, finished his genteel appearance.

A Battle with Stage Robbers.

On Sunday a week ago, the Yuma, California, stage coach, when between Yuma and San Diego, was attacked by stage robbers. The coach was in a narrow road, the brush on either side being quite thick. The robbers appeared in the road, and called on the driver to halt and give up the treasure on board, one stepping into the road in front of them, and the other three surrounding the coach. The stage not halting promptly, the man in the road fired and killed the off wheeler. There were six passengers on board, and when the horse was shot, a man by the name of W. Richard, of the firm of Richard & Co., of Pinos Villages, fired a shot-gun load of buck-shot into the stomach of the robber in front of the team, who threw up his hands, exclaiming, "My God, I am shot!" whereupon the fight commenced. The passengers were poorly armed; there were only three revolvers and a shot-gun aboard, but the owners used them in a lively manner—driving the robbers off, and getting away with the treasure. One man on board the coach named Davis got a scratch on the leg. The coach received several shots. After the highwaymen were driven off, their coats and spurs were found hanging on the bushes. A horse was found next day tied to a tree, supposed to have been left by the party for the use of the man who was shot, and who is believed to be hid away in the vicinity of the attack. A message was sent back to Yuma for a party to go in search, and the Indians were put on the trail. Their capture is nearly a certainty.

Men-of-War—Some Big Ships that are Building for John Bull.

The keel of one of the typical first-class British war ships for the future has just been laid at Portsmouth. She bears the suggestive title of Devastation, and along with her consort, the Thunderer, to be shortly commenced, will take precedence of all the existing grades in the British navy. Her length is 285 feet, her extreme breadth 62¼ feet, mean draft 26 feet, and tons burden, 4,406, old measurement. She is to be worked by two engines of 800 horse power, and her estimated speed is set down at 12¼ knots per hour. She will be able to carry 1,600 tons of coal, sufficient for a three weeks' cruise.

She is to be constructed on the granite turret principle, without any attempt to unite, by the addition of masts and sails, the characteristics of two distinct varieties of fighting ships. Being, then, neither adapted for a cruiser nor a guardship, she is simply a floating battery of enormous power. She will carry two turrets, and on each will be mounted two thirty-ton guns, capable of throwing shot of six hundred pounds weight. Her sides are to be composed of teak and iron of nearly three feet in thickness, constituting an armor plating which is intended to make her the most impenetrable ship of any navy, while her armament is claimed as the heaviest yet attempted. Owing to the absence of any work aloft, a crew of two hundred and fifty men will, it is said, be sufficient to work her. She is to cost $1,450,000 in gold.

Anecdote of Dandy.—There still lives [sic, and died,] among the Winnebagoes an old Indian, named "Dandy," who was a member of the first delegation from that tribe that ever visited Washington city. While en route to the National Capital the party was detained at Galena, some time in waiting for a steamer to descend the Mississippi, and they were strolling about the town one day they came near a Methodist church, where service was being held during the season of a revival. Greatly astonished at the first glance at this strange novelty they hastily drew up around the windows, and saw the house crowded with people, many of them, under the influence of the preaching, becoming intensely excited, some clapping their hands, others stamping, jumping, and making mysterious gestures and contortions of limbs and body, while at the same time the entire congregation were shouting at the highest pitch of their voices—all of which was perfectly incomprehensible to the Indians, who looked on the spectacle with wonder and amazement, and made various random conjectures as to the meaning of these unusual proceedings.

One of them suggested that the "Big Medicine man," (the preacher) might be exerting his powers of incantation to exercise and drive away bad spirits which had got possession of the people. Another one surmised that possibly this was a big pale-face war-dance. And one even went so far as to pronounce the whole company stark, raving mad. But none of their opinions seemed to meet the concurrence of the majority of the party until Dandy, who had looked on with great interest for some time, at length assumed an air of importance, and exclaimed: "I have it—I have it; I'll tell you what's the matter!" Then pointing his finger to his head, he added: "Whisky too much! Whisky too much!" And they all walked off in disgust, verily believing that the good disciples of Wesley were on a terrible spree.—*H. B. Morey, in Harper's Magazine for December.*

The statistics of immigration in this country for the three months ending September 30 show the number of arrivals to be as follows: Whole number of persons arrived, 116,371. Of these there were 101,343 permanent immigrants; 11,998 returning United States citizens, and 3,030 temporary visitors. Of the immigrants 60,960 were men, 40,383 women, and 23,291 under fifteen years of age. There arrived at the port of New York 70,980; 10,581 at Port Huron; 10,238 at Boston; 4,803 at San Francisco; 1,414 at Detroit. The remaining arrivals were principally at Philadelphia, Portland, New Orleans and Key West. A majority of these immigrants were Germans. The Chinese arriving at San Francisco numbered 5,105, showing a slight decrease from last quarter. A larger portion than usual of the immigrants is made up of professional men, tradesmen and skilled mechanics.

—A circular is issued from the Indian office forbidding visits of delegations of Indians to Washington for the purpose of transacting the business of their respective tribes before the Department.

—Geo. W. Harris, known as "Sut Lovengood," the humorous writer, died near Knoxville, Ky., on the 13th, of apoplexy.

A CHICAGO GIRL OF THE PERIOD.

Her Little Toes Offend Her, and She Has Them Cut Off.

Chicago Tribune, 11th.

There lives on Wabash avenue, in a house of highly respectable exterior, a young lady, the pride of her mother and the joy of her papa. She is, or rather she was, in every respect, an attractive, graceful and accomplished girl; and so thought young Mr. ——, to whom she is engaged, and who, looking at her with the eye of a lover, could see, of course, no blemish in her.

Yet there was one little defect, one small imperfection, which was said to mar the symmetry of her otherwise perfect form. Nature had given her a pair of wonderfully small feet, but although in length they were all that a Chinese beauty might have adored, they were just a little too broad in proportion to their size. But for this little oversight of Nature's they would have been the most ravishing pair of little feet that ever "twinkled" beneath a petticoat. The young lady often sighed as the bootmaker took the measure of them, and thought how she might have dazzled the world, and her adorer particularly, had Nature been a little less liberal. She adopted a variety of expedients in order to pinch and squeeze those rebellious little toes into a proper attitude. Like Cinderella's sister, she did her best to crush them into the glass slipper, but the wicked fairy always put the screw on and punished her sorely for the attempt. In short, her feet gave her no rest by night or day. She was about to be married, and, in view of that event, she resolved to make a double sacrifice.

A few months ago she visited an eminent surgeon of this city, and made a proposal which caused the practitioner to shudder. He at once declined to accede to her strange request; and there the matter dropped for a time. More recently the young lady renewed her proposition, expressing her firm determination to have it carried out, and so persistently did she cling to her resolution that the Doctor was at last prevailed upon to comply with her wish. This was nothing less than the amputation of the small toe of each foot, which would reduce the member to a size exactly proportioned to its length. The operation was one demanding the nicest skill on the part of the surgeon, and a few days since was successfully performed, with the consent of the young lady's relatives and friends. The obnoxious toes have been extracted just like teeth leaving the feet somewhat disfigured for a time, but suited to fit into the smallest, daintiest little boot that can be fashioned. The young martyr is now in bed, waiting patiently for the wound to heal. The operation has cost her a pang, perhaps, but only think what she has gained (what she has lost) by it!—Two small fantastic toes! Many a victor has lived long, honored and happy, with one foot in the grave. This courageous little heroine has achieved a victory which the fashionable world will delight to honor, and she can now walk abroad in midday weather without trailing her skirts—Doubtless she is aching for the next evening party, where her little feet will be exhibited as a triumph of art over nature.—The young lady has boldly put into practice the scriptural precept, "If thy small toe offend thee, cut it off."

The two little offenders should be buried with great pomp and ceremony in the back yard. Peace to their ashes, and may the corns press lightly on the survivors.

Crime in the British Army is increasing. The average number of effective soldiers is set down at 186,506, and the number of convictions last year amounted to 25,612, or 13.73 per cent. The number of soldiers sent to military prisons at home—which was 5,470 in 1764, or 5.97 per cent. of the force—was gradually augmented in the intervening years, until it reached 7,553, or 8.88 per cent., in 1868; while the daily average number of men in military prisons at home had risen from 1.27 per cent. in 1864, to 1,241, or 1.47 per cent., in 1868.—This increase is in a great measure due to the prevalence of drunkenness among the soldiers, and a considerable diminution in this offence is anticipated from the new regulation which now punishes it by fines instead of imprisonment. After drunkenness, desertion stands prominent in the catalogue of military crimes, for which 1,776, of the 7,553 sentences passed in 1868, were inflicted.

Talk about cats—here's one that beats anything ever heard of before. His name is George, and his love of music is remarkable. Whenever any one plays on the piano, George takes position on a chair near by, and at certain passages, that must be particularly pleasing to him, does his "meows" most enthusiastically by way of applause. Sometimes, when the parlor is deserted, and the piano left open, George will mount the stool, and properly adjusting his haunches, put the keys with his fore-paws and perform a number of remarkable involuntaries. Occasionally he plants all-fours on the keys, and, in an ecstasy of delight, dances up and down and makes music of a most original kind. Somebody ought to bring that cat out. George is no flat in music.

An Interviewer Snubbed.—Not long ago a morning paper sent a reporter to Hartford, Conn., to interview Mrs. Stowe on the subject of the Byron scandal. The gentleman saw only the young girl who opens the door of Mrs. Stowe's residence when the bell is rung. He returned to New York. A few days ago the same reporter heard that Mrs. Stowe was in the city and went in search of her again, but was so unfortunate as to see only a relative of hers who did not know when she would be open to an interview on behalf of the press. The reporter was disgusted, and straightway undertook to interview James Fisk, Jr. in relation to his views about Ida Lewis. Mr. Fisk declined the honor. Imagine the disgust of "interviewer!"

Sitting before his tent, in the glow of a camp fire, one evening, General Sherman let his cigar go out to listen to an air that a distant band was playing. The musicians ceased at last. The General turned to one of his officers: "Send an orderly to ask that band to play that tune again." A little while, and the band received the word. The tune was "The Blue Juniata," with exquisite variations. The band played it again, even more beautifully than before. Again it ceased, and then, off to the right, nearly a quarter of a mile away, the voices of some soldiers took it up, with words. The band, and still another band, played a low accompaniment. Camp after camp began singing, and the music of "The Blue Juniata" became for a few minutes the oratorio of half an army.

—It is a somewhat remarkable circumstance that the original proprietors (after the Indians) of lands now held by the government at Newport, R. I., lie buried on those grounds, with only a simple slab lying horizontally on the ground to mark their resting place. Jahleel Brenton, the original proprietor of the grounds now occupied by Fort Adams, and also of the thousand acres, more or less, lying south and east of that fortification, and from whom Brenton's Point, Brenton's Cove and Brenton's Reef derive their names, is buried on the eastern slope of the fort lands. No member of his family is buried near, nor indeed are there any other graves in the vicinity. Samuel Carr, the original proprietor of Goat Island, lies buried on the eastern slope with his daughter "Wait," who died the same day, as recorded on the slab covering their grave, and both were buried in the same grave. He died the same year as Brenton, 1799.

A gentleman had just taken his seat at the dinner-table the other day, when the servant reported a beggar at the door. Feeling in his pocket for a "stamp," but finding none, he replied, "Tell him I haven't a shilling with me," and resumed his dinner. Presently the servant returned with, "please sir, he says he can change a note." "Well," responded the gentleman, "you tell him if he isn't off my steps in half a minute, he'll have something to make a note of!"

—The late John A. Roebling bequeathed $30,000 to the "Trenton Society for the relief of respectable aged indigent widows and single women," and a like sum to the "Union Indigent Home Association for destitute [illegible]."

CHICAGO CORRESPONDENCE.

Business—Lower Prices—The Wheat Market—The Secular and Religious Press—The Advance—The Little Corporal—The Weather—New City and County Officers—Amusements.

Chicago, Dec. 13, 1869.—The year is drawing to a close, and business men are beginning to calculate its profits and losses. There has been a larger amount of business done during the past year, than in any preceding year, but it has been done at less profit, and in the case of wholesale dealers, whose goods are largely sold on trust, the balance sheet cannot be struck till the collections are made, which, in the present scarcity of money in the country, is a slow and difficult work. Money is close at the banks, and none but the best customers are accommodated with all the loans they require.

LOWER PRICES

obtain for almost all fancy goods, with a prospect of their going still lower, and our retail merchants are selling off their stocks as fast as they can, at a great reduction on the prices of the early fall; a proof of the want of money to meet maturing obligations, and of the downward tendency of prices. Every one knows that there must be a great shrinkage in nominal value before we can reach a specie basis.

The general reduction in prices, and the decline of gold—or rather the appreciation of greenbacks—shows that we are approximating the specie standard. A few weeks will reveal the disposition Congress will make of the tariff, taxes and finance. If these questions are settled satisfactorily, business men and capitalists will have a new point of departure, and feel that they have a stable basis for the establishment of new enterprises, and greater activity in old ones. In the meantime, the leading business men are preparing for increased activity another year.

THE WHEAT MARKET

is inactive, receipts are light, shipments by water have ceased, and prices continue low. The dull season is fairly upon us, as far as trade is concerned.

There is nothing new here in the line of [illegible]. The Agitator has bidden us farewell and begins a new life in Boston with the opening year. There is talk of a new woman's paper here of a broader character than the Agitator, but nothing is yet matured.

THE SECULAR AND RELIGIOUS PRESS

flourish here in the greatest perfection, and are types of western progress and enterprise. The changed relations which business, politics and religion have been made to sustain to each other, within a single generation, is marvelous. In the early history of secular journalism in this country, religious topics were regarded as foreign to the secular press, and the proceedings of religious bodies, and the progress of religious revivals secured but a meagre notice, as matter of news—often accompanied by an apology, as if the press were treading on unusual, if not forbidden ground. Gradually, however, the secular journals attained to greater freedom, and broader views of their duties, till now nothing of human interest escapes their notice.

The change in religious journals has been quite as marked. From being devoted solely to religious topics, and thus giving a quasi sanction to the practical heresy that religion was rightfully divorced from business and politics, these papers, beside giving religious news, discussing religious questions, and enforcing religious truth, now publish a summary of the current news, chronicle all important events, give full commercial reports, and discuss, with marked ability, financial and political questions. Taking a lively interest in all that concerns human well-being, they seek to mould the government and business of the country, in its national aspects as well as in the details of private life, into harmony with the laws of God. The leading religious presses of the country not only command a large circulation and influence, but are sought for by business men and politicians, as indices of the tone and guides of a healthy public sentiment, in relation to trade and politics. The infusion of a healthy moral sentiment into channels of business and politics is a public benefaction. In this connection I cannot forbear noticing a recent flagrant breach of good manners—not to say good morals—in a widely circulated religious journal, with which I have been familiar from its origin—the New York Independent. For the last four years it has watered its columns largely with commercial advertising and wholesale puffing of railroad bonds and mortgages, banks, insurance companies, &c., and prospered pecuniarily in so doing. Independent of all religious organizations and representing only its editor and publisher, it had a right to use its columns as it chose, subject only to the laws of morality, and to the courtesies and amenities which are observed by all the decent portion of the secular press. But in its issue of December 23, it has two cuts occupying half of the first and last pages of a triple sheet, representing—the first—the principles of the Independent, and what it claims to have accomplished, and—the last—the Birthday Banquet of the Independent on attaining its majority of twenty-one years. In this last cut are represented the publisher, editor and contributors of the Independent, at a feast, while in one corner the waiter is driving out a lean, hungry dog, on whose collar is printed, in capitals, the name of its Chicago contemporary, the "Advance." Its self-glorification is a matter of taste, but its pictorial vilification of its neighbor is unworthy of a Christian newspaper. What is the character of the contemporary which the Independent caricatures and contemns?

THE ADVANCE

is a religious family journal, published by the Advance Co., in Chicago, at $2.50 a year. It has a very able editorial corps, and a long array of contributors, embracing the best religious and literary talent in the country. Rev. Dr. Patton, its editor-in-chief, is the peer in ability, character, qualifications, and in all the attributes of a Christian gentleman, of any editor in the land. The Advance has all the excellencies without the egotism of the Independent, never sells its opinions to corporations or individuals, discusses public questions ably and fearlessly, is free from bigotry and sectarian controversy, actively promotes the cause of Sunday schools, temperance and every good work, and circulates widely among the members of all religious denominations. The progressive Henry Ward Beecher says, "I regard it as standing fairly on the highest ground yet reached by religious journals in America," and the conservative Dr. Bushnell declares, "the Advance is the ablest, best and most outspoken religious journal published." I am glad to learn that, since the publication of the Independent's indecent cartoon, the mails from all parts of the country have brought hosts of subscribers who have quit the Independent in disgust to take the Advance. Its able political, financial and commercial articles commend it to business men and statesmen, and its Agricultural, Scientific and Literary departments, its full market reports and its admirable synopsis of current news, give it the breadth and scope of a first-class secular paper. Whoever wishes a first-class religious journal, representing the genius, spirit and enterprise of the Great West, should subscribe for The Advance.

SUBSCRIBERS FOR THE LITTLE CORPORAL

come pouring into the publishers, Alfred L. Sewell & Co., Chicago, by thousands, as those who subscribe for 1870, before the 1st of January, get the November and December No.'s free. So excellent a Juvenile Magazine cannot be found in the wide world, save this, for one dollar.

THE WEATHER

has been moderate for the past week, with occasional slight rain falls. Navigation is nearly suspended, a few boats only running short distances. The new

CITY & COUNTY OFFICERS

have been installed, and the people are looking anxiously for the promised retrenchment and reform, and hope to see it.

AMUSEMENTS.

Dominick Murray has been the reigning star, for two weeks, at McVicker's, and justifies his high reputation. Maggie Mitchell begins an engagement here next Tuesday.

Emerson & Manning's minstrels at the Dearborn draw full houses.

The Lydia Thompson troupe of blondes finish their engagement at the Opera House this week. Next week the Parepa-Rosa concert troupe reappear for four nights and one matinee.

At Aiken's Museum a new American comedy, entitled "Rogue," draws a real crowd. One is always sure of entertainment at the Museum. S.

The wheat growers of California complain bitterly of the want of sufficient vessels to export their produce. There are now 10,000 tons of wheat in store on the banks of the Tuolumne River in Stanislaus county, and more than 5,000 tons in Napa county, awaiting shipment. The farmers who refused in the early part of the season to accept $2 a bushel for their wheat, would now be glad of an offer of $1.50 per bushel.

—The Pope, fearful that the Ecumenical Council will kill him, has issued a bull, ordering that in case of his death his successor shall be elected by the assembled prelates of the church.

—A vigilance committee called "Law and Order Regulators" has been organized in New York.

CONGRESSIONAL SUMMARY.

Senate.—Dec. 9.—Several communications and petitions relating to Cuban independence, and removing disabilities from participants in the rebellion, were presented.—A plan of forming a map [illegible] of the land resources of the country was discussed.—Mr. Carpenter introduced a bill fixing the salary of the Chief Justice of the Supreme Court at $10,000, and Associates at [illegible], referred to Judiciary Committee.—By Mr. Sumner, a bill putting medical practitioners on a footing of equality in the District of Columbia, without distinction of color.—By Mr. Trumbull, a bill relative to the appellate jurisdiction of the Supreme Court. By Mr. Stewart, a resolution restoring to private entry the land withdrawn for the benefit of the N. P. R. R.—By Mr. Drake, a bill to establish a uniform time for holding elections for electors for President and Vice President of the United States and Representatives to Congress in all the states of the Union.—By Mr. Sawyer, exempting the property of charitable institutions from tax or duty. Referred.—A bill removing disabilities from certain persons was passed.

House.—A petition was received asking a repeal of the tax on [illegible]; asking removal of duties on coal; by Mr. Banks, a bill for the reconstruction of Georgia according to the plan recommended by President Grant; by Mr. Stevenson, to place the following articles on the free list: Tea, coffee, molasses, syrup, Melada, or cane juice, rice, salt, lumber, hides, stains for printing paper, and iron in pigs; by Mr. Fox, a resolution creating a committee to inquire into the recent Wall street panic; by Van Trump, a resolution from the Ohio legislature, respecting the proposed 15th amendment; by Mr. Loughridge, a bill to continue the supply of artificial limbs to soldiers. The census bill was then taken up and considered. Mr. Butler was in favor of having the census taken by the officers of the internal revenue.—Mr. Garfield thought the old mode of taking it by U. S. Marshals was better, as many had had experience.—Mr. Butler argued in favor of the revenue officers; they had a plenty of trained clerks with little to do.—Mr. Maynard thought well of Butler's proposition.—Mr. Garfield said that the "tax gatherer" was odious to the people, and he said it would be necessary also to appoint as many new assistants as under the marshals.—Mr. Allison said it would seriously interfere with the duties of the assessors for six months at least.—Mr. Wood, of New York city, was at first inclined to favor the idea of Mr. Butler, but he considered the census work too important to be prejudiced, as it would be, by putting it in the hands of the revenue collectors.—Mr. Butler closed the debate with sharp reference to the peculiarities of New York city. His proposition was lost—only 22 favoring. Mr. Lawrence introduced a bill to punish election frauds, and Mr Davis, a bill to impose a tax on fictitious and gambling sales of gold. The House then adjourned.

House—Dec. 10.—Bills introduced by Mr. Rogers to remove political disabilities from some lately in rebellion; by Strickland, to extend the time for completing military road from Copper Harbor, Michigan, to Green Bay, Wisconsin; by Lawrence, to abolish certain fees required of pensioners; by Hay, to repeal so much of the internal revenue law as requires farmers and gardeners to have a produce brokers' license to sell their own products at market stalls or stands; by Coleman to provide for the sale of gold in the Treasury. Resolutions were offered by Mercur, to retrench in the funeral expenses of Congressmen; by Ring, to enquire into the expediency of recognizing Cuba; a bill by Ingersoll, in relation to increase of the greenback issue. The House then went into Committee of the Whole to consider the census bill, which was discussed during the remainder of the sitting. Several amendments thereto were adopted, one imposing a fine of $5,000 on any corporation refusing to give any information required by the act. Schofield urged the striking out of the existing clause of the bill which required a multiplication of Federal officers—the amendment was rejected. A petition from New York containing over 7,000 names was presented for the independence of Cuba. Adjourned till Monday.

Senate.—Dec. 13th.—Carpenter, from the Judiciary Committee, reported Morton's Georgia reconstruction bill, with amendments.—Corbett introduced a bill to establish a department of Indian affairs; also a bill to fund the maturing debt of the United States by a self-funding bond. It provides for the issue of $1,000,000,000 in coupon registered bonds, of $1,000 each, to bear interest, the first three years at 6 per cent., the next three years at 5 per cent., next decade 4½ per cent., and next twenty years at 4 per cent.; to be free from all tax, and to be used in redeeming the 5-20 bonds.—Wilson introduced a bill for the regulation of immigration, declaring invalid all contracts whereby immigrants pledge their labor after arrival, and making it a misdemeanor to extort such pledges.—Conkling, a bill to repeal the franking law.—Carpenter, a bill providing for the [illegible] of Supreme Court Judges when incapacitated from performing their duty, and for continuing their salary for life.—Harlan, a bill for quarterly payment of pensions.—Scott, a bill to extend time for filing pension claims. Referred.—Carpenter submitted a resolution that the Spanish gunboats should not be permitted to depart during the continuance of the Cuban rebellion. Laid on the table.—The Senate took up the bill regulating and defining the powers of United States courts, which prohibits any judge or court constituted by Congress from holding any act of Congress invalid because of a supposed repugnance between such act and the Constitution of the United States. Drake supported his bill at length, which, after discussion, was referred to the Judiciary Committee.

House.—A large number of bills were introduced and referred, among which were, to provide for the construction of the Niagara ship canal; dividing Wisconsin into two districts, and for withholding money from Indians who hold white captives.—Butler offered a bill that Virginia having complied with all requirements was entitled to representation in Congress. Referred to Committee on Reconstruction.—Peters offered a resolution declaring the House to be in accord with the President on Canadian reciprocity. Adopted.—A resolution for adjournment from Dec. 22d to Jan. 5th was adopted.—Butler reported a resolution instructing Ways and Means Committee to prepare a bill taxing U. S. bonds 3 per cent., to be deducted from the interest; this with other resolutions being [illegible] went over.—A resolution was adopted authorizing the Committee on Banking to investigate the causes of the recent gold panic.—A petition for the recognition of Cuban belligerency, signed by 71,000 persons was read and referred to Committee on Foreign Affairs. Butler, from the Judiciary, reported the bill for repeal of the tenure of office act, which was ordered printed.—The Senate bill removing disabilities from certain persons was taken up, and led to considerable discussion, and was finally adopted.—A number of other unimportant bills were presented, after which the House proceeded to the consideration of the Census bill.

Senate.—Dec. 14th.—Trumbull offered a resolution looking to dispensing with land offices in states where there was no public land for sale.—By Howard, a resolution of enquiry as to the propriety of dispensing with certain penalties in the internal revenue act.—By Cole, to enquire into the expediency of increasing the tax on distilled spirits to $1. Laid on the table.—Bills were introduced, by Drake, to increase the mail service with China and Japan; also to fix the terminus of the Western Pacific Railroad Company.—Morrill, of Maine, announced the death of Wm. Pitt Fessenden. Eulogies were pronounced by Mr. Morrill and other Senators.—Adjourned.

House.—A resolution was introduced by the Committee on Ways and Means to inquire into the expediency of abolishing the offices of collectors, assessors and other agents of the Internal Revenue Department, and apportioning the amount of tax required to be raised from domestic sources among the several states in proportion to their population. Referred to the Committee on Ways and Means.—Also concerning the treatment of American citizens held as prisoners under the English government. Referred to Committee on Foreign Affairs.—A bill by Paine, looking to an establishment of a system of meteorological signals for the protection of marine disasters.—By Banks, for furnishing, at cost to War Department, clothing to needy and indigent soldiers, sailors and marines in Soldiers' Homes.—Schenck presented a report from Alaska, relating to the disposition of Seal Islands.—Kelly presented a petition from National Colored Labor Convention, praying that public lands in the Southern States be given to Freedmen in tracts of 40 acres each.—The President sent in a message approving a bill for the removal of disabilities.—The House then took up the Census bill. Garfield proposed to strike out the section fixing the number of representatives, which was agreed to; he also proposed adding statistics of Telegraph, and Life, Fire and Insurance Cos. A discussion followed, in which Woodward characterized Life Insurance a stupendous fraud.—An amendment was adopted requiring statistics from bankers and brokers.—Cox thought the bill was already so laden with inquisitorial requirements that it would delay the census for two years.—Cobb, of Wisconsin, offered an amendment requiring statistics of U. S. bonds held by corporations and individuals, in hopes the Ways and Means Committee would devise a plan of taxing the interest thereof.

A Sewing Machine which is sold for only Five Dollars.—For the benefit of our lady readers, we copy from our files the following suggestive extracts:

"A Sewing Machine has become an absolute necessity in every well regulated family. The "Fairy" will work a complete revolution in an article of so much utility, and commends itself wherever used.—*N. Y. Herald.*

"Those who depend on their needle for a living will give the "Fairy" a hearty welcome.—*Henry Ward Beecher.*

"Possesses every requisite for family use.—*N. Y. Observer.*

On receipt of P. O. Order for amount $5, the Company that has this valuable invention, will ship by Express, a Sewing Machine, perfectly adjusted, that they warrant will do equally as good work as the higher priced ones—or it can be sent C. O. D, by addressing the Fairy Sewing Machine Co., 85 and 87 Dearborn Street, P.O. Drawer 5787, Chicago.

One of the most singular member of the Ecumenical Council will be a Chinese Bishop, who is at the same time a manufacturer of umbrellas. This is M. Louis Faurie, Bishop of Kong Tcheon, a native of Bordeaux, in France, but since, nineteen years a resident of China. The Bishop wears a long mustache and goatee, and from his crown dangles the queue of the Celestials; he is dressed in Chinese costume. The Bishop has a large orphan asylum in his charge, and in order to support it, he has started an umbrella factory, giving employment to a good many hands.

Hall's Vegetable Sicilian Hair Renewer. Hall's Vegetable Sicilian Hair Renewer. Sold by all druggists.

The New Era, Atlanta, Ga., one of the leading papers in the South, thus endorses Hoofland's Bitters. "Hoofland's German Bitters is well known to the invalid. For many years it has been in use, and its reputation is unimpaired. It is not claimed for it that it is competent to perform miracles, but there are many diseases and disabilities which it can reach more readily than any other known remedy, and in all such cases it is an excellent remedy. Dyspepsia and Diseases resulting from a disordered Liver, or a derangement of the digestive faculties, comes within its scope, and persons suffering from such diseases have found great relief from a fair trial of this celebrated Bitters. This remedy is not alcoholic, contains no rum or whisky, and cannot make drunkards. Its reputation is backed up by testimonials from many eminent clergymen and others."

Hoofland's German Tonic is a combination of the ingredients of the bitters, with pure Santa Cruz Rum, orange, anise, &c. It is used for the same diseases as the Bitters in cases where an Alcoholic Stimulant is necessary. It is a preparation of rare medicinal value, and most agreeable to the palate.

De Soto, when he visited the shore of America, sought long and sedulously for the "spring of perpetual youth," that those who bathed therein might never grow old in appearance. People of our day have in part discovered a substitute for this unfound spring in Ring's Vegetable Ambrosia, a few applications of which gives to white or gray hair that dark, strong and glossy appearance peculiar to youthful beauty. If any of our readers doubt this, let them try a bottle, and be convinced of the truth of the assertion.

Quinine will break Chills and Fever, but the disease will almost invariably return on the seventh, fourteenth and twenty-first days, while Dr. F. WILHOFT'S ANTI-PERIODIC or FEVER AND AGUE TONIC, cures the disease, together with its peculiar tendency to return again. Made in New Orleans by Wheelock, Finlay & Co., and sold at wholesale by Fuller, Finch & Fuller, Chicago, Ill.

An Established Remedy. — "Brown's Bronchial Troches" are widely known as an established remedy for Coughs, Colds, Bronchitis, Hoarseness, and other troubles of the Throat and Lungs. Their good reputation and extensive use has brought out imitations, represented to be the same. Obtain only "Brown's Bronchial Troches.

Magic Oil cures as if by magic, rheumatism, neuralgia, toothache, earache, sorethroat, colic and all external and internal pains. This liniment has been used with astonishing success by thousands of sufferers during a period of fifteen years. A single trial will insure its permanent use in the family. Ask for Pratt & Butcher's Magic Oil. Sold at all drug stores.

A Prime Article.—Johnson's baking powder is the purest and best article of its kind in the market. One-half the housekeepers of Milwaukee will testify to its excellence. For sale by all grocers.

From One of the Oldest Printers in the State of Illinois.

Office of the Whig and Republican, Quincy, Illinois, August 21, 18[illegible].

Messrs. Prince, Walton & Co., Cincinnati, Ohio—Gents: I find your Roback's Bitters, after using two boxes in my family, to be a "good egg." Send me another dozen by United States Express, and if you don't want local notices to the amount, charge it to me on advertising account. Regards to Mr. Walton. Yours in haste, James L. Langdon.

Agricultural.—The New York Weekly Tribune is a great Farmer's Paper. Its Agricultural Department, valuable always, containing as it does Full Reports of The American Institute Farmers' Club, and articles written for its columns by the most eminent Agriculturists of America, is about to be enriched by other attractive features in a Horticultural Department, which will comprise Management of Small Farms, Fruit and Vegetable Culture, and how to make them pay. Also, a Veterinary Department, for which Prof. James Law, Veterinary Surgeon in Cornell University, has been engaged to answer questions concerning diseases of Cattle, Horses, Sheep and other domestic animals, and prescribe remedies through the columns of The Weekly Tribune. See advertisement in another column.

See Advertisement of Dr. Butts' Dispensary, headed Book for the million—MARRIAGE GUIDE—in another column. It should be read by all.

A most perfect regulator of the whole human system is found in Dr. Pierce's Alterative Extract, or Golden Medical Discovery. It cures Female Weakness, Weak Back, and all irregularities. It is a great restorative tonic, and nerve force generator, and hence in all cases of Nervous or General Debility, nothing can equal it. Sold by Druggists, or send three dollars and twenty-five cents to Dr. R. V. Pierce, Buffalo, N. Y., and get three bottles, free of express charges.

Thousands of men connected with the Washington Life Insurance Company are, by this better way, laying up money. Many of these take out policies which are payable to themselves on arriving at a specified age.

The other day a panther entered the dwelling of Eli P. Whidden, of Manatee, Fla., and attacked a little daughter of Mr. Whidden. The father rushed to the rescue of his child, whereupon the panther turned on him, and compelled him to retreat. The animal followed him into the yard, where Mr Whidden seized a foot-adze and, with one blow, killed the beast. It is supposed that hunger urged the panther to make the attack. The little girl was not seriously injured.

Delays are Dangerous.—Mothers as you love your offspring don't fail to use Mrs. Whitcomb's Syrup, for soothing children. Read the advertisement in another column.

The Best and Original Tonic of Iron Phosphorus and Calisaya, known as Caswell, Mack & Co.'s Ferro Phosphorated Elixir of Calisaya Bark. The Iron restores color to the blood, the Phosphorus renews waste of the nerve tissue and the Calisaya gives a natural healthful tone to the digestive organs thereby curing Dyspepsia in its various forms, Wakefulness, General Debility and Depression of Spirits. Manufactured only by CASWELL, HAZARD & CO., successors to Caswell, Mack & Co., New York. Sold by all Druggists.

Private medical aid. Read Dr. Whittier's advertisement.

Persons in want of Trusses, Supporters, Artificial Limbs, or Surgical Instruments, can be supplied at [illegible]

The best policy—The Washington Life Insurance policy.

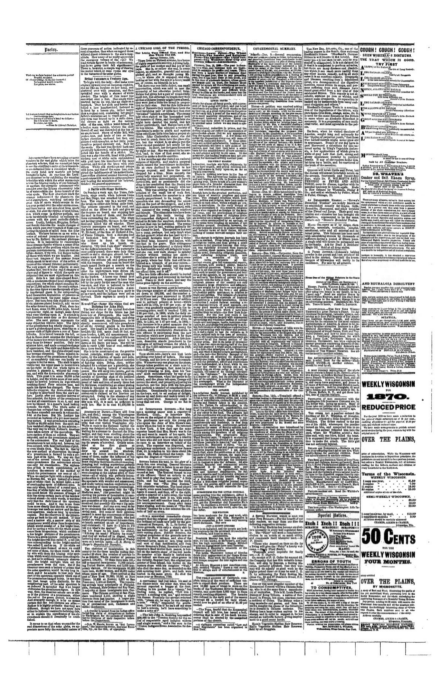

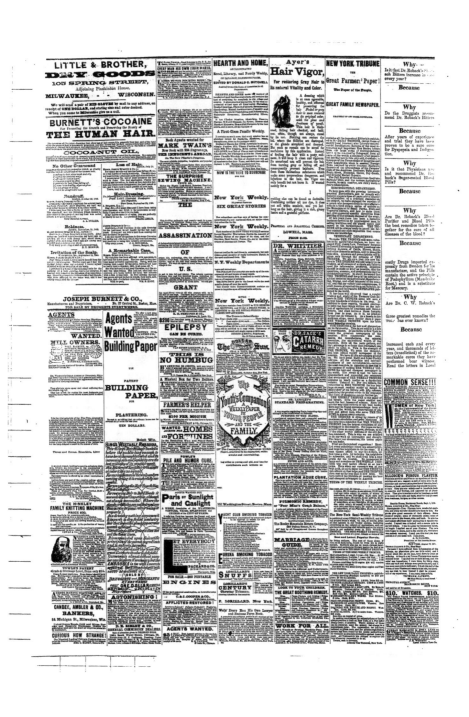

The Chaska Herald.

RATES OF ADVERTISING

1 Square one time	[illegible]
each subsequent insertion	50
One column one year	80 00
Half " " "	45 00
Fourth " " "	25 00
Business cards not over 3 lines	5 00
over 5 lines and unde 10	7 00
over 10 lines and under 15	10 00

Legal Advertisements pr square, first insertion, 75 cents, each subsequent insertion 40 cents. Leaded notices 10 cents per line 1st insertion, each subsequent insertion, 5 cents per line. All notices less than five lines, 50 cents.

MINNESOTA IRON WORKS.

Cor. First and Marshall Streets.
Minneapolis, Minn.
SUPPLIES MILL-MEN

With Steam Engines and Boilers, both Portable and Stationary, Flouring Mill Machinery, complete, Saw Mill Machinery complete, Planing Mill Machinery complete, Water Wheels, Grate Bars, Hangings, Shaftings, Pulleys, &c.

Farmers.

With Horse Powers, Hay Presses, Sorghum Mills, Wind Mills, Force Pumps, Reaper and Mower Castings, Jack-Screws, Iron Kettles, from 15 to 300 gallons, Sledge Hammers, &c.,

Builders.

With Architectural Castings, as Iron Columns Fluted and Plain, Iron Caps, ornamental and plain, Iron Stair Plates and Railings, Iron Grates and Doors, Iron Doors and Fire Shutters, Iron Fencing, Iron Cornices, Iron Conductor Shields, Sash Weights, &c.

Pittsburg, Youghiogheny and Lehigh Coal.

IRON AND BRASS CASTINGS OF ALL KINDS.

All communications, letters of inquiry or orders, must be addressed in full,
"MINNESOTA IRON WORKS"
Minneapolis.

J. R. BARRETT & CO., Proprietors,
MANCHESTER, N. H.
LORD & SMITH,
CHICAGO,
General Agents for the Northwestern States.
G. A. DU TOIT, Agent for Carver County.
E. H. BIGGS, State Agent, St. Paul, Minn.

WALTHAM WATCHES

For a few months past we have advertised the above Watches at extremely low prices, and the result has been most satisfactory. Our plan has been to sell the genuine Waltham Watch, in Solid Gold or Silver Cases only, and at a very small profit; giving the purchaser every opportunity of examination and comparison, and with the understanding that if the Watch does not prove satisfactory, it can be exchanged or the money refunded.

These Watches are, without exception, the most perfect specimens of fine mechanism ever produced in any country. Each and every part is made by machinery of the most delicate and elaborate construction.

Compared with foreign watches, they possess many advantages, excelling not only in principle and finish, but still more in their reliability as time-keepers. As an indication of the prices we submit the following:

Silver Hunting Watches,	$18 00
Gold Hunting Watches, 18 karat case,	80 00
Gold Hunting Watches, ladies size	70 00

We often receive orders direct from our advertisement, but prefer that every one should send first for our descriptive price list, which explains all the different kinds, tells the weight and quality of the cases, and gives prices of each. This we will forward to any one on application, and it will be found very useful in making a selection.

Every Watch is warranted by special certificate from the American Watch Co.

We send them by express to any address.—Allow the purchaser to open the package and examine the Watch before paying, and if afterwards it does not prove satisfactory, it can be exchanged or the money will be cheerfully refunded.

Please state that you saw this in the Chaska Herald.

Address, in full, HOWARD & CO.,
No. 619 Broadway, N. Y.

ERIE RAILWAY.

THE BROAD GAUGE, DOUBLE TRACK ROUTE BETWEEN THE
ATLANTIC CITIES
AND THE
WEST AND SOUTH-WEST.

THIS RAILWAY EXTENDS FROM
NEW YORK to CINCINNATI 860 miles,
NEW YORK to CLEVELAND 625 miles,
NEW YORK to DUNKIRK 460 miles,
NEW YORK to BUFFALO 423 miles,
NEW YORK to ROCHESTER 385 miles,
AND IS
22 Miles the Shorter Route

Four Express Trains daily, leave New York from Depot foot of Chambers St., and foot of 23rd St., at
8.00 a.m. 10,00 a.m. 5.30 p.m. & 6.30 p.m.
running through without change and connection with all Western and Southern Lines.

Trains leave Cincinnati by Columbus, O., time from Depot cor. 5th and Hoadley Streets, at
7.00 A. M. and 9.45 P. M.
running through to New York without change.

Leave Cleveland by Columbus, O., time from Atlantic and Great Western Depot, at
7.20 a. m., 3.25 p. m., and 10.20 p. m.

Leave Dunkirk by New York time, from Union Depot, at
11.05 a. m., 5.00 p. m. and 9.40 p. m.

Leave Buffalo by New York time, from Depot corner Exchange and Michigan Streets, at
7 00 a.m., 2.50 p.m. 6.40 p.m. & 11 30 p.m.

Leave Rochester by New York time, from Genesee Valley Depot, at
7.30 a. m., and 4.00 p. m.

New and Improved Drawing Room Coaches are attached to the train leaving New York at 10.00 A. M. and Buffalo at 7.00 A. M., running through without change, and affording a fine opportunity for viewing the varied and beautiful scenery of this line, while enjoying the comfort and retirement of a private Drawing Room.

Magnificent Day and Night Coaches, of a style peculiar to this line are run through without change between New York and Rochester, Buffalo, Dunkirk, Cleveland, Cincinnati and intermediate points.

BAGGAGE CHECKED THROUGH,
And Fare as low and time as quick as by any other Route.
ASK FOR TICKETS via ERIE RAILWAY,
Which can be procured at all principal offices throughout the country.

L. D. RUCKER, Gen. Sup't.
WM. R. BARR, Gen. Pass'r Ag't.

New Store.

At the Post Office in Carver you can get Dry Goods, Hats, Caps, Boots & Shoes, Ready made clothing and all styles of Dress Goods from Sixty to one hundred per cent cheaper than at any other store in Carver Co. We would call special attention to our stock of Glass Ware, Lamps and Looking Glasses

Groceries can be had Twenty per cent cheaper than at any other place in the County. Produce taken in exchange for Goods,

AUCTION EVERY FAIR DAY.

C. E. ROGERS & CO.

FRANK WARNER
ATTORNEY AT LAW, Chaska Minn., Office at Court House, opposite Auditors Office.

THE ST. PAUL PIONEER.

Established in 1849.

The Oldest and Best Newspaper in the State.

DEMOCRATIC IN POLITICS.

Daily, Tri-Weekly, Weekly.

The St. Paul Pioneer has already entered upon the twenty-first year of its existence, with a larger list of subscribers and more extensive patronage than it ever before enjoyed.

It is reliable democratic, progressive in its ideas, and the organ of the people.

It advocates honesty and economy in the administration of the government.

The reduction of taxation.

The repeal or great modification of the existing oppressive tariff.

The prompt payment of the debt.

The taxation of government bonds the same as other property is taxed.

The banishment of corruption from all the places where it is lodged.

The defense of the national honor at all times.

That the government shall be administered solely for the good of the people.

All the editions of the Pioneer will contain the latest telegraphic dispatches from all parts of the world, the latest news of all kinds; reliable and full market reports; official documents and the laws; political and general editorial; correspondence from all parts of our own State and from abroad, the local news from the various localities in the state; interesting tales, and general reading for the fireside.

TERMS BY MAIL,
DAILY.

One year	$10 00
Six months	5 00
Three months	2 50
One month	1 00

TRI-WEEKLY.

One year	$4 00
Six months	2 00
In clubs of six or more, each copy one year	3 00

WEEKLY.

One copy, one year	$2 00
One copy, six months	1 00
In clubs of ten or more, each copy one year	1 50

A copy of the weekly will be sent gratis to any person who gets up a club of ten, and of the tri-weekly to any person who gets up a club of twenty weekly subscribers. Address
PIONEER PRINTING Co.,
St. Paul, Minn.

"A Complete Pictorial History of the Times."

The Best, Cheapest, and Most Successful Family Paper in the World.

Harper's Weekly.

SPLENDIDLY ILLUSTRATED.

In November will be commenced "Man and Wife," a new serial story, splendidly illustrated, by Wilkie Collins, (author of "The Woman in White," "No Name," "Armadale," and "The Moonstone") New subscribers will be supplied with Harper's Weekly from the commencement of the story to the end of 1870 for $4.

CRITICAL NOTICES OF THE PRESS.

The model newspaper of our country. Complete in all the departments of an American Family paper. Harper's Weekly has earned for itself a right to its title, "A Weekly Journal of Civilization."—New York Evening Post.

Harper's Weekly may be unreservedly declared the best newspaper in America.—New York Independent.

The articles upon public questions which appear in Harper's Weekly from week to week form a remarkable series of brief political essays. They are distinguished by clear and pointed statement, by good common sense, by independence, and breadth of view. They are the expression of mature conviction, high principle, and strong feeling, and take their place among the best newspaper writing of the times.—North American Review, Boston, Mass.

SUBSCRIPTIONS. 1870.

TERMS:

HARPER'S WEEKLY, one year, $4 00

An extra copy of either the Magazine, Weekly, or Bazar will be supplied gratis for every club of Five Subscribers at $4 each, in one remittance; or, Six copies for $20, without extra copy.

Subscriptions to Harper's Magazine, Weekly, and Bazar, to one address for one year, $10; or, two of Harper's Periodicals, to one address for one year, $7.

Back Numbers can be supplied at any time.

The annual volumes of Harper's Weekly, in neat cloth binding, will be sent by express, free of expense, for $7 each. A complete set, comprising 13 volumes, freight at expense of purchaser. Volume 13 ready Jan 1, 1870.

The postage on Harper's Weekly is 20 cents a year, which must be paid at the subscriber's post-office.

Address HARPER & BROTHERS, N. Y.

INSURANCE.

We would respectfully notify our friends and patrons that the

UNDERWRITER'S AGENCY
OF NEW YORK.

(Composed of the oldest German Insurance Co. in the U. S. and three other Companies,) is now represented by F. E. Du Toit, who will be prepared to insure Farm property and Stocks of Goods in this and the surrounding Counties at the LOWEST RATES.

Cash Assets, $3, 555 000

Losses promptly paid.

Germania, Hanover, Niagara, and Republic Ins. Cos., of New York.

A. STODDARD, Gen'l. Agt.
F. E. DU TOIT, Local Agent, Chaska.

NEW STORE.

WACONIA - - - - MINN.

Louis Gothelf pays the highest price for farmers produce as well in cash as in trade, and sells goods of every description at St. Paul prices and respectfully solicits patronage and guarantees satisfaction. Give me a call.

LOUIS GOTHELF.

INSURANCE

F. E. DU TOIT.
AGENT

of the following Insurance Co's,

ÆTNA
Hartford, Con.—Assets 5,052, 000,00

UNDERWRITER'S AGENCY
New York City,—Assets 3,555,000,00

CHARTER OAK LIFE INS CO
OF
Hartford, Conn.—Assets, 4,000,000.00

Policies of Insurance issued against loss or damage by fire and perils of Inland transportation.

Losses Adjusted and Paid promptly at the place where the *Policy is Issued*.

Will attend promptly, to collections. Paying of Taxes, &c.

OFFICE, AT THE "HERALD" OFFICE.
CHASKA MINNESOTA

FORTIETH YEAR.

GODEY'S LADY'S BOOK FOR 1870.

THE
CHEAPEST OF LADIES' MAGAZINES,
Because it is The Best.

It has always been the care of the publishers to combine in its pages whatever is useful, whatever is elevating, whatever is pure, dignified, and virtuous in sentiment, with whatever may afford rational and innocent amusement. For its Literary Department, in past years,

THE BEST WRITERS,

In the literary world have contributed, and will continue to furnish articles for the year 1870. Such names as Marion Harland, Ion Churchill, Louise Dorr, Mrs. Victoria Victor, S. Annie Frost, Mrs. Dennison, and Mrs. C. A. Hopkins, cannot be found on the Prospectus of any other magazine.

Beautiful Steel Plates.

Of these the Lady's Book contains fourteen each year, superior (we challenge comparison) to any publisher in this country, either in book or periodical.

Our Fashion Plates.

Have a reputation for correctness the world over.

Embroidery Patterns.—We give frequently a presentation sheet to our patrons containing twenty, thirty, and sometimes forty designs in embroidery.

Original Music.—Godey's is the only magazine in which music prepared expressly for it appears.

Model Cottages.—The only magazine in this country that gives these designs is the Lady's Book.

Drawing Lessons.—In this we are also alone.

We have also a Childrens, a Horticultural and a Health department.

GODEY'S INVALUABLE RECEIPTS, upon every subject for the Boudoir, Nursery, Kitchen, House, and Laundry.

Tinted Engravings.—This is a series of engravings that no one has attempted but ourselves. They give great satisfaction.

Ladies' Fancy Work Department.—Some of the designs in this department are printed in colors, in a style unequalled.

Terms for 1870.

One copy, one year,	$3 00
Two copies, one year,	5 00
Three copies, one year,	7 50
Four copies, one year, and an extra copy to the person getting up the club, making six copies,	14 00
Eight copies, one year, and an extra copy to the person getting up the club, making nine copies,	21 00
Eleven copies, one year, and an extra copy to the person getting up the club, making twelve copies	27 50

Godey's Lady's Book and Arthur's Home Magazine will be sent one year on receipt of $4.00.

Godey's Lady's Book and Once a Month will be sent one year on receipt of $4.00.

Godey's Lady's Book and The Children's Hour will be sent one year on receipt of $3.50.

Godey's Lady's Book, Arthur's Home Magazine, and Children's Hour will be sent one year on receipt of $5.00.

Godey's Lady's Book, Arthur's Home Magazine, Once a Month, and The Children's Hour will be sent one year on receipt of $6.50.

The money must all be sent at one time for any of the clubs, and additions may be made to clubs at club rates.

HOW TO REMIT.—In remitting by Mail, a Post-office Order on Philadelphia, or a Draft on Philadelphia or New York, payable to the order of L. A. Godey, is preferable to bank notes, as should the Order or Draft be lost or stolen, it can be renewed without loss to the sender. If a Draft or a Post-office Order cannot be procured, send United States or National Bank notes.

Address L. A. GODEY,
N. E. Corner Sixth and Chestnut Sts., Phila.

Words Of Wisdom

For Young Men.

On the Ruling Passion in Youth and Early Manhood, with Self Help for the Erring and unfortunate. Sent in sealed letter envelopes, free of charge. Address, HOWARD ASSOCIATION, Box P. Philadelphia, Pa.

SAINT PAUL STEAM
TOBACCO WORKS
KEIFER & SUTHEIMER,

Wholesale Dealers in all kinds of Tobacco. Factory cor., Eagle & Washington St., [illegible], Room 333, 3d street,

St. Paul, Minn.

SALOON!

CARVER - - - MINN.

The best of Liquors, Segars and Beer constantly kept on hand. Farmers call on me.

PETER BUTTENDORF.

Wanted—Lady Agents

In every Town and Village, to sell what every lady will purchase at sight. Address Miss WILLIAMS, 180 Fulton St., N. Y.

Commissioners Notice.

Notice is hereby given, that by order of the Probate Court for Carver County, Minn., the undersigned have been appointed commissioners to receive, examine and adjust claims against the estate of Peter Thompson late of said County deceased, and will meet for that purpose on the first Monday of each month, at the Court House in Chaska in said County, at 2 o'clock P. M., for six months from August 14th 1869, and said period of six months is the time limited by said order for creditors to present their claims.

Chaska, Aug. 14th 1869.

PETER WEEGO.
G. KRAYENBUHL.
F. E. DU TOIT,

MORTGAGE SALE.

Whereas default has been made in the condition of a certain indenture of mortgage bearing date the twenty eight day of July A. D. 1867 executed and delivered by Sount Johnson and Olof Olsson of the County of Carver in the State of Minnesota, mortgagors unto Swan M. Abrahamson of said County of Carver mortgagee, whereby the said mortgagors did bargain grant sell and convey unto the said mortgagee the following described real estate situate and being in said County of Carver and State of Minnesota to-wit: The north west (¼) quarter of the north west quarter [¼] and lot number [1] one in section [3] three and lot number (5) three in section (4) four, Township (116) one hundred and sixteen of Range [25] twenty five containing one hundred and seven acres and eighty nine hundredths of an acre according to the government survey to secure the payment of the sum of seven hundred dollars and interest according to the condition of a certain promissory note for the sum of seven hundred dollars made and executed by the said Olof Olsson and Sount Johnson to the order of the said mortgagee payable on the first day of September A. D 1869 without interest and bearing even date with said mortgage and which said mortgage was afterwards on the 29d day of July A. D. 1869 duly recorded in the office of the Register of Deeds in and for said County in Book "G" of mortgages on page (48) forty eight. And whereas afterwards on the 8th day of December A. D. 1869 the said mortgagee duly assigned said mortgage by an instrument in writing of that date to Henry Shaubut and William F. Lewis of Mankato in the state aforesaid which said assignment was duly recorded in the said Register of Deeds office on the 10th day of December A. D. 1869 in Book "G" of mortgages on the margin of page forty eight and there is claimed to be due and is due on the said mortgage at the date of this notice for principal and interest the sum of seven hundred and sixteen dollars and seventeen cents and no suit or proceedings at law or otherwise having been instituted to recover the debt so remaining secured by said mortgage or any part thereof.

Now therefore notice is hereby given that by virtue of a power of sale in the said mortgage contained, and pursuant to the statute in such case made and provided, the said mortgage will be foreclosed by sale of the said mortgaged premises and the mortgaged premises herein above described will be sold by the sheriff of Carver County aforesaid at public auction to the highest bidder for cash at the front door of the Court House in the town of Chaska in said County of Carver on the 5th day of February A. D. 1870 at ten o'clock in the forenoon of that day to satisfy the amount that shall then be due on said note and mortgage with all the legal costs and disbursements.

Dated Chaska, December 24th 1869.

WILLIAM F. LEWIS & HENRY SHAUBUT,
Assignees of Mortgage.
BAXTER & SARGENT,
Att'ys for Assignees of Mortgages.

THE LADY'S FRIEND.

Two Months Gratis!!

The Lady's Friend announces the following Novelets for 1870: Did he Forget Her?" by Louise Chandler Moulton; "The Cassamena Aunt by Elizabeth Prescott author of "Between Two," &c.; "Solid Silver; or, Chrisie Dean's Bridal Gifts," by Amanda M Douglas, author of "The Deburry Fortune," &c., with numerous shorter stories by a brilliant galaxy of lady writers.

A finely executed steel engraving, a handsome double-page, finely colored fashion plate, and a large assortment of wood-cuts illustrating the fashions, fancy work, &c., are given in every number.

It will give a popular piece of Music in every number.

Portraits of Distinguished Authors.

The January number will contain portraits (engraved on steel) of Mrs. Henry Wood, Florence Percy, Louise Chandler Prescott, Amanda M. Douglas, Mrs. Margaret Hosmer, and August Bell.

New subscribers who send in their names for 1870 before the first of November shall receive the November and December numbers of this year in addition, making 14 months in all. And new subscribers sending in their names by the first of December shall receive the magnificent December holiday number, making 13 months in all.

TERMS.—$2 50 a year, two copies, $4; four copies $6; five copies (and one gratis) $8. One copy of the Lady's Friend and The Saturday Evening Post, $4.

A copy of the large and beautiful Premium Steel Engraving—"Taking the Measure of the Wedding Ring,"—engraved in England at a cost of $2,000, will be sent to every full ($2 50) subscriber, and to every person sending a club. This engraving is a gem of art. Address

DEACON & PETERSON,
319 Walnut street, Phila.
—Specimen copies sent for ten cents.—

"A Repository of Fashion, Pleasure, And Instruction."

HARPER'S BAZAR.

A supplement containing numerous full sized patterns of useful articles accompanies the paper every fortnight, and occasionally an elegant colored Fashion Plate.

Harper's Bazar contains 16 folio pages of the size of Harper's Weekly, printed on superfine calendered paper, and is published weekly.

CRITICAL NOTICES OF THE PRESS.

Harper's Bazar contains, besides pictures, patterns, etc., a variety of matter of especial use and interest to the family; articles on health, dress and housekeeping in all its branches; its editorial matter is specially adapted to the circle it is intended to interest and instruct; and it has besides, good stories and literary matter of merit. It is not surprising that the journal, with such feature, has achieved in a short time an immense success; for something of its kind was desired in thousands of families, and its publishers have filled the demand. The young lady who buys a single number of Harper's Bazar is made a subscriber for life.—New York Evening Post.

The Bazar is excellent. Like all the periodicals which the Harper's publish, it is almost ideally well edited, and the class of readers for whom it is intended—the mothers and daughters in average families—can not but profit by its good sense and good taste, which we have no doubt, are to-day making very many homes happier than they may have been before the women began taking lessons in personal and household and social management from this good natured mentor.—The Nation.

It has the merit of being sensible, of conveying instruction, of giving excellent patterns in every department, and of being well stocked with reading matter.—Watchman and Reflector.

Subscriptions—1870,

TERMS:

Harper's Bazar, one year, $4 00.

An Extra copy of either the Magazine, Weekly or Bazar, will be supplied gratis for every Club of Five subscribers at $4 00 each, in one remittance; or Six Copies for $20 00, without extra copy.

Subscriptions to Harper's Magazine, Weekly, and Bazar, to one address, one year, $10 00; or two of Harper's Periodicals, to one address, one year, $7 00.

Back numbers supplied at any time.

Vols. I. and II. of Harper's Bazar, for the years 1868-9, elegantly bound in green morocco cloth, will be sent by express, freight prepaid, for $7 00 each.

The postage on Harper's Bazar is 20 cents a year, which must be paid at the subscriber's post office.

Address HARPER & BROTHERS,
New York.

Estray.

Came into my enclosure in the town of Hancock, Carver Co. one light red cow, the owner will please come forward prove property, pay charges and take the same away.

ANDREW NILSON.

LEGAL NOTICES.

Mortgage Sale.

Names of Mortgagors, Jacob Haas and Elisabeth Haas of Chaska in the County of Carver and State of Minnesota.

Name of Mortgagee, Henry Young of Chaska aforesaid.

Date of Mortgage, May 1st A. D. 1869.

When recorded, May 11th A. D. 1869 at 10 o'clock in the forenoon of that day in Book "H" of mortgages on page 147 in the office of the Register of Deeds of said County of Carver.

Amount claimed to be due at the date of this notice, one hundred and seventy five dollars & ninety seven cents.

Discription of mortgaged premises. The east [½] half of the south east [¼] quarter of section [34] thirty four in township [116] one hundred and sixteen, Range [23] twenty three west, excepting fifteen [15] acres described as follows: Begining at the south east corner of section [34] thirty four and running thence westerly along the south line of said section [20] twenty chains to a post in the south west corner of the south east [¼] quarter of the south east [¼] quarter of said section; thence northly along the west line of said south east quarter [¼] of the south east quarter [¼] of said section [34] thirty four two [2] chains and [70] seventy links to the center of the Yorkville and Bloomington State road; thence north [43] forty three degrees east along the center of said road [22] twenty two chains and [50] links to a point on the east line of said section thirty four; thence south twelve chains and thirty links to the place of begining.

Default having been made in the payment of the said sum due on said mortgage as aforesaid and no proceedings at law or otherwise having been instituted to recover the same or any part thereof; now therefore notice is hereby given that by virtue of the power of sale contained in said mortgage and of the statute in such case made and provided the said mortgage will be foreclosed by a sale of said mortgaged premises at public vendue to the highest bidder for cash at the front door of the Court House in Chaska in said county of Carver on the 8th day of January A. D. 1870 at eleven o'clock in the forenoon of that day for the purpose of satisfying the sum then due thereon and secured by said mortgage together with the costs and disbursements of sale and additional sum of twenty five dollars attorneys fees according to the terms of said mortgage.

Chaska, Nov. 22d 1869.

HENRY YOUNG, Mortgagee.
BAXTER & SARGENT, Atty's for Mortgagee.

SUMMONS.

State of Minnesota, District Court, 4th Judicial Dist. County of Carver. } S. S.

Johannes Anderson, vs. J. F. L. Jetter.

The State of Minnesota, To the above named defendant:

You are hereby summoned and required to answer the complaint in this action which has been filed in the office of the Clerk of the District Court at Chaska in said County, and to serve a copy of your answer to the said complaint on the subscriber, at his office in Watertown in said County within twenty days after the service of this summons upon you, exclusive of the day of such service, and if you fail to answer the said complaint within the time aforesaid, the Plaintiff in this action will apply to the Court for the relief demanded in the Complaint.

Dated Watertown, Dec. 4th A. D. 1869.

H. J. PECK,
Plaintiff's Attorney, Watertown Minn.

SHERIFF SALE.

By virtue of an execution issued out of and under the seal of the district court of the Fourth Judicial District in and for the County of Carver in the State of Minnesota, to me directed & delivered upon a judgment in an action in which Florian Linenfelser was Plaintiff and George Kranzbuhle and Berthold Hertz were defendants. Said execution bearing date December fifteenth A. D. 1869. I have levied on all of the following described land and real estate as the property of the said defendant, Berthold Hertz and all of the right title interest and estate which the said defendant Berthold Hertz had thereon on the fourteenth day of December A. D. 1869, the day of the docketing of said judgment or at any time since have levied on the same, to wit: Lots [7, 8, 9, & 10] seven, eight, nine and ten and the south west [¼] half of lot [11] eleven in Block 56 fifty four in the townsite of Carver in the County of Carver aforesaid according to the plat thereof on record in the office of the Register of Deeds of said county carver. Now therefore, notice is hereby given that by virtue of the said execution, I will sell the said above described premises at public auction to satisfy said execution and the costs thereon, on the 29th day of January A. D 1870 at one o'clock in the afternoon of said day, at the front door of the Court House in Chaska in said County of Carver to the highest bidder for cash.

Chaska, Dec. 15th 1869.

FREDK. HECKLIN, Sheriff Carver Co Minn.
Baxter & Sargent, Plff's Attys.

State of Minnesota, County of Carver, In Probate Court, } S, S,

In the matter of the estate of Hermann Koopmann late of said County deceased.

On reading and filing the oath and petition of Luther L Baxter whereby it appears to this Court that said Hermann Koopmann died intestate on or about the 1st of August 1869 being at the time of his death an inhabitant of said County of Carver, and being seized in fee of about forty acres of real estate in said county, and it further appearing that said deceased left no relatives in this State entitled to the administration of the estate of said deceased. And it further appearing that none of the creditors of said deceased are willing to accept the trust as administrator of the estate of said deceased. And it further appearing that it is necessary and would be for the interest for all concerned in the estate of said deceased that an administrator be appointed upon the estate of said deceased.

Now therefore it is ordered that Saturday the 5th day of February 1870 at 2 o'clock in the afternoon of said day, at the Probate court room in Chaska be assigned as the time and place for hearing said petition.

And it is ordered that notice be given to all persons interested in said estate to appear before the Probate court of said county on the said 5th day of February 1870, at 2 o'clock in the afternoon in Chaska aforesaid, to show cause, if any they have why the said Luther L. Baxter should not be appointed administrator of the estate of Hermann Koopmann deceased.

And it is further ordered that notice be given of the pendency of said petition, by publishing copies of above orders in the Valley Herald a weekly newspaper published in Chaska in said county four weeks previous to the said day of hearing.

Dated Chaska Dec 14 1869.

J. A. SARGENT,
Judge of Probate carver co., Minn.

UNION HOTL.

CHASKA, - - - - - - - MINN

A good bar in connection with the hous. Also good Stabling.

WM. OCHS, Propr.

COMBS & WHITNEY.
WHOLESALE & RETAIL
Booksellers and Stationers
AND THE

Emporium for views of Minnesota and other Scenery, Brackets, Engravings, Frames, Chromos, &c. &c.

174 Third, Corner Cedar Street
Saint Paul. Minn.

Dr. C. B. AMES

PHYSICIAN AND SURGEON.

WATERTOWN . . . MINN.

Office at Lewis Drug Store. Offers his services to the citizens of Watertown and vicinity, and can always be found day or night ready to attend calls.

FALL & WINTER GOODS
Just Received From
Chicago
And Milwaukee.
AT THE
The New Store
OF
HENRY YOUNG

DOMESTIC AND FANCY
DRY GOODS
CLOTHING
Hats, Caps, Furs, Boots, and Shoes, &
Groceries. Cash paid for farmers produce.

Call At
"THE OLD POST OFFICE STAND"

G. A. DUTOIT.
Whole-sale and retail dealer in
Drugs, Paints, Oils,
Perfumery, patent Medicines
Etc. Window Glass, Fancy Articles, toys and Notios,
Pure Wines and Catawba Brandy for medical purposes.
CARVER MINN.

Fresh Arrival
At
LINENFELSER & FAB'R
OF
DRY GOODS
Clothing, Hats, Caps, Boots and Shoes &c.
GROCERIES & PROVISIONS
AT
"At the Brick Store."

Valley Herald.

F. E. DU TOIT Proprietor. TERMS, $1 50, Per Annum.

VOLUME 8 CHASKA, MINNESOTA, FRIDAY, DEC. 31, 1869, NUMBER 19

The Valley Herald

Official County Paper.

BY F. E. DU TOIT.

CHASKA FRIDAY DECEMBER 31 1869.

Minnesota Western Railroad.

There is a contemplated road from Minneapolis to Iowa, via the crossing the Minnesota river near Shakopee or Carver, and Albert Lea. The route has been recently surveyed by Col. Clough, of Minneapolis, and his report is regarded as very favorable as to cost, &c. At a meeting of the stockholders, held in Minneapolis on Monday, the following gentlemen were elected directors for the ensuing year:

H. T. Wells,	John Martin.
D. Morrison.	L. Butler.
W. D. Washburne.	R. P. Russell.
Richard Chute.	Isaac Atwater,
John Rollins,	E. C. Stacey, of
S. W. Farnham.	[Al]bert Lea,
John S. Pillsbury,	Isaac Lincoln,
R. J. Baldwin,	Shakopee.
W. W. McNair,	

We announced last week that we would publish the report of the Surveyor Col. Clough, in this issue, but from some unaccountable reason the Minneapolis Tribune containing the same was mislaid and we were unable to obtain a copy of the report in time for insertion in this issue. We will attempt to remedy the matter next week.

The Red River Rebellion—Dates to the 16th inst.

We have a long and interesting letter from our correspondent at Pembina, which gives us a sort of running account of affairs in the Red River insurrectionary district, down to the night of the 6th inst.

He informs us that Gov. McDougall, the new Canadian Vicegerent, is about packing up for a return to Fort Abercrombie, on his way back to Canada.—We may, therefore, expect him in St. Paul in a few days from now. It will be seen that our correspondent is a warm partizan of the insurgents, but his statements may be accepted as reliable.—*Pioneer.*

ADVERTISING.

Testimony of Successful Men,

Keep a good article; be honest, and let the people know what you have.—Advertise.—*P. T. Barnum.*

Without advertisements, I should be a poor man to-day.—*H. T. Helmbold.*

My success is owing to my liberality in advertising.—*Bonner.*

Advertising has furnished me with a competence.—*Amos Lawrence.*

I advertise my products, and make money.—*N. Longworth.*

Constant and persistent advertising is a sure prelude to wealth.—*Stephen Girard.*

He who invests one dollar in business should invest one dollar in advertising that business.—*A. T. Stewart.*

The man who pays more for shop rent than for advertising, don't understand his business.—*Horace Greeley.*

Important to Homestead Claimants,

It may be well to remind those who have taken claims under the provisions of the Homestead Law that said law went into effect on the 1st day of January 1863. It requires a residence on such claim for five years, at the expiration of which time the claimant has two years in which to perfect his title and securing his homestead, failing to do which within the said two years will work a forfeiture of his rights. A large number of persons in this State took advantage of the provisions of the Homestead act as soon as the law went into effect, to wit: in January 1863. It is important to those that they prove up their claims prior to the same time in January 1870 or they will lose their homestead, as the law contains no provisions for the relief of those who fail to do so.

—Col. George W. Dent, of California brother-in-law of President Grant, has instituted 21 ejectment suits against that number of parties, to recover some 250 acres of land in Carondolet township St. Louis county, and $13,000 for rents and damages. This is the old Dent family claim, which has been in litigation some 20 years.

A Suez letter to the New York *News* says the work on the canal has been stopped but the passage is still hazardous to vessels drawing more than 24 feet.

Fred. Cozzens, the famous wine merchant and author of New York, and central light of the Century Club, is dead.

How the Debt is Being Reduced.

"Mack" to the Cincinnati Enquirer.

Nothing is more simple than the process by which Mr. Boutwell is enabled to issue his bulletins every month, telling the people how the National debt is being reduced. I have suspected all along, but never knew until to-day, what was the modus operandi. Adapted to private business, it would enable the worst bankrupt in the United States to "stand erect," as Mr. Micawber did after he had given his I. O. U. to Traddles. The secret is this. An order has been given to the accounting officers of the Treasury to allow no claims whatever against the Government,—to pay nothing, to repudiate everything. There are just two exceptions made to this general rule,—the bond holders and the officeholders. These gentlemen are paid to the utmost farthing. All other classes of Government creditors are denied even a hearing. And so, for the sake of appearing to pay off the dept, hundreds of millions of just and equitable claims are repudiated.

The Way Congress Opens.

From the New York Times (Rep.)

If we may judge from the way in which the session of Congress has opened, we should be forced to the conclusion that we are destined to witness a repetition of an old and tiresome farce. There have already been prolonged discussions ending in nothing, mingled with the usual proportion of personalities of which everybody but Congressmen are heartily ashamed and weary. We are obliged to admit that nothing more barren or dreary can be offered to the public than the ordinary reports of Congressional debates. They are not often instructive, and no one can pretend that they are amusing.—Matters will mend, it is to be hoped, after Christmas, but garrulous Senator and Representatives must try to conquer their passion for hearing their own voices before any practical work can be done. There are some men who will speak on every subject, and the natural consequence is that it is never worth while to listen to them. Unless members of Congress wish to cause their proceedings to be altogether neglected by the public, they will try to suppress the "bores" and encourage the business men. There is a great danger at present of Congressional reports being carefully skipped by the large body of the public.

The Building of the North Pacific Railroad a Fixed Fact.

The Minneapolis Tribune of Saturday contains the following important announcement:

We learn by a private telegram received yesterday from a well informed quarter, that all necessary arrangements have been concluded, and that the Northern Pacific Rail Road will be built the coming year from Lake Superior to the Red River. This is important and gratifying news, which will be received by our citizens with unalloyed pleasure. We have already, upon several occasions, referred to this undertaking as one vast moment to this State and City, and it is a gratification to know that it is in the hands of parties having the pecuniary ability to press it on to completion with all possible energy and speed.

No Chance for Hoar,

A dispatch of the 20th, from Washington to the Chicago *Tribune*, says:

The death of Mr. Stanton has lead some persons to think that Attorney General Hoar may be confirmed as Associate Justice of the Supreme Court. Their idea is to have some Southern man appointed to the vacancy in that circuit, and let Mr. Hoar have one of the northern circuits. A talk with several of the Senators in opposition to Mr. Hoar leads to the conclusion that this project will not work. The feeling among politicians who have not been able to get such favors as they wanted from him, is very bitter, and they declare that he shall never be confirmed. Pensylvania, moreover, will present another man for Mr. Grier's vacancy, probably Judge Strong, whom they were going to put into the Cabinet if Hoar went out.

On the 14th of January, the citizens of Mankato will vote on the proposition for loaning its bonds to the amount of $75,000, bearing 7 per cent. interest, to run twenty years to aid the Minnesota & Northwestern Railroad Company to construct a line from that city to Wells and Blue Earth City byway of Good Thunder's Ford; the whole to be constructed, with cars running thereon, by the first day of August, 1872. It is believed that the proposition will be approved by a very large majority of the citizens of Mankato, who are thoroughly awake on railroad matters, and do not mean to be "left out in the cold" by railroades, or any other appliances of progress.

Land Office Removal,

Orders have been received for the removal of the Land Office from Greenleaf to Litchfield. In pursuance to these orders the office will be closed at Greenleaf on the 23th of January and reopened at Litchfield on the 29th.

HOME ITEMS.

HERALD AGENT CARVER—G. A. Du Toit.

Time Table of M. V. R. R

The following indicates the time for the arrival of trains at Merriam Station:

Up Trains	10:32 A. M.	5:30 P. M.
Down Trains	9:06 A. M.	3 08 P. M.

J. F. Lincoln, Supt.

CHRISTMAS FESTIVAL.—The S. S. Festival at the Moravian Church on Christmas Eve was in every respect a success. Preceeding the Festival, a short and appropriate discourse was delivered by Rev. C. L. Reinke, after which there was singing by the children of the School. The singing was excellent and reflected much credit upon the Superintendent Mr. Mix and the teachers of the School generally.—The children seemed to take great interest in the proceedings throughout, from which we infer that, the Superintendent, has the happy faculty of making the Sabbath School hours, hours of pleasure to them—which is not often the case.

But probably the chief attraction of the evening, to the children, was the "tree" situated in the Academy building and its "load" of *bon-bons*, and Santa Claus with his load of candies &c., to picture the delight of the children at his appearance, would take a more *facile* pen than ours. To say the least, the room presented a lively appearance during the distribution of presents.

The occasion was a pleasant one and was highly appreciated by our citizens. The Church was crowded to its utmost capacity—and many could not gain admittance, ye local among the latter. To Supt. Mix and the ladies belongs the credit of getting up the affair and carrying it through successfully. The citizens of Chaska are also entitled to "thanks" for liberal contributions to furnish few of the "necessaries" requisite for a proper "Christmas" for the Children.

THEATER & BALL.—The "Concordia" have issued "posters" informing the community at large that they intend to give one of their unrivalled performances at the Hall on January 9th 1870. They are re-hearsing a comical piece, entitled "Wellington's Uniform," which will be played on that evening. They will also sing a number of songs in their usual good style.

After the close of the theater the Shakopee Brass Band will discourse music, and those who feel inclined may "trip" around the room to their hearts delight. Admission fee $100 per couple or 50 cents per person.

HAPPY NEW YEAR!—Ere another issue of the HERALD reaches our readers, the hour hand of time, will have proclaimed the advent of a new year.—We will not now memorize upon the events of the present year, but leave our readers pass their own judgment upon past events. We merely wish upon this occasion, to bid each and every one of our readers a Happy New Year! May fortune and health smile upon them with the advent of 1870, is the sincere wish of the editor. Again, Happy New Year!!

CARVER.—We made our neighboring city—Carver, a visit on last Monday and found business quite brisk, owing in a measure, to its being fair day. Holmes, Du Toit, Denny, Zanger and Funk, were unusually crowded with customers. We also had the pleasure of meeting with a number of old "settler friends." among whom were Robert Patterson and Jos. Willmann of Benton; Herman Logering and Anthony Clesgens of Waconia; Hugh Hoy and C. Dougherty of San Francisco, each of whom were as pleasant as ever, notwithstanding the hard times. Stock business was not very active, although there were a number of buyers present. Still the Carver fairs are a success beyond a shadow of doubt.

OUT AGAIN.—We are pleased to learn that our genial Register of Deeds Fred Greiner, has so far recovered from his late attack of sickness as to be about. We wish him a speedy recovery.

WOOD.—We hope our delinquent subscribers won't forget that we take wood in payment of subscription to the HERALD. Please bear the fact in mind and govern yourselves accordingly.

Co. Commissioners

The Board of County Commissioners convene on Tuesday the 4th day of January next. Much business of importance will be up for transaction, such as acceptance of bonds, appointment of School Supt. and the usual business relating to roads, school districts &c.—Commissioners Barthel and Weisbecker assume the function of their offices at that time. We place every confidence in the ability, honesty and capacity of the board, and look for a good management of our County affairs during the ensuing year.

ACKNOWLEDGEMENT.—We gratefully acknowledge the receipt of a beautiful and useful "Editors Ink Stand" from Geo. A. Du Toit of Carver.

We likewise acknowledge the receipt of a handsome "pocket book" as a new years gift, from the "Underwriters Ins Agency of New York."

We also render thanks to E. Holmes for a Christmas present, consisting of an "illustrated handkerchief."

CATHOLIC CHURCH.—Services at the Catholic Church in this place, was largely attended during the Holidays. Father Magnus also visited Victoria and St. Hubert during the week.

PORK.—The price of pork has slightly advanced. The ranging price in our market is now from 9 to 9½ per lb.

If your horse is lame, sore or galled, you should use Johnson's Anodyne Liniment; wash the part with castile soap and warm water, rub dry, with a clean cloth, then apply the Liniment, rub in well with the hand.

Have the readers of the Valley Herald ever used any of Parsons' Purgative Pills? if not, why not? they are the best family physic, besides being the greatest anti-billous remedy there is in this country.

Carver Items.

Correspondence.

A SUCCESS.—On Christmas night there was a beautiful tree at the Church for the benefit of the Sabbath School Children. We were not present, but gather a few "items" from one who was.

The tree itself was a large one and completely loaded with various articles, such as, books beads book-marks, pincushions, S. S. Cards, Dolls, apples and candies, together with numerous other articles to please the children. The tree was well lighted and presented a really beautiful sight. The citizens of Carver turned out enmasse, and as a consequence the Church was jamed, The Church Choir did some splendid singing and Supt. Holmes delivered the address, which is highly spoken of by those who heard it. To him is due great credit, he being the "getter up" of the affair, and has worked hard to make it a success, which he did. The citizens of Carver contributed money freely to purchase the necessaries, and the ladies, are deserving of praise for the time and labor they have given in getting things in readiness.

ANOTHER.—We understand that the members of the German Lutherian, and Methodist Church, also had trees on Christmas eve at their Churches.—Those that saw them say that they were very pretty and amused the children a good deal.

USE THEM.—We mean "Allens Bitters" for sale by Geo. A. Du Toit, for loss of appetite, Dyspepsia &c it cannot be beat, Try them.

CHRISTMAS.—Christmas passed by very pleasantly and quietly in Carver. Most of our citizens attented divine service in the morning, and in the afternoon did justice to Roast Turkeys, at least we did, having been so fortunate as to receive an invitation to "dine out" or we might not have fared so well.

PERSONAL.—Col. L. L. Baxter, was in town on Wednesday and made us a "fare well call." He will leave for St. Paul on Saturday morning, to be at his post Tuesday at the opening of the Legislature.

Hon J. K. Cullen our Representative will leave on Monday. Again we say no County in the State is more ably represented in the Legislature than ours.

Sheriff Hecklin and F. E. Du Toit of the "Herald" were around on "Christmas day."

Our friend Truman D. Strait of Shakopee made us a pleasant call during the week. Call again gents.

FREE HACK.—L. H. Griffin our enterprising and liberal Hack man, ran a "free back" to and from Merriam on Christmas, as a consequence he was "loaded."

A CALL.—Freeman James of Chaska gave us a call on Monday. Mr. J. reports Chaska in a flourishing condition Call again.

MATRIMONIAL.—Rumor has it that one of our bachelor friends will take unto himself a wife about New Year. How is it?

EPITHALAMIUM.

Ring for the beautiful a knell,
A knell for the young and fair,
Who starts to the sound of her marriage bell
On a life-long walk with despair.
Swing and ring in your belfry high,
Clamor, O bells, to the sunny sky,
But your voices are liquid,
And the peal that swells
Is only a mocking [illegible]!
Ye should sing of joy, but in tones most clear
Ye are shouting lies to the listening ear,
Sold! sold! sold!
Sold for a million of glittering gold!

A thousand eyes are agape to see
The glittering cortege pass,
But the sweet bride walketh wearily,
And her eyes they are dim, alas!
Hand, not heart, is the gift she brings,
Duty, not love, is the strain she sings,
And her visions are fraught,
With hankering thought
And dire fal imaginings;
Her heart should be light, but its beat is slow,
Sobbing and throbbing, sad and low—
Sold! sold! sold!
Sold for a million of glittering gold!

Orange flowers in her shining hair,
Half concealed by gossamer lace;
Oh, she is lovely beyond compare,
Fresh and sweet is her girlish face;
Starry jewels on hand and breast,
Gems of the Orient, gold of the West,
In glimmering play
Seem, laughing, to say
—"We are the price of unrest."
Till the song is sung and the rite is read
The pageant awaits the [illegible]—"
Sold! sold! sold!
Sold for a million of perishing gold!

We clip the following paragraph from a London letter to the New York Herald:

"It is needless to inform any American who has seen our large towns in England, how fearfully we are behind you in the matter of education for the poor. If any American correspondent of an American paper, or any American writer resident in England, was to walk down or through a single district of a score I could point out in London, and was to give his fellow-countrymen a simple but faithful account of what he saw, Englishmen would put down his words as being untrue, exaggerated, unfair and the like. And yet I would defy him, or any one who was merely a word painter, and who never colored his pictures, not to astonish his readers with the drawing he set before them, provided it was only true to the life. When I tell you that we have here in London upwards of 25,000 "gutter children" who live in the streets who never hear the name of their Maker but in a blasphemous oath, and who have no occupation but what they make for themselves, no teaching but that which educates them for the prison, the reformatory, the thieves' kitchen and for ultimate penal servitude; when I tell you this as a simple statistical fact you will hardly wonder if I say education for the million is somewhat needed in this land. But when I add also as a statistical fact that to these 25,000 wanderers there is an addition of 3,000 women of bad character under 15 years of age, and 5,000 professed thieves of the same tender years, you will wonder now, with the immense wealth of London, God does not visit us for our sins and that this huge overgrown Babylon of bricks is not destroyed by Him as were the cities of the plains. Has no effort been made to redeem these children? Has no one, no set of men or women ever put on foot an undertaking to educate them in some measure, to teach them something of honesty and of their relative duties to God and man?

Efforts have not been wanting, but we divide our forces, we will not pull together, and so the evil goes on and is every year increasing. The established Episcopal Church has many schools, and might have the funds at its disposal to have many more. The Baptists, the Wesleyans, and the Roman Catholics have also their schools; the latter the most energetic, and, for the limited number of their community, the most efficient of all. But with the great many of the well-to-do classes in England there is a most unaccountable apathy upon that all important subject. Our strength is divided; there is no law by which parents are obliged to send their offspring to school, and from the thieves, roughs, and fallen women one can only expect that they should, as they do, greatly prefer that the children pick up here a little and there a little—by odd jobs, by selling matches, by thieving, and by worse—which adds something, no matter how little, to the general funds of the household.

The radical party in England propose, as a remedy for this, that an act of Parliament should be brought forward by which rates should be levied from all householders for the payment of common schools; that to these common schools it should be made imperative for all persons who are too poor to educate their children to send both boys and girls of their families; and that at these schools no religious teaching be either enforced or even allowed, so that upon the score of different creeds no objection should be raised. But to this there is the opposition of religious denominations. The Anglicans, the Wesleyans and the Catholics say alike that education without religion is worse than no education at all. What they demand is that the scheme, now practiced on a comparatively small scale, and called the denominational system, should be greatly enlarged, and that to each religious persuasion a grant of government money should, under certain restrictions, be given, with which to build schools, pay teachers and general work out, under government inspection, a system of education upon a large scale.

The Roman Catholic Church in this country has, up to the present time, shown more energy, more activity, and has been more successful in its schools than any other denomination. And the clergy as well as the laity of that church are, more than any others, determined to oppose anything like a system of secular education. They say, "increase the funds you allow us; where you have one Catholic school enjoying government assistance, we will establish five or six, if you will only extend the help you give us. Then, if you like, make it compulsory upon all the children of our faith to attend these schools, and punish the parents who don't obey your order."

The liberal press object to this. They say that they will not pay any sect more than another. They don't want and will not have religious teaching mixed up with secular education, and as to "forcing children to be taught Popery" that would be against the rights of Englishmen.

"Very well," say the Catholics, "at the next election, and even during the next Parliament, we will help the tory side on this question, and if you persist in your bill, and it is made a government measure, we will turn the political tide by voting with the tories."

Mr. Gladstone is fully alive to the gravity of the position. Personally, he objects very much indeed to education of the poor without religion, and would be inclined most decidedly to take part with the Anglicans, Wesleyans and Catholics, by bringing in a measure which would allow each denomination to educate their own poor, and augmenting greatly the government grants for that purpose. But the Premier is, in a great measure, helpless. He is surrounded by ministers who are already pledged to the proposed measure, and who will hear of nothing but their favorite scheme. But now another element has been brought to play. There is no doubt but that the Ecumenical Council will take action on this question, and that both in England and in Ireland the "thunders of the Church" will be evoked against all parents who send their children to schools at which religion forms no part of the teaching. At a large meeting of Roman Catholics, held last week at Birmingham, the Earl of Denbigh, a leading man among the Catholics of this country, declared that he would rather see children sent to schools where Protestantism was taught than to schools where no religion at all was inculcated; and the meeting, of which the Roman Catholic bishop of the place was chairman, cheered him heartily when he made this remark.

See "Little Corporal," among advertisements.

Plants in Sleeping Rooms.

Though the air is dependent for the renewal of its oxygen on the action of the green leaves of plants, it must not be forgotten that it is only in the presence and under the stimulus of light that these organisms decompose carbonic acid. All plants, irrespective of their kind of nature, absorb oxygen and exhale carbonic acid in the dark. The quantity of noxious gas thus eliminated is, however, exceedingly small when compared with the oxygen thrown out during the day. When they are flowering, plants exhale carbonic acid in considerable quantity, and at the same time evolve heat. In this condition, therefore, they resemble animals as regards their relation to the air; and a number of plants placed in a room would, under these circumstances, tend to vitiate the air.

While the phanerogamia, or flowering plants, depend on the air almost entirely for their supply of carbon, and are busy during the day in restoring to it the oxygen that has been removed by animals, many of the inferior cryptogamia, as the fungi and parasitic plants, obtain their nourishment from material that has already been organized. They do not absorb carbonic acid, but on the contrary they act like animals, absorbing oxygen and exhaling carbonic acid at all times. It is, therefore evident that their presence in a room cannot be productive of good results.

Aside from the highly deleterious action that plants may exert on the atmosphere of a sleeping-room, by increasing the proportion of carbonic acid during the night, there is another and more important objection to be urged against their presence in such apartments. Like animals, they exhale peculiar volatile organic principles, which in many instances render the air unfit for the purpose of respiration. Even in the days of Andronicus this fact was recognized, for he says, in speaking of Arabia Felix, that "by reason of myrrh, frankincense and hot spices there growing, the air was so obnoxious to their brains, that the very inhabitants at some times cannot avoid its influence." What the influence on the brains of the inhabitants may have been does not at present interest us; we have only quoted the statement to show that long ago the emanations from plants were regarded as having an influence on the condition of the air; and, in view of our present ignorance, it would be wise to banish them from our sleeping apartments, at least until we are better informed regarding their true properties.—*Dr. J. C. Draper in January Galaxy.*

A Brain Atmosphere.

A new theory is propounded to show why one happens to think of persons he has not seen for years just before meeting them. A similar phenomenon often happens when one has impressions of the death of friends who may be thousands of miles away, and subsequently learns that they died at that particular moment. A writer in the London Spectator thinks that there is a brain atmosphere extending through space, more subtle than the air or even than the electric fluid. As the undulations of the air occasion sound, and the undulations of the ether give the impression of light, so the undulations of this brain atmosphere may convey impressions between sympathetic minds. The theory is a very ingenious one, and there are certainly many facts which it will explain very satisfactorily, but these different atmospheres must be curiously constituted, if so many different vibrations, moving from so many directions, do not interfere with one another. The theory of light, with its hundred of millions of ethereal vibrations every second, through the vast space between the earth and sun, or between the earth and a distant nebula, has always been a tough morsel for our mental digestion. The masters of science lay down the law, and we submit, but our faith is weak. And now comes in a new atmosphere, with a new sense of motions. It is a little too much for us, we confess, and looks "aw'a muddle," as the world did to poor Stephen Blackwell. With vibrations of air, vibrations of ether, vibrations of brain atmosphere, and vibrations of electricity, (we suppose that must vibrate too), things will get mixed up badly. 'Tis no wonder insanity is increasing, for so many vibrations are enough to addle any weak brain, and make it difficult to distinguish one from 'tother. We must beg our scientific friends to hold up, and keep their discoveries of any more atmospheres to themselves. We shall be crushed under the load, if the number is increased. There is a limit to human endurance.—*Providence Journal.*

How Divorces are Obtained.

A writer in the New York Telegram tells how divorces are obtained:

A wife, for instance, unrestrained by any virtuous compunctions, has a husband greatly her senior, in whom there is an absence of congeniality, or perhaps imagining she fancies some one else more, makes application to the ever complaisant "divorce lawyer." He hears a statement of her grievances, and promises her speedy relief for a big fee.

Regularly in his employment are a set of vile creatures whom, I beg the sex's pardon, I must call women. Possessed of some capital in the shape of personal attractions, but poor indeed in virtue, though comely to the eye, they are putrescent in their souls. They are eager performers in any act of turpitude. Instructed minutely as to the foibles and follies of her intended victim, she familiarizes herself with his favorite haunts, and gradually insinuates herself into his acquaintance. Perhaps she begins with opening an apparent innocent flirtation, or by asking a question, proper in itself. An acquaintance formed, she then inaugurates a system of siren-like blandishments, artfully weaving her meshes, until her victim is bound, hand and foot. Few men care to resist temptation when it becomes in such bewitching form, and many take a pleasure thus in falling. About this time the lawyer(?) places a shadower in his employ on the track of the unsuspecting dupe, who is discovered entering an abode of gilded infamy. The law presumes the rest. The wife then, through the lawyer, enters her complaint, the proof of the husband's guilt is conclusive, and the wife, triumphant in her baseness, leaves the court with the air of an injured woman.

Caught in His own Trap.

An individual, whose name we should certainly make public if it could be obtained, was served a well-deserved although dishonest trick yesterday, in front of the Burnet House, on Vine street. Rushing along in search of a dollar or two, he noticed a newsboy, or a gamin whose general appearance was that of a newsboy or bootblack, pick up, turn over and scrutinize carefully a large sealed envelope. Looking over the lad's shoulder he read the address "John Burton, Burnet House," and in a corner the attractive mark "$100."

"Boy," said he, "what are you doing with that?" at the same time grabbing a corner of the envelope.

The boy looked startled and alarmed, and stammered out that he was looking for the owner. That clinched it.

"My name's Burton, and there's a hundred dollars in there that belongs to us; give it here said Greedy Grab.

The boy whined and demanded ten dollars for finding it.

"Get away," said Greedy Grab.

"Give me five dollars, or I'll yell," said the boy.

"Well, here, there's a dollar," replied Greedy Grab; "now get out, or I will kick you."

The boy scampered off, with a dollar in his fist and a grin on his face. The man who had purchased one hundred dollars with one, rushed into a corner of the Burnet House bar-room, tore open the envelope, found in it a fragment of yesterday's Gazette, and rushed out again, followed by a "ha! ha!" yell from a trio of bootblacks who had followed and watched him.—*Cincinnati Commercial.*

—Samuel Hutchinson, of the ship Sonora, is in custody in New York, charged with inhumanity to five of his seamen, whom he first drove to desertion, and then, having captured them, chained them up for ten days in the hold, between sacks of camphor. Three of the men are in the hospital at Manilla; the other two are in New York, prosecuting the captain.

FARM, GARDEN AND HOUSEHOLD.

Ditching and Draining.—These important items in farm management cannot be too frequently placed before the farming community. Many are deterred from underdraining on account of the heavy expense, although it may be safely affirmed that the entire expense of underdraining land is always returned to the farmer in the three following crops, and often in the first.

Tiles are, of course, the best means with which to form the water way, but tiles are so expensive that they are comparatively little used. Good serviceable drains can be made either with lumber, sawed for the purpose, into five or six inch widths, or even with brush and poles; in either case, however, the expenses of the drains are heavy, and what has its effects also, the work is hard and disagreeable, and where the labor of a farm depends on the farmer himself or on the members of his family, it is difficult to get work of that nature performed; then again, to dig drains properly is a trade, and requires considerable experience and special tools, the farmer often loses ten times the value of them in a single season.

Draining cannot be recommended too strongly, but where draining cannot be done, ditching can, and this is the second best thing. Few farms require ditches of more than two feet deep from the adjoining level, and where ditches are not deeper than that, the entire work can be done with the plow and the road scraper, thus putting the hard labor on the horses and not on the man, and rendering the task an easy one.

If water is got off the land quickly in the spring when the snows melt, the land is never wet during the subsequent season; whereas, if the winter's rain and snow are allowed to lodge on the ground, and soak away, it puts the crop back for a considerable time, renders the land cold and sour, and throws the earliest and best sown fall wheat into the midge season. Where a field is wet or flat there ought to be a ditch all around it, the earth thrown out by the plow in forming it on one side being made up into a bank for the fence, and on the other, spread out on the adjoining land as evenly as possible, and so as to prevent the water from forming a lodgment. For forming such ditches as these nothing can be better than the plow; nothing moves earth so fast or so cheaply, and by proper management the greatest portion of the earth in the future ditch never requires touching with any other implement. When the earth can no longer be profitably heaved out of the ditch with the plow, that implement should be used, without a mold-board to loosen the soil, and the earth so moved carried out of the ditch on the adjoining land with the road scraper. No ditch ought to be of less width at the bottom than the ordinary road scraper; if it is, the poaching of cattle searching for water and treading down the banks, soon fills it up.—*Canada Farmer.*

Farm Wages Must come Down.—"The laborer is worthy of his hire," and we are decidedly in favor of paying all good, faithful workers the highest wages that can possibly be afforded. The farm cannot pay beyond a reasonable per centage of its products for workmen. The cost for freightage and other marketing expenses is about the same for wheat at 75c per bushel as for that sold at $1.50. But making no allowance for this, let us reckon the wages of laborers in wheat or other produce which he must buy for his family. Suppose we put the wages of good workmen at four bushels of wheat per week with board, or five and a half without board. This, with wheat at $1.50 per bushel, is $26.00 or $34.37 per month. If the employer sells his wheat and pays money. Is it just that he should pay the same money wages when his wheat brings only 75? The plain truth is he cannot afford it. He cannot give eight or eleven bushels of wheat for a week's work.

If the laborer could feed his family two years ago on four bushels of wheat per week, he can get along on less than double the quantity now, while the employer is straightened for the means to pay interest, purchase machinery or implements, stock, etc. If laborers do not appreciate these facts, and moderate their demands accordingly, farmers will, from absolute necessity, be compelled to shorten sail, and a large number of laborers will be thrown out of employment. Every farmer will, of course, do the best he can to retain his well-tried men, and to keep some improvements going on. By the way, we would like to receive from our readers in different parts of the country, statements as to the number of bushels of wheat, and of corn also, that have been equivalent to the average wages of farm hands, with and without board, during each of the years 1866, 1867 and 1869; we refer to men employed by the month during the entire year.—*American Agriculturist.*

A Bushel of Wheat for a Pound of Butter.—In some of the interior places of our state we learn that wheat is down to forty-five cents per bushel, while in St. Paul a good article of butter sells readily at retail for the same price. After paying harvest hands from two to three dollars a day there is but little left for the farmer who raises the great staple, after deducting price of seed, threshing, &c. The expense of marketing is decidedly in favor of dairy products, since the forty-five cents' worth of wheat weighs some sixty times as much as the butter. Here is another argument in favor of mixed husbandry, instead of all going into one kind of crop until the market is completely over-stocked. If our farmers had raised only half as much wheat and a good crop of butter, cheese, pork, and beef, to say nothing of the great variety of little things that bring the cash, there would have been four times the money saved this year, as the wheat would have brought double the price, with one-half the cost.—*St. Paul Press.*

Beet Sugar in Wisconsin.—The Fond du Lac, Wis., Commonwealth gives a description of the Beet Sugar Manufactory of Messrs. Bonesteel & Otto, in that city. It appears that Mr. Otto has been foreman of such factories in Europe for 20 years. In 1868 he hired a few acres of land near Fond du Lac and from the beets raised made some satisfactory experiments in beet sugar making. In the spring of 1869 Mr. Bonesteel entered the firm. A farm was rented and 80 acres planted to beets. Ten tons per acre was the lowest product. All the beets were secured, and recently the process of manufacture was commenced. The machinery is said to be of the best. The factory has a capacity for making 1000 pounds of sugar daily, and has material enough to keep it employed until April next. It is now run night and day 24 persons being employed. Next year the proprietors expect to plant 160 acres of beets, and to enlarge their establishment.

To Bake Beans.—Boil a quart of white beans in two or three quarts of water until they begin to crack. Put in a teaspoonful of saleratus while they are boiling. Then drain off all the water in which they have been boiled, and put them in a pan or basin large enough to hold them and a piece of nice fat rib of corned pork, which weighs two pounds or so; score the pork and settle it in the middle of the beans, so that the fat is a little higher than the beans; cover all with water and add two tablespoonfuls of molasses, and bake in a moderate oven three hours. When done the top should be a nice brown. Don't forget the molasses, or you won't know Yankee baked beans.—*Ger. Germantown Telegraph.*

Cleaning the Cellars.—Every cellar should at least have a thorough cleaning out. Everything movable in it should have its position changed with this view; and the sides and ceiling of the cellar should be carefully brushed down and one or two heavy coats of whitewash applied. Early winter—we may say at this very time when out-door labor is pretty much over—should be appointed for the first cleaning. The other should take place in April, when the vegetable matter, and meat pickle imperatively require attention.

In both cases the cleansing should be thorough, and the cellar made to appear as clean and sweet as any room in the house.—*Germantown Telegraph.*

CONGRESSIONAL SUMMARY.

Senate—Dec. 15th.—The bill relating to an International Industrial Convention was discussed, and laid over for the present.—Kellogg offered a resolution, which was agreed to, directing the Committee on commerce to inquire into the expediency of repealing the laws relative to the [illegible] customs laws; and also for increasing the salaries of collectors, surveyors and naval officers at the principal ports.—The Senate concurred in the House resolution to adjourn from the 22d instant to the 5th proximo.—Brownlow occupied a half hour in personal explanation of his course in the Tennessee canvass. He heartily supported the administration, and was not in favor of Andrew Johnson for Senator.—Carpenter called up his resolution declaring that the Spanish gunboats should not be permitted to depart. He argued that their detention would be the only course consistent with our avowed neutrality. Mr. Sumner took a contrary view, and thought he or the Senator from Wisconsin misapprehended the statute on the subject. Considerable discussion followed on the question, participated in by Carpenter, Sumner, Howard and others. No action was taken on the resolution.—The joint resolution regulating hours of labor by government employes was taken up. Morrill moved an amendment repealing the act making 8 hours a day's work, which he supported in a long speech, declaring that as the act only applied to men in the service of the government it was anti-republican, and offensive to all laboring men.

House—Prosser introduced a bill to provide for specie payments; Clarke, a resolution that public lands should be open to settlement as soon as the Indian title was extinguished; Conger, one instructing the Committee on Commerce in relation to the establishment of a harbor of refuge on the shore of Lake Huron, between Point au Barques and the St. Clair river. Adopted. [illegible] introduced a bill increasing tax on National banks; [illegible] offered a resolution looking to inquiry into the [illegible] disaster. The House then took up the Census bill. The amendment requiring the collection of statistics on bonds held by corporations and individuals was rejected, and the amendment of Garfield adopted. [illegible] moved to strike out the Agricultural schedule; rejected. The bill was then reported to the House. The amendment for the collection of social statistics was agreed to.

Senate—Dec. 16th.—Wilson offered a resolution, which was adopted, looking to the protection of public meetings in the District of Columbia.—Thurman, a resolution of inquiry as to the designs of the United States in the Yerger case, which went over.—Cooper introduced a joint resolution to close the account of John W. Forney, late Secretary of the Senate, which was adopted after explanation by Cameron, in which he said the accounts of Forney had been fairly adjusted.—The Georgia reconstruction bill was taken up, and discussed at length, without coming to any definite action.—Sherman introduced a bill to establish a Bureau of Customs and Revenue; Sumner, a bill providing that the acts of the several departments shall not be called in question by the other departments, and fixing the limits of the judicial power; also, a bill to encourage the carrying of United States mails to foreign countries in American steamships, and for the encouragement of emigration from Europe to the United States.

House—Bills were introduced, to apportion the Representation of the several states for the 42nd Congress; to amend existing revenue laws; to repeal the tax of ten per cent on notes of state banks.—[illegible] presented letters from Secretary of Navy, asking authority to enlist 1,500 more men for the Navy. Some further amendments to the Census bill were disposed of and the bill passed.—Allison introduced a bill to fix the number of members in the House of Representatives.—Brooks reported a bill to furnish, at government expense, artificial limbs and other supports, to honorably discharged soldiers during life. Ordered printed. A message was received from the President declining to furnish correspondence on Cuban affairs as asked by a resolution of the House.—House went into Committee of the Whole on the President's message. Munger, (dem.) of Ohio, made a speech criticising the financial policy of the government, and advocating repudiation of the debt. He was followed by Brooks of New York, Kerr of Indiana, Sherman of New York, Randall of Pennsylvania, and others—all democrats—in sharp rebuke, declaring that the national debt never can be, and never will be, repudiated. Garfield then offered a resolution declaring that a proposition for repudiation, direct or indirect, was dishonorable, and that the House sets its seal of condemnation upon it, without distinction of party. The resolution was passed, by only one dissenting vote.—A message was received from the President, announcing the ratification of the 15th amendment by Alabama.

Senate—Dec. 17th.—The bill relative to telegraphic communication with foreign countries [illegible] land in the United States. Some discussion took place as to the constitutional right of the general government to supervise the question, in which Sumner and Sherman were the chief disputants.—Bills were introduced, to abolish the franking privilege, and to provide for a reduction of army officers.—The Georgia reconstruction bill was taken up, which occupied the remainder of the afternoon and evening session, the discussion turning chiefly on Morton's amendment requiring the ratification of the 15th amendment before Senators and Representatives are admitted. At a late hour a vote was reached, and the amendment agreed to—yeas 38, nays 12. An amendment, by Howard, was agreed to, by which persons who aided the rebellion would be excluded from seats in the Legislature of Georgia, except such as were forced into the service. The bill was then passed—yeas 47, nays 9.—Adjourned till Monday.

House—Not in session.

Senate—Dec. 20th.—Schurz introduced a bill to reform the civil service, providing for a board to examine all applicants for office, and for a year of probation. Referred.—Trumbull introduced a joint resolution declaring Virginia entitled to representation in Congress; Pomeroy, to charter an American and Holland cable company; Sumner, a resolution asking the President for Cuban correspondence; also a bill to provide for the adjustment of claims of American citizens for spoliations committed by the French prior to 1801.—Morton reported favorably on the bill repealing the duties on canned and preserved fish.

House—Bills and resolutions were introduced by Bingham granting pensions to surviving soldiers and widows of the war of 1812; by Williams relative to the power of Congress to regulate tariffs by rail on roads extending through two or more states; by Hay to distribute the number and rank of government employes among the several districts and territories; also to require agricultural societies to take out fair licenses; by Burdett to regulate labor contracts with immigrants; by Loughridge to provide for payment of bounties to soldiers who were discharged for sickness contracted in line of duty; by Cobb to grant certain islands in Wisconsin as swamp lands; by Cox, a resolution setting forth the necessity of an immediate return to specie payments; by Moore, as to further legislation to suppress polygamy in Utah; adopted; by Getz, instructing P. O. committee to incorporate in a bill for abolishing the franking privilege a provision allowing newspapers to be sent to actual subscribers free of postage; by Woodward, asking the President if any citizens were in military custody, and asking information concerning them; Washburn of Wis. from committee on Appropriations, reported a bill appropriating $200,000 for improving Des Moines Rapids, on the Mississippi River. Passed.—The House refused, by a vote of 106 to 80, to suspend the rules to admit a joint resolution declaring Virginia entitled to representation.—The Georgia bill was taken up, and a lengthy debate followed, but no vote was reached when, at 11:30, the House adjourned.

Senate—Dec. 21st.—Cragin reported an amendment to the bill for enforcing the law against polygamy.—Warner introduced a bill for the more equal distribution of national banking capital.—The census bill was taken up, and, after discussion, a joint resolution suspending all existing laws relative to taking the census until February 1st, 1870, was passed.—After considerable discussion on the ocean telegraph bill, it was re-committed to the Committee on Foreign Relations.—A joint resolution was taken up, and passed, reimbursing owners of steamboats and other vessels, in loyal states, taken by the government during the war. The amount applied for under the bill was $213,000.

House—Consideration of the Georgia bill was continued, and after a sharp debate in which Bingham of Ohio, (rep.) spoke against, and Butler in its favor, the bill passed—yeas 121, nays 51.—Bingham and Farnsworth (reps.) voted in the negative.—A concurrent resolution, extending the recess of Congress from the 5th to 10th of January, was agreed to.—A resolution was passed after some opposition authorizing the President to make such preparations for the reception of the remains of George Peabody as his decease merited, and commensurate with the justice and magnanimity of a great nation.—Logan offered a joint resolution directing casting for the erection of an equestrian statue of bronze of Gen. Grant, to be placed on the south terrace of the Treasury. Passed.—Mungen introduced a resolution allowing retired army and navy officers to hold civil offices.

New Postage Stamps.—The Post-office Department has completed its selections of designs for the new series of postage stamps to take the place of those now in issue which were adopted by the late Postmaster General Randall, about one year ago. The new design will be about one-third larger than the present stamp, or the size of the old stamps, and consist entirely of profile busts taken from standing original marbles executed by artists of acknowledged reputation. Some of the stamps have already been engraved, proofs of which have been approved by the Post-office Department, as well as by the President and Cabinet, as the most appropriate and elegant in all respects of any hitherto issued by any nation. They will comprise the heads of the following distinguished Americans: One cent—Franklin, by Barton, of Franklin Institute, Philadelphia; two cents—Jackson, by Powers; three cents—Washington, by Houdon; six cents—Lincoln, by Volk; ten cents—Jefferson, by Powers; twelve cents—Clay, by Hart; fifteen cents—Webster, by Clevenger; twenty-four cents—Scott, by Coffee; thirty cents—O. H. Perry, by Wolcott.

—A charge of "habitually sleeping at a house of ill-fame" has been preferred against a member of the Indianapolis night police force.

Personal Items.

—John P. Hale is in poor health.

—Father Hyacinthe will return to America.

—Dan Rice is with his show in Mississippi.

—Bonner owns $200,000 worth of horse flesh.

—Richardson's brain weighed fifty-four ounces.

—Liszt says Alida Topp is the queen of lady pianists.

—Agnes Strickland is writing up the Tudor princesses.

—Rosa Bonheur not only smokes, but carries a pocket pistol.

—President McCosh has abolished "hazing" at Princeton College.

—Anna Cora Mowatt Ritchie is writing a story for the Boston Advertiser.

—The widowed Marchioness of Hastings is illustrating a book of fairy tales.

—The late Earl of Derby left behind him a fortune of about $1,000,000 a year.

—Isabella is the guest of the ex-King of Naples at the Farnese palace in Rome.

—It is said that Long John Wentworth throws a shadow twenty-seven feet long on a clear day.

—Mrs. Fanny Moore, a widow lady, died in Weare, N. H., recently, aged 100 years and 9 months.

—A daughter of Professor Agassiz is in the insane asylum at Somerville, Mass., a monomaniac.

—Rev. John Quincy Adams is instructing Young Mens' Christian Associations on "Mental Culture."

—Admiral Farragut has sent valuable presents to the physicians who attended him while sick in Chicago.

—Chief Engineer Damrell, of the Boston Fire Department, has been presented with a diamond ring valued at $1,000.

—Rossi, the Italian tragedian, who is expected in this country next September, is now creating a great furore in Palermo.

Capt. Dahlgren advocates the establishment of a National School of Mining in the centre of the great mining regions of the West.

—The mistress of Venancio Lopez has been reinstated in the possession of her property at Asuncion, by order of the Brazilian Minister.

—An old man of 82, who peddles on the railroad train that arrives at East Conneaught, Pa., is the father of 32 children by one wife, who is now 64.

—The Pope sent a special invitation to Dr. Newman to attend the Ecumenical Council, but the latter was compelled by age and bodily infirmity to decline the honor.

—Miss Jennie Collins is the leader of the "strikes" and "co-operative unions" among the mill girls of Massachusetts and New Hampshire. She belongs to the Labor League, and travels and makes speeches.

A Model Printing Office.

In the Union Building is located one of the most attractive job printing establishments in the entire west, of which Messrs. P. L. Hanscom & Co. are the proprietors. Not least among those men who have sought and secured a hold upon the confidence and patronage of the business public, and achieved a success in Chicago as merited as it is solid, is Mr. Hanscom. Some five years ago he opened a small office on Dearborn Street, and, in a modest way, commenced business, obtaining customers here and there, steadily making friends. His plan of conducting business was then, as it always has been, to give perfect satisfaction, and send out work unsurpassed in point of finish and workmanlike execution. The result was that friends and customers multiplied, and his business soon necessitated more room, as well as increased facilities, to keep pace with its demands. Farwell Hall Building was selected as a new base, and there he opened and operated upon a much more extensive scale; when in the midst of prosperity he lost his entire stock of materials and presses with the disastrous fire which occurred to that building two years ago. It required, however, only a few hours to secure new quarters, and, with a new outfit, settled down to business again—this time at Nos. 120 and 130 LaSalle street. An important branch of his business then, as now, was that of gummed and cut labels for druggists' use, and while at the last named place he very largely extended his facilities for procuring business, soon succeeding in obtaining customers in all parts of the country. The rapid growth of the business made it evident that still more room was needed for the prompt and efficient execution of his many orders. For this purpose he secured the magnificent hall over the Union National Bank, occupying 100 feet on Washington street and 60 feet on LaSalle. Seven steam presses are now kept constantly in use, and some forty of the best workmen to be obtained find steady employment. For the convenience of the public his counting-room (one of the finest offices in the building), is located on the second floor, easily accessible from both Washington and La Salle streets. Here the energetic and genial proprietor or his gentlemanly assistants may always be found in readiness to supply the wants of customers, and when desired show them through the busy establishment. If there is a job printer in Chicago who is deserving of widespread patronage it is Mr. Hanscom; but the fact that he has, from an humble start five years ago, succeeded in establishing one of the largest and finest job offices in the West, of itself speaks forcibly in his praise, and best illustrates the character of himself and his work.—*Chicago Tribune.*

The Novelty Clothes Wringer.—"Take it on trial with any and all others and keep the best," is what the proprietors of the "Novelty Clothes Ringer" say, as will be seen by reference to their advertisement in another column. Nothing but the utmost confidence in their own goods, and a full knowledge of what they had to compete with, would warrant any manufacturer in adopting so broad a platform. This company have from the commencement guaranteed their wringers perfectly satisfactory in all cases, which may to some extent account for their great success. We are informed that their sales of the "Novelty" alone amount to over a quarter of a million dollars annually. It should not be forgotten that this wringer has a place in our Premium List. Cog-wheels on both ends of the rolls, so arranged as to give them one third more power than those having cog-wheels on one end only, allowing the rolls to separate at either end—together with the patent curved clamp for fastening the wringer to a tub, are a few of the noteworthy advantages of the "Novelty." Nothing can be more appropriate for a holiday present to a wife or mother than one of these best of wringers.—*New York Christian Advocate.*

If any of our readers are prematurely gray, or are troubled with falling of the hair, dandruff, or itching of the scalp, they have to use Ring's Vegetable Ambrosia, and their trouble will soon be over. The preparation is not only a restorer of gray hair, but one of the most elegant hair dressings we have ever seen. It also, by softening and invigorating the hair, prevents premature baldness, and in many cases restores hair to bald heads.

The greatest medical discovery of the age—Pratt & Butcher's Magic Oil, used in families for the past fifteen years with astonishing success—a certain, quick cure for all rheumatic complaints, also headache, toothache and lame back, stiff joints, &c—price only 50 cents. Sold by druggists. Fuller, Finch & Fuller wholesale agents, Chicago.

The Oldest Youth's Publication.—Mr. Nathaniel Willis, father of N. P. Willis, started a Youth's paper in Boston in 1827, called the Youth's Companion. It has been published weekly from that year until the present time (43 years), and is to-day one of the most vigorous and enterprising sheets in the country.

Hall's Vegetable Sicilian Hair Renewer is becoming a universal favorite for restoring gray hair to its original color, and making the hair grow out thick.

Brief History of "Tai-Ko-O-Kama," or the Great Wonder of the Age.

When the troupe of Japanese Gymnasts visited Chicago in 1868, Mr. Campbell, who has always an "eye to business," was struck with the peculiarly glossy appearance of their hair. One of the oldest members of the troupe, who, with a companion, was sauntering about town, chanced to drop into Mr. Campbell's store, and looking closely at his hair, Mr. Campbell became convinced that the Japanese knew something about the art of coloring hair. Consequently, on the day following he called on the Japanese Interpreter, at the Tremont House, and stated his business, saying that if he was correct in his conjecture, he would willingly pay an exorbitant price for information that would be the means of driving the poisonous and filthy Hair Dyes from the American market.

The Interpreter informed him that one of the older members of the troupe had been in former years chief hair-dresser to His Majesty the Tycoon, and that he was in possession of secrets in the art of coloring hair, but that he was under obligations to his government not to reveal them. Through the kindness of the interpreter, Mr. Campbell was introduced to this person, and made known his wishes. He was met by a refusal at once. This person, whose name, as many will remember, was O-wee-gee-wee-nah, told Mr. Campbell that there were two kinds of dyes made in Japan, one for coloring black and the other for producing a brown effect; that the former was in common use, while the latter was a "court secret," and used only in the family of the Tycoon.

Mr. Campbell determined to possess himself of this dye if possible, as nothing had ever been known in Europe or America that would color hair brown. He therefore offered O-wee-gee-wee-nah a large sum of money for the secret, but he was refused. Shortly after this the troupe left Chicago and went to New York, and Mr. Campbell followed them in a few days. He went immediately to the hotel where they were stopping, and set deliberately at work to accomplish his purpose. He became intimately acquainted with every gymnast, attended their exhibitions nightly, introduced them to his friends, drove them to the parks and places of public interest, and ingratiated himself thoroughly in their favor.

At length gaining their confidence he succeeded in obtaining a promise from O-wee-gee-wee-nah—that whenever they left the country he should have the secret, but only on condition that it should never be communicated to a third party. The amount to be paid on surrender of the secret was fabulous. Mr. Campbell remained in New York until the troupe was ready to sail. The hour was set for communicating the desired information, and a bag, of twenty dollar gold pieces, was ready for delivery when O-wee-gee-wee-nah was taken suddenly ill, and as he was like all his countrymen, superstitious, he regarded his sickness as judgment on him for the act he was about to commit, and here Mr. Campbell was foiled again.

The troupe sailed for Europe, but Mr. Campbell was not to be defeated. His agent started in the next steamer and overhauled the gymnasts in London, and followed them to Paris. Here their exhibitions were not as profitable, as they had been, and here Mr. Campbell's agent boldly renewed his offer, increasing it by more than a thousand dollars in gold, and at last, in Paris, he was successful—he laid hands on the mighty secret and at once started on his return trip.

Mr. Campbell after thoroughly experimenting with the dye has put it upon the market. Persons have only to try it to be satisfied. The account here given reads more like fiction than truth, but a head of gray hair changed to the soft, glossy brown of youth, will convince the most skeptical that Mark Campbell in this, as in other things, does not humbug the people. This is the eighth wonder of the world. "Japanese Hair Dye" is prepared only at Mark Campbell's Hair Emporium, 81 South Clark St., Chicago, Ill., and is sold by all druggists everywhere.

More Testimony.—From the Times New Point, N. Y. "We take pleasure this week in calling the attention of our readers to the advertisement of "*Hoofland's German Bitters.*" It is the only Tonic for the Invalid that commends itself. Our Druggist, E. Van Wagenen, in this village has sold two gross the past six months, and in every instance it gave satisfaction. Now is the time to use the Bitters. *Hoofland's Bitters is entirely free from alcoholic admixture.*"

Hoofland's German Tonic is a combination of all the ingredients of the Bitters, with pure Santa Cruz Rum, orange, anise, &c. It is used for the same diseases as the Bitters, in cases where an alcoholic stimulant is necessary. It is a preparation of rare medicinal value, and most agreeable to the palate.

We call the especial attention of all those of our readers interested in the knitting of socks, stockings, drawers, hoods, shawls, under clothing, &c., to the advertisement of the American Knitting Machine Co. of Boston; who have reduced the price of their machines to $25, which places them in these close times, within the means of every one.

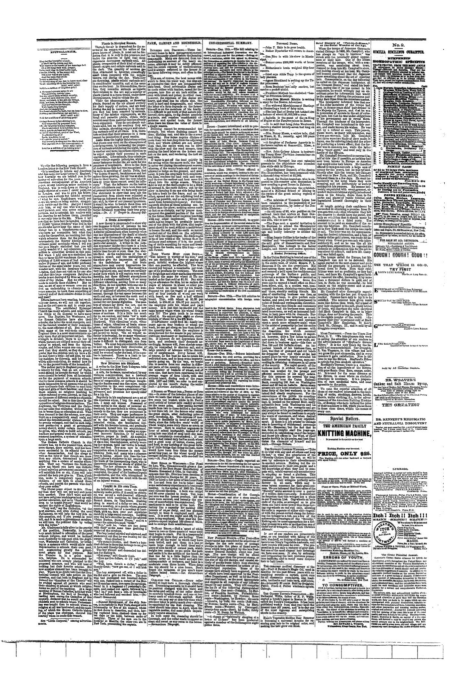

No. 28.

THE HINKLEY

THE SURPRISE SEWING MACHINE.

$10. WATCHES. $10.

D. R. SIBLEY & CO., GENERAL COMMISSION DEALERS.

The Sun.

THE LITTLE CORPORAL

THE MOST POPULAR JUVENILE MAGAZINE IN THE WORLD!

FREE FOR TWO MONTHS!

ENTIRELY ORIGINAL AND FIRST-CLASS.

ALFRED L. SEWELL & CO., Publishers, Chicago, Ill.

BURNETT'S COCOAINE

For Promoting the Growth and Preserving the Beauty of

THE HUMAN HAIR.

COCOA-NUT OIL,

Dandruff.

A. FULLER.

Baldness.

Irritation of the Scalp.

JOSEPH HILL, JR.

SUSAN R. POPE.

Hair-Dressing.

FRANK LESLIE.

A Remarkable Case.

WM. S. EDDY.

JOSEPH BURNETT & CO.,

FOR SALE BY DRUGGISTS EVERYWHERE.

ASTONISHING!

BLOOMINGTON, ILL. NURSERY.

FOR SALE.---200 PORTABLE

ENGINES

C. & J. COOPER & CO.,

$290

EPILEPSY

CAN BE CURED.

THIS IS NO HUMBUG

A Musical Box for Two Dollars.

FARMER'S HELPER

$100 PER MONTH

WANTED AGENTS FOR HOMES AND FORTUNES

ACENTS WANTED.

RAGS.

All kinds of Paper Stock bought, and sacks furnished when required, by

H. G. BRADLEY & CO., MILWAUKEE, WIS.

GOLD WATCHES! AND JEWELRY. Collins Metal

No. 335 Broadway, New York.

Agents Wanted

RING'S VEGETABLE AMBROSIA.

RING'S AMBROSIA RESTORES GRAY HAIR TO ITS ORIGINAL COLOR

RING'S AMBROSIA ERADICATES DANDRUFF, Cures Humors, AND Itching of the Scalp.

RING'S AMBROSIA Prevents Baldness, And frequently causes New Hair to grow on Bald places.

SOLD BY DRUGGISTS And MERCHANTS Everywhere

Price One Dollar per Bottle.

E.M. TUBBS & Co. Proprietors MANCHESTER N.H.

LET EVERYBODY

PACKARD & CO.

Building Paper

USE

PATENT

BUILDING PAPER,

FOR

PLASTERING.

TEN DOLLARS.

Beloit Wis.

MILL OWNERS.

"BE NOT DECEIVED."

Patent Flange Cog-Wheels

ON BOTH ENDS OF THE ROLLS.

DOUBLE GEAR,

The NOVELTY

N. B. PHELPS & CO., Gen. Ag'ts.

17 Cortlandt St., N.Y.

COMMON SENSE!!!

WOMEN of New York;

FOR THE

THE PEOPLE'S FAVORITE JOURNAL.

New York Weekly.

New York Weekly.

N.Y. Weekly Departments

AN UNRIVALLED LITERARY PAPER IS THE

New York Weekly.

STREET & SMITH, Proprietors,

THE

ASSASSINATION

OF

U.S.

GRANT

SEMINAL WEAKNESS

DR. WISHART'S

PINE TREE TAR CORDIAL.

Consumption of the Lungs, Cough, Sore Throat and Breast, Bronchitis, Liver Complaint, Blind and Bleeding Piles, Asthma, Whooping Cough, Diptheria, &c.

ALLCOCK'S POROUS PLASTER

THOMAS JACKSON.

A Book for the Million.

MARRIAGE GUIDE.

LOOK TO YOUR CHILDREN.

AFFLICTED RESTORED!

AGENTS WANTED FOR

Paris BY Sunlight and Gaslight

TOWLE'S PATENT

Grade & Drainage Level, Price only $15.

NEW YORK TRIBUNE

THE

Great Farmers' Paper!

The Paper of the People,

GREAT FAMILY NEWSPAPER.

NOW IS THE TIME TO FORM CLUBS.

The New-York Weekly Tribune

HORTICULTURAL DEPARTMENT.

VETERINARY DEPARTMENT.

TERMS OF THE WEEKLY TRIBUNE.

The New-York Semi-Weekly Tribune

ROBACK'S

Roback's Stomach Bitters, unlike all other Bitters in the market, possess intrinsic merit. Most Bitters, so called, are merely wishiwashy stuff, sold as a beverage. Dr. Roback's Bitters are not a beverage in any sense of the word, but contain the most expensive drugs known to science for the radical cure of Indigestion and Dyspepsia, and for all cases where a tonic and stimulant are required. They restore the vital forces in a remarkable degree, and give tone to the system.

STOMACH

BITTERS

It is now eleven years since Dr. Roback, the celebrated Swedish physician, from Stockholm, Sweden, came to this country and introduced the Scandinavian Blood Purifier; since which time thousands have been cured, by its use, of Scrofula and other blood diseases. It contains, besides the Iodide of Potassa and Syrup of Stillingia, drugs imported from Sweden for its express manufacture, unknown and not kept by apothecaries in this country. A single trial will convince the most skeptical of its wonderful value.

BLOOD

PURIFIER

Dr. Roback's Blood Pills are unsurpassed by any Pill manufactured for a similar purpose. One trial invariably establishes them as favorites with all who use them.

The reasons why Dr. Roback's Blood Pills should be kept in every family are: Because they can be employed in all cases where a "family physic" is required, and are perfectly safe in their administration at all times; Because they are made both with and without sugar-coating, thus adapting them to the use of everybody: Because they can be purchased at any drug store at the extremely low price of twenty-five cents per box.

BLOOD

PILLS

For Sale by Druggists and Dealers in Patent Medicines every-where.

Ayer's Cherry Pectoral,

For Diseases of the Throat and Lungs, such as Coughs, Colds, Whooping Cough, Bronchitis, Asthma, and Consumption.

Ayer's Ague Cure,

PRICE, $1.00 PER BOTTLE.

DR. WHITTIER.

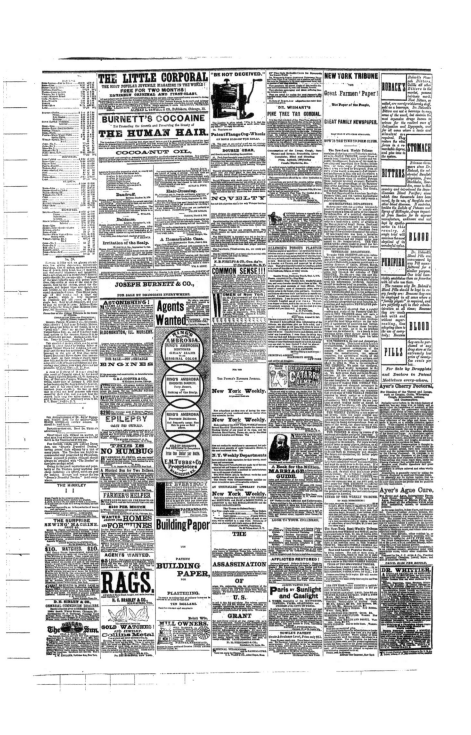

The Chaska Herald.

RATES OF ADVERTISING

Legal Advertisements per square, first insertion, 75 cents, each subsequent insertion 40 cents. Leaded notices 10 cents per line 1st insertion, each subsequent insertion, 5 cents per line. All notices less than five lines, 50 cents.

New Store.

At the Post Office in Carver you can get Dry Goods, Hats, Caps, Boots & Shoes, Ready made clothing and all styles of Dress Goods from Sixty to one hundred per cent cheaper than at any other store in Carver Co. We would call special attention to our stock of Glass Ware, Lamps and Looking Glasses

Groceries can be had Twenty per cent cheaper than at any other place in the County. Produce taken in exchange for Goods.

AUCTION ,EVERY FAIR DAY.

Cor. First and Marshall Streets.

Minneapolis, Minn.

SUPPLIES MILL MEN

With Steam Engines and Boilers, both Portable and Stationary, Flouring Mill Machinery, complete, Saw Mill Machinery complete, Planing Mill Machinery complete, Water Wheels, Gate Bars, Hangings, Shaftings, Pulleys, &c.,

Farmers.

With Horse Powers, Hay Presses, Sorghum Mills, Wind Mills, Force Pumps, Reaper and Mower Castings, Jack Screws, Iron Kettles, from 15 to 300 gallons, Sledge Hammers, &c.,

Builders.

With Architectural Castings, as Iron Columns ...

Pittsburg, Youghiogheny and Lehigh Coal.

"MINNESOTA IRON WORKS" Minneapolis.

LORD & SMITH, CHICAGO, General Agents for the Northwestern States.

WALTHAM WATCHES

Every Watch is warranted by special certificate from the American Watch Co.

Please state that you saw this in the Chaska Herald.

Address, in full, HOWARD & CO., No. 619 Broadway, N. Y.

Plow And Wagon Factory AT WACCKA FRED LUTZ PROPRIETOR.

I would respectfully inform the citizens of Carver County that I now manufacture as good and durable plows as are made in the Union, and offer them as cheap as can be purchased at St. Paul. Also Wagons, Blacksmithing done to order on short notice.

We would respectfully notify our friends and patrons that the

UNDERWRITER'S AGENCY OF NEW YORK.

(Composed of the oldest German Insurance Co. in the U. S. and three other Companies,) is now represented by F. E. Du Toit, who will be prepared to insure Farm property and Stocks of Goods in this and the surrounding Counties at the LOWEST RATES.

Cash Assets, $3, 555 000

Losses promptly paid.

Words Of Wisdom For Young Men.

On the Ruling Passion in Youth and Early Manhood, with Self Help for the Erring and unfortunate. Sent in sealed letter envelopes, free of charge. Address, HOWARD ASSOCIATION Box P. Philadelphia, Pa.

SAINT PAUL STEAM

TOBACCO WORKS

KEIFER & BUTHEIMER,

Wholesale Dealers in all kinds of Tobacco. Factory cor., Eagle & Washington st. ...

St. Paul, Minn.

THE CHEAPEST OF LADIES' MAGAZINES, Because it is The Best.

THE BEST WRITERS.

Beautiful Steel Plates.

Our Fashion Plates.

GODEY'S INVALUABLE RECEIPT.

Terms for 1870.

HOW TO REMIT

L. A. GODEY, N. E. Corner Sixth and Chestnut sts., Phila.

SUBSCRIPTIONS. 1870.

TERMS:

HARPER'S WEEKLY, one year, $4 00

Address HARPER & BROTHERS, N. Y.

Insurance.

For reliable indemnity against loss by Fire apply to Fred E. Du Toit, Agent of the following old and reliable companies at Chaska, Minn.

Aetna, Hartford, capital $5,050,000

Underwriters, New York, 4,000,000

Western Buffalo, 700,000

Charter Oak, Hartford Life 5,000,000

All of the above companies insure property at reasonable rates and pay their losses promptly.

Commissioners Notice.

Chaska, Aug. 14th 1869.

PETER WEEGO, G. KRAYENBUHL, F. E. DU TOIT,

Finkle & Lyon, S. M. Co.

H. J. PECK

AVOID THE QUACKS.

MORTGAGE SALE.

Dated Chaska, December 24th 1869

BAXTER & SARGENT, Att'ys for Assignees of Mortgagee.

Mortgage Sale.

SUMMONS.

State of Minnesota, District Court, 4th Judicial Dist. County of Carver. } S. S.

Johannes Anderson, vs. J. F. L. Jetter.

Dated Watertown, Dec. 4th A. D. 1869.

H. J. PECK, Plaintiff's Attorney, Watertown Minn.

SHERIFF SALE.

FREDK. HECKLIN, Sheriff Carver Co Minn.

Baxter & Sargent, Plff's Attys.

State of Minnesota, County of Carver, In Probate Court, } S. S.

Now therefore it is ordered that Saturday the 5th day of February 1870 at 2 o'clock in the afternoon of said day, at the Probate court room in chaska be assigned as the time and place for hearing said petition.

And it is ordered that notice be given to all persons interested in said estate to appear before the Probate court of said county on the said 5th day of February 1870, at 2 o'clock in the afternoon in chaska aforesaid, to show cause, if any they have why the said Luther L. Baxter should not be appointed administrator of the estate of Hermann Koopmann deceased.

And it is further ordered that notice be given of the pendency of said petition, by publishing copies of above orders in the Valley Herald a weekly newspaper published in chaska in said county four weeks previous to the said day of hearing.

Dated chaska Dec 14 1869.

J. A. SARGENT, Judge of Probate carver co., Minn.

FRANK MINSLER, mortgagee, BAXTER & SARGENT, Att'ys for mortgagee.

CARVER BREWERY

BERTHOLD HERTZ, Proprietor.

UNION HOTL

CHASKA. - - - - - - MINN

A good bar in connection with the hous. Also good Stabling.

WM. OCHS, Propr.

COMBS & WHITNEY.

WHOLESALE & RETAIL

Booksellers and Stationers

AND THE

Emporium for views of Minnesota and other Scenery, Brackets, Engravings, Frames, Chromos, &c. &c.

174 Third, Corner Cedar Street

Saint Paul, Minn.

Dr. C. B. AMES

PHYSICIAN AND SURGEON.

WATERTOWN . . . MINN.

Office at Lewis Drug Store. Offers his service to the citizens of Watertown and vicinity, and can always be found day or night ready to attend calls.

HENRY YOUNG

DRY GOODS

CLOTHING

Hats, Caps, Furs, Boots, and Shoes, &

Drugs, Paints, Oils,

At

LINENFELSE

OF

DRY GOODS

Clothing, Hats, Caps, Boots and Shoes &c.

GROCERIES & PROVISIONS

AT.

"At

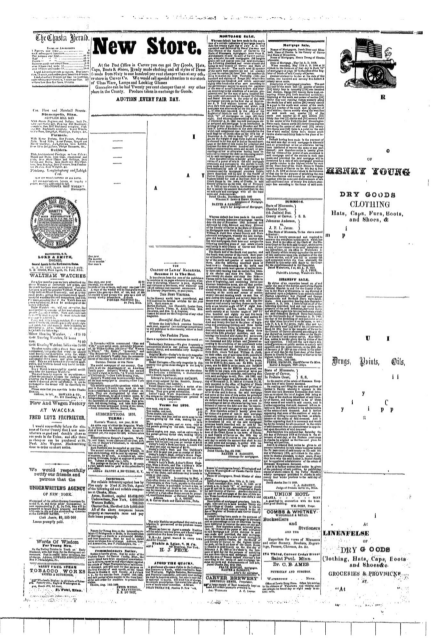